The Ethics of Gender

NEW DIMENSIONS TO RELIGIOUS ETHICS

Series Editors: Frank G. Kirkpatrick and Susan Frank Parsons
Trinity College, Hartford, US, and Margaret Beaufort Institute of Theology, Cambridge, UK

The aim of this series is to offer high-quality materials for use in the study of ethics at the undergraduate or seminary level, by means of engagement in the interdisciplinary debate about significant moral questions with a distinctive theological voice. Each volume investigates a dimension of religious ethics that has become problematic, not least due to the wider climate of reappraisal of Enlightenment thought. More especially, it is understood that these are dimensions which run through a number of contemporary moral dilemmas that trouble the postmodern world. It is hoped that an analysis of basic assumptions will provide students with a good grounding in ethical thought, and will open windows onto new features of the moral landscape that require further attention. The series thus looks forward to a most challenging renewal of thinking in religious ethics and to the serious engagement of theologians in what are most poignant questions of our time.

Published

1. *The Ethics of Community*
Frank G. Kirkpatrick

2. *The Ethics of Gender*
Susan Frank Parsons

3. *The Ethics of Sex*
Mark D. Jordan

Forthcoming

The Ethics of Nature
Celia Deane Drummond

The Ethics of Race
Shawn Copeland

The Ethics of Gender

Susan Frank Parsons

Margaret Beaufort Institute of Theology, Cambridge

BLACKWELL
Publishers

First published 2002

2 4 6 8 10 9 7 5 3 1

Blackwell Publishers Ltd
108 Cowley Road
Oxford OX4 1JF
UK

Blackwell Publishers Inc.
350 Main Street
Malden, Massachusetts 02148
USA

British Library Cataloguing in Publication Data

A CIP catalogue record for this book is available from the British Library.

Library of Congress Cataloging-in-Publication Data

Parsons, Susan Frank.
The ethics of gender / Susan Frank Parsons.
p. cm. — (New dimensions to religious ethics)
Includes bibliographical references and index.
ISBN 0–631–21516–6 (alk. paper) — ISBN 0–631–21517–4 (pbk. : alk. paper)
1. Christian ethics—Roman Catholic authors.   2. Feminist ethics.   I. Title.
II. Series.
BJ1278.F45 P365 2001
170′.82—dc21
2001001140

Typeset in 10½ on 12½ pt Bembo
by Graphicraft Limited, Hong Kong
Printed in Great Britain by Antony Rowe Ltd, Wiltshire

This book is printed on acid-free paper.

For Andrew

Contents

Preface

In the process of writing this book, I have been venturing to follow the trail of thinking with gender through its critical engagement with ethics and with theology. My interest has been held, initially by a rather vague discomforting sense that ethics, and in particular theological ethics, may have come to some kind of an end, and that thinking with gender has been the way in which that end has been encountered. These discomforts have arisen through my teaching of ethics, in which I became aware of such a concentration on the business of solving practical problems and learning the techniques of valuing, that ethics was in danger of losing this opportunity to investigate its own philosophical foundations and its place as a discipline of modern western thinking.

The more closely I considered what was being said in critical theories of gender, initially found in various kinds of feminism and in arguments about sex, the more profoundly I heard this discomfort articulated. For it seems that the discourse called "theory" has arisen in the weak spot of a certain kind of ethical humanism that has become comfortable and resistant, in places, to a self-critique. Thinking with gender is the practice of a hermeneutic of suspicion which renders vulnerable this humanism, and it is the call for reinterpretations and revaluations by which humanity may be set on its way again. Whether this is the way we should go is one of the questions with which this book is concerned.

In taking on this question, I found that a strong wind blew through my mind, generally wrecking the place, so that nothing has been quite the same as before. I have been thrown into the human situation, and into my own living of it, to find myself gripped by an anguish and upheld by a love that are both more profound than I would otherwise have known. For the question of gender reopens the fundamental issues of philosophy in a way that allows nothing to be assumed without thinking, and reaches into the vocation of theology to attend to the things that most trouble humanity and turn them into the love of God. By locating the problematic, critical gender theory may return our philosophical thinking to the matter of truth, and our theological thinking to the cry for redemption as it is heard in the modern, and now postmodern, idiom.

This road is a hard one to take and, although I have tried to smooth out most of the bumps along the way, there are many that remain in my thinking, and thus also in this writing. There is so much I have come upon that I only begin to understand and to be able to articulate, so the text bears some awkwardness of speaking in ways that are new to me. I have tried simply to say what is coming to be known in this thinking today, and to put it into some kind of order for others to follow. If I may accompany those whose desiring of truth also takes them into difficult places, and asks of them that they too become the crucibles in which mercy is to be formed, then this writing will have served its purpose. May the poor pots in which such truth comes to birth be shaped into godly beings for the sake of love.

I am especially grateful to those who have befriended me on this way. My thanks are due to the Margaret Beaufort Institute of Theology, Cambridge, for hospitality in providing a place of study and of prayer in the Lent term of 1998 during which this book began to form; to the Cambridge Faculty of Divinity for its welcome to seminars; to the Peterhouse Theory Group for such interesting discussions; to ordained women in the Church of England in whose various gatherings around the country I have been invited to think aloud; to students of the East Midlands Ministry Training Course and St. John's College, Nottingham for helping me to teach this subject; to Alex Wright (formerly) and Rebecca Harkin (presently) of Blackwell Publishers; to the anonymous reader for such thoughtful attention to the text; and to my friends who have discussed many of these matters with me, especially Chris Cottrell, James Hanvey, Laurence Hemming, Frank Kirkpatrick, Ferdinand Knapp, and Mark Parsons. The book is dedicated to our son, in hope, that his own adventure of living will bring him much joy, that his thinking will always call upon truth, and that his laughter and his tenderness, shared so generously, will keep him in the way of love.

Advent 2000

Introduction

In many ways, the question of gender has become a troubled dimension of contemporary life. It is here that there is an ongoing wonder of our humanity, and in particular of what it is to be woman and what it is to be man. To begin to think about this dimension of our lives is already to anticipate trouble. Some of this is learned from experience. Those who raise questions about gender often find themselves in a place of serious discomfort as their comments are spoken and ramify through the dynamics of a group, and at great cost to themselves, they find that their own ways of life and integrity are placed on the line. Those who have not raised those questions often find that they are under attack for not having done so, and their presumptions and their complacency are challenged, so that their lives too are put at risk. We cannot seem to help the fact that our personal values and behaviour are deeply implicated in the questions gender raises. In addition, by now, few of the groups to which we belong or the institutions of our daily lives have been untouched by gender questions. Most of us live, work, study, and play within contexts that have been affected by some form of a critique of gender, and by a reaction to this critique as these contexts adapt to the challenging questions. Gender disturbs when it appears, and our lives have become shaped by this disturbance. We learn from experience the trouble we can expect from the question of gender, for in it we are asked to be reflective about who we are.

Some of this is learned through attention to contemporary culture. Representations of gender appear in all sorts of artistic expressions that find their way into the culture of our time, and thus into our consciousness as participants in that culture. Novels tell stories of the formation and discovery, of the hiding and blossoming of gender identity. Dramas enact the confusions, the breakdowns, the dynamics, the play of gender relationships. Films portray, paintings reveal, songs express, sculptures embody the issues of gender, that is, those things that issue forth from the raising of the question of gender. These things indicate that gender has come to be an important and a common way of representing ourselves to ourselves. Gender has become an aesthetic avenue through which the human self is being expressed, human relationships are explored, and dilemmas of human living revealed. We absorb these things as we grow up and later become aware of ourselves as persons shaped by culture. What it is to be woman and what it is to be man features in our enculturation in a big way, so that part of the trouble we anticipate as we begin to approach this dimension for consideration is that our own becoming engendered persons within these cultural expressions is itself going to be examined, challenged, and opened to question, and thus also put at risk. For in the question of gender, we are asked to be reflective about who we have come to be as women and men within our common cultural life.

When we seek to examine this cultural phenomenon of gender representations in any depth, to attend to it critically, we encounter a tangled, multilayered and dense complex of issues. It is this complexity that has made gender studies such a richly variegated area for academic enquiry. The emergence of the human sciences, and more recently of critical and cultural theory, has enabled this enquiry in particular ways. By means of these investigative tools, we are encouraged to step back from our involvement in culture, to distance ourselves from what is all around us in the water we swim in, and to raise critical questions about the structures and the forces that determine the characteristic features of the culture to which we belong. Thus we may examine the path of its historical development, the role of its geographical locations, the workings of its ideological persuasions, the formations of its distinctive institutions, the functions of its economy – all of which help us to appreciate how our culture is situated in and amongst other cultures of the world. In each of these dimensions of culture, the question of gender has been opened for examination and critique, a fact to which the growing number of books on gender studies attests. Through these studies, the cultural construction of gender is impressed upon us. We begin to appreciate that we think gender in cultured ways, that we embody cultured gender ideals, and that we hold cultural political and social expectations of gender behavior. The trouble gender brings here is a critical awareness of our being made, of our fabrication, as products of our cultures.

The study of culture brings further trouble as there is a digging deep into the foundations of our ideas and practices. For critical and cultural theories are excavating the groundwork of culture, examining the roots of our thinking. In this archaeological work, we uncover the ways in which present thinking about our humanity has been formed, exposing the underlying structures that support and shape our thinking about gender. We begin to wonder about the history of our understandings of gender, and about how it is that the ideas we now have have been formed, and about how it is that gender has come to be so important for us. In western culture, gender holds a particular fascination. Gender seems to be making itself known and demanding to be made known as a significant dimension of our humanity. Somehow, issues simply are not fully addressed until the matter of gender has been raised and resolved in some way. So gender is part of our contemporary intellectual scene, requiring visible signs of its presence, such that even when it is not declared to be there, or declared not to be there, our critical theoretical apparatus challenges us to uncover what is hidden from view. There is something of an expectation, that something fundamental, essential even, about our humanity will come to be revealed in gender. By means of questioning gender, we seem to expect a breakthrough to a true understanding of our humanness, a full revelation of ourselves to ourselves and to the world. Excavations follow the traces of these hopes that through the trouble of thinking with gender, we will come to know our humanity more fully.

With knowledge may come revaluations. Developing theories seem to promise that with this new critical thinking, we will be able to pry open our ideas and practices today. So we mine the past to provide the resources for changing the present. We examine how ideas and practices of gender have been formed so that we may discover the possibilities, the openings, the ways through into new formations in our day. We investigate the structures of gender thinking to help us to rethink how it is with gender, to find a supply of political and ethical resources for our use now. So, critical studies of culture have brought to our attention the texts of gender that seem everywhere to be scribbled over the fabric of our encultured lives. We weave our individual ways precariously through their traces. To ask about gender is to become aware of, but also importantly to reassess these gendered texts that have already been written. Gender thus comes to be as a sign of the emergence to power of the human person, power over determining texts, so that gender comes to be expressed as the taking of authority over, the right to author one's own texts. In this power, the capacity of human beings to transcend the given is being realized. Every enquiry into gender comes into being bearing this history, and every raising of the question of gender comes to exist in the presence of this question of power, and thus of disputes over power and of encouragement for an empowering. We engage in this enquiry, and are persuaded of the significance of so doing, because by means of it, we believe that we will be enabled to make ours a better culture. Our anticipation of trouble as we approach the dimension of gender in our lives appears as a question about the power of revaluations, and as a question about how this association of gender and power has come to be.

So gender causes trouble in our thinking. It asks us to reflect on who we are as individual women and men. It asks us to consider what we have become in our common cultural heritage. It asks us to think about the ways we are fabricated as cultural products. It asks that we dig into the foundations of our ideas and consider how they have come to be important to us. It asks us to reflect upon the place of gender as the location of a promise for a better culture and a better human life. So Judith Butler was wise in selecting this word for the title of her book, *Gender Trouble*, and for understanding that in considerations of gender, there are subversions of our thinking at work.[1] For the notions of causing trouble and of being troubled are themselves indications that matters of gender lie in a place of brokenness in our culture. These words begin to signify a realization that all is not well in our understanding, that the difference of women and men has become the rift of gender into which modernity has plunged, rendering problematic the thinking of a common humanity. Yet these words signify a hope too, an expectation of a mediation, that in finding another way of speaking and thinking gender we might break through into something new. Gender takes the trouble to bring us to the edge of this promise by subverting our thinking.

Something of an examination of these subversions of our ethical thinking, and of the task of a theological ethics, is what this present book undertakes. For this is a book which seeks to investigate the interface of gender with ethics, and to consider the ways in which a Christian theological ethics informed by gender might come to be shaped. As a preliminary definition, we might suggest that ethics is a discipline of thinking that draws my attention to what might be called good. In so doing, it opens up a way of the shaping of my life in accordance with that which is deemed good, and asks that I play some part in that shaping, and that I give myself over to it. Gender questions challenge nearly every dimension of ethical thinking, and it will be part of our task to investigate these challenges. Thinking with gender puts a question mark over the content of ethical vision and recommendations for practice, by asking in what ways our notions of good are already shaped by assumptions about what women and men are. We are asked to examine these assumptions and to question

---

[1]   Judith Butler: *Gender Trouble: Feminism and the Subversion of Identity* (London: Routledge, 1990).

whether they are themselves ethical. Thinking with gender challenges our modes of ethical reasoning by suggesting that women's ways of thinking may be different from men's ways of thinking. So we are asked to consider for whom ethical deliberation is intended. Thinking with gender calls into question our assumptions about what ethics is, and what the purposes of ethics might be, and thus about the role of ethics in our formation as women and men. We are asked to reflect upon the place of ethics in human life. In all of these challenges, gender raises questions about the ethics of ethics. One of our central concerns will therefore need to be – what is it to engage in a discipline of thinking that attends to what might be called good in such a time as this?

So too, there are subversions of our understanding of theology. Again, we may begin by suggesting that theology is a discipline of thinking myself into the faith I am given. Theology opens to me a way of understanding how it is that I come into a knowing of God, and how it is that in this knowing, there is a being-met by that which is beyond my knowing, and how it is that my life can be gripped by this knowing which will not let me go. As I engage in its ways of thinking, what I think about comes to matter in my life and the mysterious gracefulness of this coming together of humanity and God never ceases to amaze the heart of the theologian. Once again, gender challenges theology by asking in what ways our knowing of God is already a gendered knowing, and our faith already a thoroughly gendered phenomenon. In so doing, it asks whether and in what ways the divine has been made in the image of the human. Thinking with gender looks to the cultural formation of theology and investigates its entanglement with ideas and practices of gender. Thinking with gender excavates the underpinnings of theology to consider the roots of these ways of thinking, in the hope of opening up new ways for the contemporary world. Thinking with gender seeks a liberation of humanity into a more authentic relation with God in which each of us, woman and man, may find ourselves more truly reflected in the presence of God. In all of these ways, theology is challenged to ask whether its thinking about God can be purified of its idolatry through the hermeneutic of suspicion that is gender. These questions too lie within our task here, for another of our central concerns needs to be – what is it to engage in a discipline of thinking myself into the faith I am given through what is being said in the question of gender?

The interface of these two questions forms the matrix for this book. The disciplines from which they arise guide its proceedings. Our central concerns both have to do with thinking, with ways of thinking, with patterns of thinking – all of which is to presume that we cannot help ourselves thinking. Thinking happens. It is what human beings do, perhaps it is even what human beings do best, and in a book which offers a thinking about thinking, we encounter both its unavoidability and its givenness at once. Our questions here have to do with the ways in which we will enter into this thinking. They have to do with believing that somehow in the clarifying of how we go about our thinking through the question of gender comes a sensitivity of friendship, a kindling of generosity, and a pastoral responsiveness to our neighbours. They have to do with risking that in an engagement with the question of gender, with what is so very troubled in our midst, a deepening of understanding may bring us to ourselves in our common humanity. They have to do with trusting that precisely in what we cannot help ourselves to do, the disciplines of ethics and of theology may be turned into their own best efforts. They have to do with hoping that in our thinking the way of a redeeming may come to be opened to us. These questions may thus awaken the vocation of our humanity in an other way, by calling us into what is a reflecting that finds its heart continually thrown open to the coming of God. So this book sets out to examine the interface of gender and ethics. It seeks to engage in a thinking of what might be called good through the enquiry that gender theory has undertaken, and it does so with a mind and heart of faith.

Outline of the Book

In the first chapter we take a preliminary look at the discipline of ethics and at the more recent discourse of gender theory. Some consideration of the key terms and assumptions of each will be needed. We may then become more attentive to what it is that is being said in these ways of thinking, to the strands of overlapping interest and concern, and to those difficult and challenging issues that emerge between them. In this way, the questions and themes of this book may begin to come into focus.

The next two chapters take up the challenges of gender thinking that emerged with the Enlightenment, in the time called modernity. In the first of these, we will explore the challenges of modern feminism, three forms of which have in different ways attempted to work within the terms of the discipline of ethics as understood within modernism. Liberal, naturalistic, and constructionist feminisms have made use of ethical vocabulary and ideas, in order to discover the particular meaning and place of women, and to propose changes that would be consistent with the best potential of ethics for guiding our attainment of the good for human life. A feminist ethics of gender provides one model of the relationship between ethics and gender, so it will be helpful to summarize the ways in which present ethical debate involving questions of gender has been shaped by the trouble feminists have taken.

In the second of these, we will explore the question – Is ethics a man's subject? This question appearing in feminist thinking begins to unravel the modernist ethical project, and demonstrates that feminisms are already anticipations of postmodernity. The opening up of questions regarding the gendered subject of ethical thinking and acting begins to require of us some new thinking about our humanness which can no longer be woven within the fabric of modernism. Thus gender and ethics enter a new time of postmodernity, in which different questions of gender are posed.

Following that sketch of modern developments, there are three chapters which take up some of the changes being wrought within postmodern thinking. These have to do with our thinking about the body and embodiment, about language and subjectivity, and about power and agency. Each of these has to do with a fundamental dimension of our humanness that thinking with gender touches upon. In each of these areas of thinking, there is an overturning of the patterns in which modernity has conceived of these things, and the assumptions that have guided modern enquiries about them. So some investigation of what is being said in postmodern theory may illuminate our considerations of the ethics of gender.

In postmodern theory, there appears a question about what it means to say that the body is a natural biologically given reality, and an investigation of the ways in which the body comes to be as a social construction. In this reversal of modern humanist assumptions, the matter of the appearing of gender with the body may need to be thought in new ways. So too there is a questioning of the existence of a human subject independent of language, and an awareness that the subject may not be the speaker of language but rather the one that is spoken by it. Again this reverses a key dimension of modern humanism, and its implications for the subject of an ethics of gender will need to be considered. Thirdly, there is a challenging of the model of action which appears with the humanist subject, as a producer of deeds, an empowered being, a self as agent. Understanding ourselves to be ones through whom there are enactments taking place turns our thinking over in a way that requires a rethinking of what it is to act ethically.

With these developments, we may begin to appreciate the ways in which the issue of gender lies across the fault lines of the shift from modern to postmodern, in the midst of which we still have to think. The next chapter will consider three forms of an ethics of gender that have been proposed for this context. There is the new humanist universalism of Martha Nussbaum, which places gender into the broader context of human capabilities and flourishing, where it may take its place and discover its guidelines. There is the ethics of transformative practice of Elaine Graham, which finds gender to be an important locus of the work of liberation for full human empowerment. There is the revised natural law ethic of Lisa Sowle Cahill, in which a premodern form of ethical reasoning is adapted and rendered flexible for our newer dilemmas and questions of gender. A comparison of these three forms of the ethics of gender, and a consideration of their different strengths and weaknesses, will help us to summarize some of the main implications of the gender critique of ethics in a postmodern context.

The final three chapters turn to our guiding questions. What is it to engage in a discipline of thinking that attends to what is to be called good in such a time as this? What is it to engage in a discipline of theological thinking through what is being said in the question of gender? It is a key assumption of this work that the event of postmodernity in which we are living opens up to us new ways of thinking for a theological ethics. Thinking with gender contributes to the disruption of modern metaphysics and the ethics derived therein. In so doing, it may free up our thinking in ways that are both more authentic to the human beings that we are and more open to the coming to be of the divine in our midst. The ethics of gender touches upon and brings us towards the three dimensions of a theological ethics – faith, hope, and love – as these have come to the surface in postmodern questions about origins, about subjectivity, and about what it is to interpret. In considering each of these in turn, we may attend to this event and begin to develop a way of thinking for a theological ethics that may faith the redeeming love of God into the hope of our lives.

1

On Ethics and Gender

In this chapter, we undertake a preliminary exploration of the discipline of ethics, which has a long and well-established place in the tradition of western thinking. By bringing some of its major characteristics into focus, we can begin to appreciate its distinctiveness as a way of thinking. We then describe the emerging interest in questions of gender, a modern concern for understanding our humanity that has come to be expressed in gender theory and gender studies. We hope through this exploration that some sense of the interface between these two, this discipline of thinking which is ethics and this theory of our humanity which the question of gender probes, can be clarified.

Entering into Ethics

Three characteristic features of ethics may serve as a framework for our considerations here. First, ethics is a discourse concerning good. It has been a way in which individuals have reflected upon what is to be called good, and in so doing, have drawn others into conversation around this subject, bringing their reflections too into the discussion. To enter into ethics is to learn to participate in this discourse ourselves. Secondly, ethics can be identified as a textual field, now comprising a great many writings that are available to us to read and study, of writings that have played some part in the shaping of western culture and understanding. To enter into ethics is to walk through this field, as persons whose lives have already been written into its thinking. Thirdly, ethics is a deliberative practice. To direct our attention to what is to be called good opens a way for the shaping of our own lives accordingly. Ethics helps us to build the bridges between ourselves and what we call good, and it does so by helping us to think about what we are doing. To enter into ethics is to learn a deliberative practice. Giving a somewhat fuller description of these three features may take us further into this way of thinking.

Ethics as a discourse concerning good

First, then, ethics may be characterized as a discourse, directing our attention toward what is to be called good. In so doing, it draws us into asking ultimate questions of ourselves and of the world. We are brought to wonder about what has been our origin and what is to be our goal, about why it is that our lives have come to be at all and for what purpose we seem to be here. We are drawn to wonder about the wide horizons within which our individual lives happen, and about our human place within this context. In these wonderings, ethics calls us into a thinking about what is so good about living. It asks that we take this question with great seriousness, since in working through its meaning for ourselves, we come to embody the good we are seeking. It asks that we attend to this question of what is to be called good with great care, since the light shed by its beauty and its truth comes to matter with much delicacy of patience and of discernment. The reflections that are nurtured within this discipline of thinking are ways of approaching something that is believed to transcend us, that stands out beyond us, at the same time as this is something to which we ultimately belong, and into which our lives are finally to be given over. This elusive "something" which is to be called good is what ethics draws us towards. It invites our participation.

In the western tradition, there have been two major lines of approach to this good, around which the discourse of ethics has been shaped. One of these has been to enquire into the essence of our humanness. By asking the question – What is it that makes and keeps us human? – it has been thought that we could discover that core essential being that belongs with our humanness, that defining character of our being human, and thus we would know what is good. Once we are able to discern the outlines of this essence that belongs universally to all human beings, once we know who it is that we most fundamentally are, then we will be able to sketch out for ourselves a way of being good in conformity with this essence. Understanding the essence of our humanness gives us what Gerard Hughes has called a "Principle of Humanity."[1] It provides us with a basic ground of

---

[1]   Gerard Hughes, SJ: "Is Ethics One or Many?," unpublished paper given to the Association of Teachers of Moral Theology, UK, cited in Kevin T. Kelly: *New Directions in Moral Theology: The Challenge of Being Human* (London: Geoffrey Chapman, 1992), p. 20.

respect for all human beings and challenges us to find ways of affirming the goodness of all humanity, even across very wide diversities of culture and ways of life. For basically, to know what it is that we essentially are is to discover that element or that substance which holds all human beings in common, and it is this which provides the conception of a good that transcends time and place.

With the emergence of the human and natural sciences during the modern era, it has become more typical for ethicists to locate what makes and keeps us human within the natural rather than the supernatural world. Our humanness comes to be understood less as a kind of ultimate metaphysical essence that transcends time and place, and more as a set of characteristic behaviors or capacities that distinguish the human as a being amongst other beings. What belongs to our humanness distinctively has thus been variously formulated as our ability to reason, as our capacity for using language, or as our formation of a culture. These capacities have been singled out as the good which it is the task of ethics to sustain. Today, for example, there is much investigation of the roots of human ethical thinking and acting in our animal nature, as illuminated by ethology and by sociobiology. Here the truth that "we *are* animals," as Mary Midgley has put it, is understood to be the ground in which our ethical lives can take root.[2] Modern humanism, while more naturalistic in focus, has nevertheless maintained this concern for the upholding of what is distinctively good about human being.

Another line of approach to the good within the western ethical tradition has been to enquire into the end of things. By asking – In what is life fulfilled? – ethical thinkers have sought to discover the purpose of existence, the goal which life is in the process of realizing. It is this which may then be called good. With some conception of this end that holds all things in its direction, it becomes possible to formulate the purposes of individual things, and to shape our human lives toward their own appropriate fulfilment. John Macmurray has called this "thinking the world as one action," and through its conception, human intentions and actions can be set into an overall context of meaning.[3] We can direct our lives in hope towards an end that harmonizes the multiplicity of our choices. This kind of ethical thinking which is teleological, that is, concerned with the *telos* or the end of life, sets before us a conception of the final good as that toward which our own actions are to aim. It is concerned not so much with what

[2] Mary Midgley: *Beast and Man: The Roots of Human Nature* (London: Methuen, 1980), p. xiii.
[3] John Macmurray: *The Self as Agent* (London: Faber & Faber, 1969), p. 204.

we are essentially, than with what is to become of us in the end. By setting before us a vision of ultimate good, our actions are directed into the farthest reaches of the ethical imagination.

This route of enquiry into good has also been affected by developments of thinking during the modern period. As doubt is cast on the belief that there is some intrinsic purpose written within the fabric of nature, so the focus has come to be on the role of the human will itself in establishing the end for which each of us is to strive. To be able to set these goals requires freedom of choice for each individual and some confidence in the efficacy of our decisions. The demand for personal empowerment ensues. Modern ethical thinking about purposes bears the marks of the techno-logical revolution with its emphasis on productivity, so that today we need to justify much of what we do in terms of its practical outcome. We are required to be pragmatic about our decisions, so that we consider their efficacy in bringing about the changes we have chosen to implement. Thus the setting of aims and objectives becomes the accepted practice of the institutions of our common life, and holding all of this in some kind of overall order and system of laws becomes the task of government. Notions of finality become limited to the particular sphere of action for which we are each accountable. So it may be that our best hope in this reading of our historical situation is for the development of an ironic sensitivity one to another.[4]

Through these two questions, ethical enquiry has sought to draw our attention to what is to be called good. In each of them, we come upon an underlying concern of ethics in the western tradition, namely a concern that what is good be located closely within and alongside what is true. Vardy and Grosch express this in claiming that "Before questions about morality and ethics can be addressed, there are prior issues of the nature of truth to be considered."[5] Their book on the puzzle of ethics sets out on an initial exploration of ways in which truth is approached, as a preamble to their consideration of theories and applications of ethics. An enquiry into truth is believed to precede ethical considerations, for truth is to provide something of a foundation for the construction of good, or something of the ultimate horizon within which good can be identified. It becomes the discipline of ethical thinking to remain attached to the light of this truth which then in turn illuminates the good for us. In this way, ethics has

---

[4]   See Richard Rorty: *Contingency, Irony, and Solidarity* (Cambridge: Cambridge University Press, 1989).
[5]   Peter Vardy and Paul Grosch: *The Puzzle of Ethics* (London: HarperCollins, 1994), p. 15.

come to call good that which is in conformity with truth, that which embodies truth, that which is to complete truth in us by the living of our lives. It is the discernment and maintenance of these close links between truth and goodness that has shaped the discipline of thinking that is ethics.

Ethics as a textual field

Entering into ethics as a discourse concerning good is learning to participate in these kinds of questions and searches. We are able to do so today by means of texts that have been written, published, translated, and circulated, and it is these which give us a way into the discussion. This field of texts comprises writings from across a span of many centuries and a diversity of societies. Locating and collecting these together has been a feature of the teaching and study of ethics in the modern period. At first, the interest was in reproducing the texts of classical Greece and Rome, and setting these alongside texts from the Judeo-Christian tradition. Together these still serve as something of a standard of judgment for later works, and provide both the basic vocabulary and broad frameworks of argument with which ethics has to do. Today this textual field has become very wide indeed and its sources more varied than were envisioned in the early days of the Enlightenment. Now texts are gathered into this field from such a very broad range of contexts, that what might constitute a canon of ethics is becoming harder to describe and to locate with any specificity.[6] What has happened is that ethics is becoming both a study of texts, and a study of the field of texts that are available to us, and this is bringing new insights.

One of these new insights has to do with a recognition that there have been developments within ethics throughout history, that ethics is an enquiry which itself is subject to historical changes.[7] While within the

[6] The sheer size of the volumes now being published for the study of ethics gives ample evidence of this growing body of texts. See, e.g., Peter Singer, ed.: *A Companion to Ethics* (Oxford: Blackwell, 1994); Wayne G. Boulton, Thomas D. Kennedy, and Allen Verhey, eds.: *From Christ to the World: Introductory Readings in Christian Ethics* (Grand Rapids, MI: William B. Eerdmans, 1994); William Schweiker and Charles Hallisey: *Companion to Religious Ethics* (Oxford: Blackwell, forthcoming); Robin Gill: *A Textbook of Christian Ethics*, 2nd ed. (Edinburgh: T. & T. Clark, 1995); Ronald P. Hamel and Kenneth R. Himes, OFM, eds.: *Introduction to Christian Ethics: A Reader* (New York: Paulist Press, 1989).

[7] The work of Alasdair MacIntyre, beginning with his *A Short History of Ethics: A History of Moral Philosophy from the Homeric Age to the Twentieth Century* (London: Routledge & Kegan Paul, 1967), has been important here, as in another way has been John Mahoney: *The Making of Moral Theology: A Study of the Roman Catholic Tradition* (Oxford: Clarendon Press, 1989).

discourse of ethics there appears to be an impulse toward what is timeless, what is permanently identified as the end of human life or what stands for all time as the truth of human essence, an awareness of the historicity of the texts makes this less naively plausible. Ethics, like other disciplines of thinking, becomes itself subject to historical investigation, so that it becomes important to us today to ask when a particular text appeared. This historical awareness raises new questions. Doubts arise about whether any historical document, any written text, can or should claim to be more and to know more than it is possible in fact to be and to know from within human history. The historicity of texts can then be used as a reason to debunk their own truth claims, and our claims in using them, for the establishment of what is true beyond history.[8] We may also develop a keener awareness of our own historicity, by asking what it is to think ethically immersed in our time.

Another of these new insights has to do with the contextuality of ethics, in which we note the relationship between the texts of ethics and the wider context in which they are set and out of which they are formed. In his *Textbook of Christian Ethics*, Gill argues for a "sociologically minded approach," which requires consideration of the social determinants and the social significance of particular texts before we compare one set of ideas with another.[9] It has become important to know where texts have originated, in the midst of what political concerns and economic structures they have been formulated, and to what ongoing developments they contribute. Because ethical discourse has expressed a certain impulse toward the universal, toward what is applicable and of relevance to all humanity, this insight raises questions regarding the authority which should be given to texts that are formed in such contingencies. To ask whether these texts can speak for everyone, is to become suspicious that issues and values arising in one context are insinuating themselves into quite different contexts, and may even subdue the particularly different features that lie there. To remind ourselves of the contextuality of ethics becomes a way of seeking to limit the power of texts to speak univocally. Again this brings us to question anew what it is to think ethically within our own place and perspective.

---

[8] For many of us who have studied ethics, the debunking of Aristotle by MacIntyre stands as a model for this kind of critique. When one reads that "All Aristotle's conceptual brilliance in the course of the argument declines at the end to an apology for this extraordinarily parochial form of human existence," ethical enquiry cannot quite be the same again. MacIntyre: *Short History*, p. 83.

[9] Gill: *Textbook*, p. 24.

A third new insight has to do with the intertextuality of ethics, in which the relationship between what is written in this textual field and elsewhere in other fields of enquiry is uncovered and rendered significant. Overlapping concepts and vocabulary become the signals for investigations of the connections between one set of texts and others. On the trail of these connections, we may begin to speculate about the influences that flow between texts, about the patterns that emerge within them separately and between them together, and even about possible common sources which might explain or make sense of these connections. Gender has proved to be a particularly rich theme for this kind of intertextual exploration, since the presence of certain images of gender, of distinctive words about gender, of particular conceptualizations of gender – all of these provide us with material for speculation about the mutual influences of texts and about their common roots or purposes. Insofar as ethics relates intertextually to other kinds of writings, we may again question whether there is unique and important insight to be gained within its own texts, or whether it represents variations on the same themes. Pulling at a single complicated thread, like that of gender, may make the garment of ethics alone unwearable, or it may provide us with a thread which helps us to weave new intertextualities in our conversations and writings for the future.

This consideration of ethics as a textual field is one manifestation of our move into a postmodern time, in which we have begun to ask questions about the formation of our culture during the modern period. We are able to attend to how it is that ethics has been a manifestation of that culture, and how we have been formed within it as ethical thinkers. We come to attend to the ways in which our lives have already been written into the texts within this field, so that we come upon moments of familiarity and of strangeness as we walk into it. Once our critical awareness of the shaping of this field has been raised, we are no longer able to go back on ourselves, to repeat naively the ways of thinking that these texts speak. Before us then lies a question about what it is to be thinking ethically in our time.

Ethics as a deliberative practice

This brings us to ethics as a deliberative practice for the leading of a good human life. The discourse concerning good which has shaped its discipline has been held within a certain space, a territory that was given to it to explore, a location within what some now call the domain of truth. Where truth has reigned, there ethics could provide its maps, opening up its two routes to the good which truth sustains, along which ethical thinkers could travel freely back and forth, in conversation as they journey. The expectation has been that a certain knowledge would be available along these routes, which could be transported from one site to another. What I would learn as I explore the matter of the essence of being human, I could then translate into my actions, by using the knowledge of human nature as a guide in the formulation of principles for my decisions. What I might learn as I consider how it is that the world is gathered up into a fitting end, I could use in a practical way for the reorienting of my life in a healthy direction, keeping this end in view as I go forward purposefully. Ethics has negotiated this move from the good that truth upholds to my personal life and decision-making. Its value has been in this work of mediation which deliberates first before doing anything, thinks before acting.

Such an understanding of the deliberative practice of ethics reveals the extent to which ethics has been a loyal servant of truth, carrying out its assigned duties diligently and forming human lives according to the certainties of its vision. To think ethically has been to be drawn into this obedience personally, to give the good that truth sustains our own allegiance. Yet all is not well in the kingdom of truth. There is a restlessness around the place indicative of a certain lack of peacefulness and good order. This comes about partly through philosophical disputes regarding the nature of truth that now bother the work of ethical thinking in its reliance upon this authority. Whether truth is one or many, whether the knowing of it is relative or absolute, whether it yields knowledge of what is real or expresses the human will to know it – these unresolvable debates unsettle the deliberative practice which ethics is to embody. This comes also through theological critique of ethics, which wonders about the relationship of God and the good. Whether God is understood to be bound to an autonomously established order of truth in which goodness stands, or whether God is its author and ultimate source, is a continuing question for theological ethics. In asking it, we are trying to understand what it is to have a mind and heart of faith as we enter into ethics.

So it is that the deliberative practice which is ethics enters into a postmodern time, in which there is an undermining of the settled landscape of the moral life. The destruction of the regime of truth and of its divine authority has been well underway since Friedrich Nietzsche spoke the death of God at the end of the nineteenth century.[10] So, too, our

---

[10]   Friedrich Nietzsche: *The Gay Science*, trans. Walter Kaufmann (New York: Vintage, 1974).

human self-understanding has been disturbed since Søren Kierkegaard turned the question of truth, inside out, into a question of my subjectivity.[11] Today, what it is to think and what it is to act are no longer straightforward matters that can be taken for granted. The translation which ethics performed cannot be carried out in the same way as before, since, without the horizon of meaning in which its maps can be interpreted, we are turned anew into our humanity, poured out into the world to find our way by another means. Because the question of gender appears with our humanity, because it has come to be woven into the fabric of our self-understanding, to think of the ethics of gender is to be continually reminded of this exposure, this openness into which our being human is called. To follow the lines of enquiry that emerge with postmodernity, is to enter anew into an interpretative work in which the deliberative practice that is ethics may come into its own in another way.

Thinking with Gender

Gender is implicated in these matters, for it figures as a disruptive thread of argument – undermining certainties of truth, behaving badly, cutting across normal expectations, troubling what is natural, and turning over our thinking. Gender has arisen as a category of thinking in which our humanity is reflected. As such, it reveals what we understand ourselves to be and allows us to represent our humanity in particular ways. At the same time, it calls into question this self-understanding and engages in critique of these very representations. This dual character of gender thinking, which allows both a revealing in and withdrawal from representation, is perhaps the most striking feature of present debates, and the one which makes the ethics of gender such a rich and complex discourse.

To think with gender suggests in the most general sense to think with what it is to be woman and to be man, in the midst of our human situation, immersed in daily experiences, filled with ordinary dilemmas and wonderings, formed in thinking by culture and language. Gender is one of the ways in which we think differences, so that it stands as a marker of what is unique to woman and to man, and it allows us to wonder why and how it is that we are not alike. So, too, it is one of the ways in which we think our common humanity, about what it is that makes us beings

[11] Søren Kierkegaard: *Concluding Unscientific Postscript*, trans. David F. Swenson (Princeton, NJ: Princeton University Press, 1968).

who are able to live together, to communicate with each other, to love one another, and to form relationships. Thinking with gender is thus a form of human self-reflection, which has taken up its place especially within the human sciences that have attended to this outpouring of ourselves wholly into our world. Gender also is characteristic of our language. Because western thinking is conducted in the medium of Indo-European languages, the fact that our languages are gendered has its impact upon the things that we can say, think, and understand, and upon the structures of our thinking. Recognising this linguistic dimension of gender is a way of acknowledging that there is not a place outside of language where we can stand to challenge what is given to us through the languages in which we think. Because gender has to do with what we understand ourselves to be and because it has to do with the language in which we think and communicate, it touches fundamental matters of our living and being human. When we are thinking with gender, we are in the midst of these matters, unable to treat them with complete detachment because we cannot leave our humanity behind while we think about them, and unable to find another way to think about them because our language goes with us wherever we go.

At the same time, gender is a critical way of thinking our humanity, which calls into question the forms of our thinking, our assumptions, and our methods. In recent decades, there has been a growing interest in gender as a category of critical theory, as ways of understanding our humanity that have emerged with the Enlightenment in the west are being questioned. It is no longer straightforward to assume that gender is some-thing given by nature, or that it is universally the same. Suspending these assumptions, questions appear about the construction of gender within human social experience, and about the moulding of the human person within a gendered framework. Within critical thinking of the nineteenth century comes the distinction between sex, thought to be a natural char-acteristic of our bodies, and gender, thought to be a cultural characteristic of our social bodies. Around this distinction, gender theory and gender studies begin to be formed, marking out a field of academic investigation within which explorations of the formation and the influence of this cultural characteristic can be conducted. In gender studies, there is both a critique of our received ways of thinking about ourselves, and a demon-stration of the social construction of our human being in language and in cultural representations. For some, gender studies leads into a political programme of resistance and of change to social structures, and into a personal agenda of troubling and of affirming one's identity. The basic shape of this thinking with gender can be sketched here.

Gender and biology

In western thinking, biology emerged in the nineteenth century as that science of life which attends to the fundamentals of nature and of human life within a natural context. As an investigation of the physical nature of life, biology offers a way of understanding the forms and structures of physical bodies, along with their normal characteristics and functions, and suggests some explanations of their origins and of their patterns of living. Because biology addresses what are considered to be foundational aspects of our very life, it has held a place of privilege in modern western thinking. To be able to ground gender in the realities of the physical world that this science opens up, to be able to demonstrate the appearing of gender in the forms of natural bodies, holds a certain promise of truth. For to know these things would be to know what is most real and most natural, and thus to be able to grasp the foundations of gender itself. Yet gender is a self-critical category, and so it is that also in the nineteenth century appears the challenge to this thought of what is natural, and the unsettling of our investment in biology as the foundational science of human life.

The work of Thomas Laqueur has been helpful here in tracing this development. He argues that the word "gender" shifted in meaning, from the notion of that which belonged to a common genus, to the notion of that which distinguishes members of the same kind, and that modern biology contributed to this shift. Here, gender appears as a sexual differentiation between the male and the female members of living species, and is understood to be a defining feature of higher forms of life, and thus especially of the human form. To study life is to come to terms with this sexual difference and to appreciate both its impact and its explanatory power. Thus, Laqueur investigates closely the invention of sex as we know it during the late eighteenth century, when "two sexes . . . were invented as a new foundation for gender."[12] The continual development of new techniques and equipment for the investigation of life opened up to biologists the connections between this sexual difference and a number of further ones, between, for example, sexual organs, muscle structure, hormonal cycles, and more recently, chromosomal patterns and genetic make-up, all of which lend themselves to empirical examination. In this sense, the delineation of sexual difference as the basis for gender could be considered a most significant element of a particularly fruitful scientific paradigm, within which humanity could find itself reflected.

[12] Thomas Laqueur: *Making Sex: Body and Gender from the Greeks to Freud* (Cambridge, MA: Harvard University Press, 1992), p. 150.

Gender appears as a critical category in the first instance, as it calls into question all that comes to be associated with this difference, and in particular, the identification of gender with sex. For along with the descriptions of physical characteristics, has come a long list of qualities, of activities, of attributes, of tendencies, of social roles, and of virtues which are held to be associated with these apparent facts of life. It is a gender question to ask about the connection between these, about the links between biological facts and social facts, and to pose the challenge that this connection is a human fabrication. These links are forged. So essential can this connection seem to be, however, that everything to do with gender distinctions can be thought to be natural, belonging somehow to the way things are, forming some kind of essence of what makes us and keeps us women and men. It is precisely this assumption of naturalness, of givenness, of essential-ness that gender questions question. Laqueur thus writes:

> The dominant, though by no means universal, view since the eighteenth century has been that there are two stable, incommensurable, opposite sexes and that the political, economic, and cultural lives of men and women, their gender roles, are somehow based on these "facts." Biology – the stable, ahistorical, sexed body – is understood to be the epistemic foundation for prescriptive claims about the social order.[13]

As a result of this kind of challenge, the word "gender" begins to be used for those qualities, activities, attributes, tendencies, social roles, and virtues that are fabricated, made up in the midst of changing social practices and structures, and that come to shape the lives of women and men within particular societies, while the word "sex" begins to be used for the difference that biology relies upon so crucially.

In the second instance, however, gender appears as a critique of thinking as it calls into question the necessity with which this distinction, this biological differentiation between male and female members of a living species, is believed to be true at all. At this point, thinking with gender turns to subvert, not the associations that are constructed upon the foundations of biology, but the substantive claims that are its own foundation. The impact of this sexual difference was believed to be profound, for it came to seem that living things depend upon it for the continuation of the species to which they belong, and for the variety of living things that do exist. Life simply would not be in the forms in which we know it, were it not for this difference, and the ultimacy with which this claim is felt and

---

[13]   Laqueur: *Making Sex*, p. 6.

believed gives the sexual differentiation a crucial place in this science. It is helpful for thinking with gender that Michel Foucault has so carefully illuminated the way in which this basic belief in Life was formed in the appearance of modern biology. Life came to be understood as the essential underlying drive that sustains us in the created order. It "becomes a fundamental force," the experience of which is "posited as the most general law of beings, the revelation of that primitive force on the basis of which they are." Life, he suggests, "functions as an untamed ontology" and in its formulation the imposition of sexual differentiation has a most crucial part to play.[14] To notice the appearance of sexual difference in modern biology is to uncover also this foundational assumption regarding life upon which it is itself constructed. For if this distinction is seen to be simply one among many possible interesting ways of understanding living things, if we begin to question the notion of life which essentially carries this distinction, then we begin to pose the possibility that this way of understanding, through this kind of biology, may have its limitations. It may not reveal us to ourselves in the ways that we had expected. The troubling of biology that is undertaken by thinking with gender brings the matter of nature and of life into consideration in the ethics of gender.

Gender and the human sciences

Thinking with gender has found an important place within the full range of human sciences through which we investigate the nature and the forms of humankind, the styles and the patterns of personal and social life. In anthropology and psychology, in sociology and political science, gender has figured in its dual capacity, both to require that the matter of what it is to be gendered be brought to the surface, and to criticize the assumptions of gender operative within these sciences. Since these ways of thinking our humanity emerge with the Enlightenment, such disciplines bear the marks of its interest in providing better explanations and in drawing better maps of humanity than had previously been available. The great energy and enthusiasm, the confident expectation in which they were born, carry their disciples out from Europe into distant regions of the world, back into times past in search of how things once were, and deep into structures of the human mind. In all of this is a belief that humanity may be revealed to itself, may come to know itself more fully, and may come to better ways of living as a result. Gender appears in three critical areas within the

---

[14]   Michel Foucault: *The Order of Things: An Archaeology of the Human Sciences* (London: Routledge, 1997), p. 278.

discourses of these sciences, the asking of its questions unsettling the humanist faith out of which they are made.

Gender raises its questions in relation to the universal scope of claims made by these sciences, as they generalize about humanity. Statements made regarding what women and men always everywhere are and do, or regarding the universal place of gender in the organization of human social life, are challenged, and we are asked to reconsider both the logic and the function of these assertions in our understanding. As empirical generalizations, they clearly serve and have served very productively in the generation of research projects to test their validity. Once they claim to be grounded in some more certain knowledge, to be known otherwise than by observation and experience, they expose their own limits as standpoints, as perspectives, from which humanity is viewed. Likewise gender raises its questions in relation to the search for origins – for the roots of economic practices, or the primitive forms of social order, or the early formations of the *polis* as a public space. Here the expectation of discovering the pristine moment, the root experience, out of which present practices and forms of life have developed is suspected of bearing existing needs and interests into the past. So while the traffic in women, or the emergence of the private household, or the taboos attached to bodies, may be granted explanatory power to illuminate the ways we now live, these discoveries may also mask the strangeness of the past and its ways to us. So, too, gender raises its questions regarding the structures of the human mind. Laqueur again argues that "if structuralism has taught us anything it is that humans impose their sense of opposition onto a world of continuous shades of difference and similarity."[15] The pattern of dualistic thinking that manifests itself in gender difference is taken to have the most profound consequences in the philosophical tradition as in the psychic life of an individual. Yet gender itself both embodies and eludes the structures meant to contain it and, in its exceeding our thought, seems still to beckon us beyond ourselves.

In each of these areas of enquiry, the human sciences have come to rely upon biology as something of a foundational discipline, through which what is real and true about humanity could be grasped and used in ethical deliberation. For gender to challenge the basis of this human understanding, to criticize the biologism that lies within the hermeneutic of modern humanism, is to begin to open a critical way of thinking about our thinking about ourselves. What we can claim to be universally true of human beings, what we believe lies within human origins, what we understand to

[15] Laqueur: *Making Sex*, p. 19.

be the workings of the human mind – gender comes in each place with its hermeneutic of suspicion to question the assumptions that shape the human sciences, and what it means for women and men to think in this way. In each of these instances, gender challenges what have been taken to be formative discourses of human understanding throughout the modern period, in terms of which human life, human nature, and human purposes could be formulated and sustained. To question these discourses is to begin to probe into the appearance of the human itself as an object of study, and to begin to wonder with Foucault why and how it is that "Before the end of the eighteenth century, *man* did not exist. . . ."[16] We have come to understand ourselves, how we have come to be during our history, what language we have used to speak our being, how these forms of knowing and speaking enfold our knowing and speaking of God – all of these are questions that gender brings with it. Gender theory provides a way of thinking with these questions as, in its diverse manifestations, we may engage through it in a critique of modern humanism.

For gender questions are shaped by a skepticism regarding our knowledge of ourselves, and by an awareness of the construction of our schemes of knowledge in history and through culture. That these questions simultaneously continue the critical thinking of the Enlightenment and unsettle the sciences that have emerged within its purview, is characteristic of postmodern thinking with gender, which is where we are today. The gender critique exposes that "instability of difference and sameness" which, Laqueur writes, "lies at the very heart of the biological enterprise, in its dependence on prior and shifting epistemological, and one could add political, grounds."[17] That this same instability is notable in the human sciences generally is the crucial nerve of our thinking that gender touches. Implicated in this critique is a further one which bears also on our interest here, namely that gender theory is questioning what has been taken to be a primary ground of ethics during modernism. To believe that ethics is founded in our biology, that those biological realities form a given human nature which expresses itself in differing social systems and makes itself powerfully manifest in the perilous life of the individual person, is part of our modern intellectual inheritance in the west. It finds expression again in collections like Peter Singer's, which opens with a chapter on "The Origins of Ethics" in the matrix of animal social life.[18] Whether this any longer can furnish a unifying discourse for all humanity, whether it is

---

[16]   Foucault: *Order*, p. 308.
[17]   Laqueur: *Making Sex*, p. 17.
[18]   Mary Midgley: "The Origin of Ethics," in Singer: *Companion*, pp. 3–13.

2

Feminism as an Ethics of Gender

Some ways of ethical thinking with gender have been demonstrated within the various forms of feminism that have been developing since the time of the Enlightenment. Participating in the political and social changes brought about in western Europe and North America, and sharing in the new movements of thought that are shaped at this time, feminisms develop their own distinctive characteristics within and contributions to these developments. Modern feminisms have presented three rather different ways of entering into ethics, and it will be helpful for us here to have a sketch of these.[1] Each way has operated with a distinctive form of discourse concerning good and has sought to direct our attention to this good and to the ways of realizing it with special reference to women. Each has offered a particular perspective on the textual field of ethics, engaging as women in critical readings of these texts that challenge what may be found or assumed to be there. Each has contributed to an understanding of ethics as a deliberative practice and has encouraged women in particular to take up this ethical deliberation as a way of making a difference to their lives. By attending to these three dimensions of feminist ethics in each section of this chapter, we can see how forms of feminist thinking address the matter of our humanity.

These forms of address are situated within the construction of a new humanism born out of the fervour for change that characterized the appearance of modernism. This humanism appears as a set of fundamental affirmations of the human being as the one who knows, the one who values, and the one who effects changes within the world. Not only is a central importance claimed for the human being in occupying such a

---

[1] Fuller descriptions of these may be found in Susan Frank Parsons: *Feminism and Christian Ethics* (Cambridge: Cambridge University Press, 1996).

pivotal role, but this claim carries with it assumptions of universality and of inclusiveness. To be able to consider that all human beings share in a set of common characteristics, or a common human nature, provides the framework within which modern ethical thinking has been constructed. It is in this context that thinking with gender becomes the predominant critical tool of feminisms. Listening to what is now a worldwide discussion taking place within these forms of feminism, one can hear a recurring question – what about women? In searching for the answer to this query, feminist thinking with gender has been formulated. Therefore, each of the forms of feminist ethics makes explicit the place and the significance of gender within an overall understanding of our humanity. In this work, feminisms are thus both dependent upon and critical of the humanism out of which they appear. The three sections of this chapter analyse and reflect upon these different ways of thinking ethically with gender.

An Ethic of Equality

The earliest works of modern feminism share in the enthusiasm for political and intellectual change that characterizes the birth of liberalism. Believing that humanity was to be freed from economic structures that benefit the privileged at the expense of the masses, from religious authority that restricts freedom of thinking and believing, and from political institutions that restrict access to power, liberalism manifests an optimism for a better future in this world that humanity can effectively bring about. Liberal feminism joins the voices of women to this reforming spirit by seeking to understand and to express the implications of such freedoms for women. The basic characteristic of this feminist ethic of gender is the requirement to bring about in reality, in the new political and religious institutions, in new forms of social organization and in our ways of thinking, the proclamation of a universal human nature in which gender seems to have no logical hold. Therefore this is an ethic of gender which asserts that there is no fundamental difference between women and men, in any of the qualities or capacities that count in what is understood to be our basic human essence, and thus which seeks to realize that belief in political and social, philosophical and theological reformations.

Indications of this may be found in the discourse concerning good which lies within liberal feminist ethics. Here our attention is drawn to the goodness of human being itself. To be fully human is the highest calling of each individual, understood both as an intellectual realization of the capacities of the human mind for knowledge, and as a spiritual vocation to become the human beings made by God in the divine image. In this there is a call for each one of us to become a person in our own right. So Mary Wollstonecraft proclaims that "the first object of laudable ambition is to obtain a character as a human being, regardless of the distinction of sex; and that secondary views should be brought to this simple touchstone."[2] Central to this notion of full humanity is a fundamental equality of human beings, such that what is understood to be human about us is, by definition, something that is shared by, or given to each one of us equally. Liberal feminists affirm that this equality is grounded in the facility we have as human beings for reasoning and for understanding, a capacity to think in which it is believed that distinctions of gender have no fundamental part to play. Emphasis on the capacity for reason may be seen as a development of the theological insight, that individual persons are created by God to be both responsive to and responsible for the hearing and obeying of the word of God. This God-given nature with which we are made to be distinctive creatures provides the foundation for the feminist affirmation that "the common possession of reason and moral conscience" now refers "to the actual capacities of men and women as finite, historical persons."[3] So liberal feminism becomes the secular form of a one-nature theological anthropology.[4]

Moving through the textual field of ethics, liberal feminists look for precedents for this way of thinking with gender, and have encouraged the use of these writings in the forming and guiding of ethical practice today. Working with the notion of a fundamental goodness of human nature shared equally by women and men provides both a perspective from which to judge the rational validity of ethical texts, and a platform upon which to criticize or reject those that fail this test. Early on in contemporary feminism, Plato was singled out as possibly the first feminist philosopher, for in the Republic it was recognized that women within the elite could be freed from various physical and social constraints on their lives in order to exercise political responsibility alongside their brothers. This suggested to feminists that Plato at least affirmed the basic capacity of women to reason in the same way as men, and thus also to be responsible citizens

[2]   Mary Wollstonecraft: *A Vindication of the Rights of Woman*, reprinted in Alice S. Rossi, ed.: *The Feminist Papers* (New York: Bantam Books, 1973), p. 42.
[3]   Rosemary Radford Ruether: *Sexism and God-Talk: Towards a Feminist Theology* (London: SCM Press, 1983), p. 103.
[4]   See Mary Aquin O'Neill: "The Mystery of Being Human Together," in Catherine Mowry LaCugna, ed.: *Freeing Theology: The Essentials of Theology in Feminist Perspective* (San Francisco: HarperCollins, 1993).

of the *polis*, and even thoughtful philosophers too. For theologians, the canonical and interpretative texts of the religious traditions are scrutinized for their attentiveness to this creation motif. For feminists in the western religious traditions of the book, this has meant close exegesis of the accounts of the creation of woman and man to determine whether and in what ways an equality of gender is written there. For Christian feminists, the proclamation of a new creation in Christ, in which St. Paul asserts there is neither male nor female and which calls people into a discipleship of equals that is to become the church, becomes the key text for an ethic in which gender difference is not to make any difference.[5]

More recent Enlightenment writings have been significant for the emergence of the deliberative practice which this ethic of equality promotes. The Kantian metaphysics of morals which requires the formulation of the moral law as a categorical imperative that is universally applicable, and which places responsibility for obedience to it upon the free will of each individual person, has become a significant text for this ethic. In particular, Kant's insistence upon freedom as the *sine qua non* of the human person, that is to be expressed morally as a respect for persons as ends-in-themselves, is taken as a foundation for the dignity of all persons regardless of any social, biological, or historical factors that shape their lives.[6] So also have the texts of utilitarianism been important for their basic affirmation of the human search for happiness in this life. That we should seek the greatest happiness for the greatest number of people was understood by Harriet Taylor and John Stuart Mill to mean, as a matter of calculation, that the quality of women's lives is of consequence for the wellbeing of the whole social order. Such notions find their way into contemporary ethical writings that provide the theoretical framework for the notions of justice within which liberal feminism conducts its political thinking. John Rawls's description of the "original position," in which the ethical decision-maker does not know the circumstances of her own life in order to ensure a dispassionate and fair result, is one significant textual presentation of this gender blindness that is important to a just and rational social ordering.[7] Likewise the art of "enlarged thinking" from Habermas embodies this concern for a

---

[5] Galatians 3:28. See Elisabeth Schüssler Fiorenza: *In Memory of Her: A Feminist Theological Reconstruction of Christian Origins* (London: SCM Press, 1983) for an account of the formation of this discipleship of equals as the church.

[6] Immanuel Kant: *Groundwork of the Metaphysic of Morals*, trans. H. J. Paton (New York: Harper Torchbooks, 1964): "Freedom must be presupposed as a property of the will of all rational beings," pp. 115–16.

[7] John Rawls: *A Theory of Justice* (Oxford: Oxford University Press, 1972), pp. 17–22.

moral point of view from which the general interest may be discovered by reasoned argument.[8]

In general, liberal feminism challenges as unjust those texts that merely reproduce the cultural context or the historical situation out of which they were written, without giving due attention to the rational formulation of principles for the enhancement of our common humanity. Because such principles are thought to be timeless and universally applicable, there is a sense in which they are not to be compromised by special circumstances or pleading, and thus a sense in which the demand for conformity to them is a stringent one. That gender justice is to extend not only throughout the public world but also into the private world of the family is an indication of this exceptionless approach to the norm of equality.[9] In theological ethics, this becomes a prophetic awareness that the will of the Creator transcends and challenges the boundaries we set up to limit its influence. Jewish and Christian liberal feminists have understood these protective borders to be assertions of male privilege that reproduce the social status and religious and political power of men over women. In this sense, they are taken to be instances of sinful impulses resistant to the will of God, which is intended for all and not for the few, and which challenges all worldly orders with its demand for obedience. Ruether's critique of the sexism of the Christian tradition is perhaps the most thorough reading of the textual field with this touchstone in mind. So her most recent book, in which she traces the history of "the Christian claim of a universal and inclusive redemption in Christ," opens with a guiding question for the investigation: "If women are equally redeemed by Christ, why has the Christian church continually reinforced sexism in society and in the church?"[10]

With this foundation in a common human nature, liberal feminists appeal for women to take up the challenge of their full humanity so that they too may be included, recognized, and accepted as persons with the same dignity and freedom as their brothers. This comes to be expressed politically as a demand for rights, and morally as a requirement for consistency in the distribution and sustenance of these rights. Setting out with the human rights to which each person is entitled, feminists encourage the

---

[8] Jürgen Habermas: "Discourse Ethics: Notes on a Program of Philosophical Justification," in *Moral Consciousness and Communicative Action*, trans. Christian Lehnhardt and Shierry Weber Nicholsen (Boston: MIT Press, 1990), p. 43 ff.

[9] See, e.g., Susan Moller Okin: *Justice, Gender and the Family* (New York: Basic Books, 1989).

[10] Rosemary Radford Ruether: *Women and Redemption: A Theological History* (London: SCM Press, 1998), p. 1.

reform of social institutions of all kinds, a vast and still uncompleted project in which women throughout the world are now involved. To fulfill it means a close and careful working-out of a whole range of equalities, specified in ever greater detail, but involving most generally, equality of opportunity, equality of representation, equality of conditions, and equality of freedoms. To develop the forms of these equalities, to challenge any resistance to their presence within institutions, and to keep a close check on the progress of equality for women become the major ethical tasks of liberal feminism. In this work, there is a continuing demand for visible signs of the affirmation of this common human nature, for tangible indicators of its presence that are measurable, so that we can assure ourselves of the progress we are making in its realization.

This very insistence intensifies the problem of evil in the form of sexist attitudes and patriarchal structures that do not live up to these principles, and that constantly render women invisible and devalued. This ethic of gender must therefore both insist upon the presence of women in particular in taking up their fair share of human freedoms and responsibilities, and at the same time affirm that the particular differences between women and men are not to be valued in themselves, but are the consequence of human failure to conform to the ideals of our own humanness. Thus women are to appear only to disappear. They are to be present as women only to efface themselves as women in particular. They are to emphasize difference as a consequence of sin, only to seek its ultimate eradication in a new order of complete equality. There are some real practical and pastoral considerations here for women whose lives are constructed out of the difference which is no difference, and thus who are to assert what is ultimately an empty affirmation of their distinctiveness only to erase it again. This reveals one of the conundrums that lies within this form of an ethics of gender. Having based itself on an understanding of our humanity in which gender cannot get a hold, in which it is affirmed that women are like men in all salient characteristics and capacities of personhood, it nevertheless works out as a special attending to and pleading for women. The question of women's difference haunts this form of feminism, making it particularly vulnerable to that pithy question of Luce Irigaray, "Égales à qui?"[11]

Yet this ethic of equality has been of profound influence in the shaping of political and moral thinking in the contemporary world. Perhaps the statements contained in a document like the UN Universal Declaration of Human Rights attempt the most full expression of its ideal of a just social

---

[11] Luce Irigaray: "Equal to Whom?," *differences, A Journal of Feminist Cultural Studies*, 1:2 (1988), pp. 59–76.

order in which differences of gender, race, nationality, or creed are not to be admitted as significant determinants of opportunity, representation, conditions of life, and basic human freedoms. Because the extension of this ideal has still so much distance to cover in order to realize its universality, and because its affirmation requires visible signs that register the changes made in favor of inclusiveness, there is a great deal yet to do in its service. That this common pledge of peoples across national boundaries may provide a framework for world order, and may develop the conditions for the peaceful and full flourishing of human life, is the hope sustaining efforts today for the elimination of all forms of discrimination based on gender.[12] So also this ethic is the one that supports efforts within religious groups for the full involvement of women in all levels of responsibility and areas of work. That synagogue, church, and mosque should also represent the affirmation of the full humanity of their adherents in their structures is the consistent regard for the common humanness of women and men which this ethic requires.

An Ethic of Difference

A feminism which lays positive claim to the differences of women and men presents another ethic of gender, opening to women a way of thinking ethically in their own terms. Contemporary with liberals have been those feminists who emphasized the natural differences of women and men, and who attempted in the recognition of these distinctive qualities or characteristics to revalue them as equal to, if not actually superior to, those of men. Naturalistic feminism arose along with Romantic notions of human nature, found also within the Scottish Enlightenment, placing greater emphasis upon the emotions in personal life and upon involvement in the natural world, as the resources for the living of a full and good human life. Fundamental to this approach is the belief that we are born as gendered persons, either as women or men, and thus that the notion of a universal humanity held within us is an abstraction. This is therefore an ethic which asserts that women and men are different all the way down, that gender is written throughout the fabric of our lives, and that what is needed is a social order of roles and relationships in which our gendered identities can

---

[12] The websites for the United Nations provide the relevant documents, including the *Universal Declaration of Human Rights*, the *European Convention on Human Rights*, and a reference guide for *The Human Rights of Women*. <http://www.un.org/Overview/rights.html>

come to be manifested. The appeal of this understanding of what is true and good about our humanness is its affirmation of what is natural, and its recommendation that a social order in which differences are allowed to flourish in a balanced and complementary way will be the most fulfilling for women and men together.

The discourse concerning good conducted within this ethic finds itself in another current of Enlightenment thinking, that locates the essence of our humanness in our embodied natures. The goodness of our human being is grounded in qualities that arise from our nature to express themselves in different ways in our reasoning and in our choosing. In these processes of thinking and deciding, we manifest the different natures that belong to us as women and men. What is good is not found therefore in the abstract exercise of self-reflection, but is known more intuitively to be interwoven with our biological makeup. This means that the forms of our bodies as sexed bodies, with differing organs and hormones, differing physical cap-abilities and bodily constructions, make a difference too to the ways in which the goodness of being human is experienced and expressed. These expressions of the good that is our essential nature become the values that shape our relationships and our actions, so there is a sense in this ethic of needing to be true to oneself, of seeking to be authentic to the gendered person that I am. Theologically, this emphasis is found in a two-nature theological anthropology, "an anthropology of complementarity, as it came to be known . . . in which the sexes complete one another, not only on the level of reproduction, but in the full range of human existence. . . ."[13] Such a "bipolar vision of the sexes," as O'Neill calls it, affords us different perspectives on what is good, different ways of addressing its practical requirements, and different spheres of activity in which we realize that good in our daily lives.

The novelty that emerges as this form of feminism appears with the Enlightenment is an insistence from women that the different nature they are be revalued. This requires of feminists a difficult and oppositional reading of the textual field of ethics, in which women have been buried alive by patriarchal writing. Because this ethic of difference is understood to be the most persistent and enduring account of gender in the western tradition, the new work brought with modern humanism requires a reassessment of the way things stand between women and men. The circulation of those texts most offensive to women, and the immensely popular writings of someone like Mary Daly, who so sharply and wittily exposes their malevol-ence, are evidence of a fitting disrespect for a tradition that puts women down in order to elevate men. So Daly argues that man-made myths of

[13]   Aquin O'Neill: "Mystery," p. 149.

procession from and return to a father-god are generated out of man's self-love, to form the necrophiliac patriarchal order that is "the prevailing religion of the entire planet."[14] Rather than taking the nature of women to be inferior or dangerous, evaluations which may be found in traditional accounts, naturalistic feminists called for a new awareness of the positive and creative capacities which belong with women's embodiment and which express themselves in life-giving and caring activities in the world. These are to be given their due. They are to be revalued as essential to the balance of a social order, to the sustenance of life itself, and to the nurturing of peacefulness in the world.

The exposure of the gendered nature of the textual field brings feminists of difference to consider the resources that might be available for a revaluation of differences by an overturning of man's rule. In this work, there are two strategies. One of these is to seek to recover those buried traditions of women's writing that have been forgotten or overwritten by men. This is archaeological work in the tradition, which digs carefully into the richly layered soil of texts and pieces together fragments that may speak another way. In theology, the recovery of "the memory of her" in biblical writings is an example of this approach which attempts "a feminist theological reconstruction of Christian origins" from the fragments. Patriarchy, Schüssler Fiorenza argues, "must not be allowed to cancel out the history and theology of the struggle, life, and leadership of Christian women who spoke and acted in the power of the Spirit."[15] This strategy also calls for work in uncovering the origins of philosophy, in which the thinking of women lies hidden, so that women today may believe of themselves that they too might be philosophers.[16] Another strategy of revaluation is for women to abandon the tradition altogether in order to engage in a new writing, in the production of texts that manifest the difference that women are. This way of entering the textual field is suspicious of what are called recoveries, since these may serve only to justify and extend the authority of the tradition. Instead, what is called for is a new thing altogether, a writing of the feminine, in which a new ethics will emerge.[17] These strategies resonate with biblical understanding that divine wisdom is a disruptive

[14] Mary Daly: *Gyn/Ecology: The Metaethics of Radical Feminism* (London: The Women's Press, 1984), pp. 37–9.

[15] Schüssler Fiorenza: *Memory*, p. 36.

[16] See, e.g., Michèle Le Doeuff: *Hipparchia's Choice: An Essay Concerning Woman, Philosophy, etc.*, trans. Trista Selous (Oxford: Blackwell, 1991).

[17] See the description of *écriture féminine* in Hélène Cixous: "The Laugh of the Medusa," trans. Keith and Paula Cohen, in Elaine Marks and Isabelle de Courtivron, eds.: *New French Feminisms: An Anthology* (Brighton: Harvester Press, 1986).

presence in the world, bringing what has been on the margins into the centre. That women as "the silent outsiders to revelation" should become its living witnesses is the hope out of which this writing is conducted.[18]

The deliberative practice within this ethic of difference requires women's own consciousness-raising, as they engage in a process of "diving deep and surfacing" with the authentic self that lies within, which is touched in its truest form apart from social conventions and traditional practices that encrust women with values that are not their own. For the ethical thinking involved here must be of such a kind as to sustain a turning over of power and an emerging new presence of women. This requires women's confrontation with their invisibility and silence in the textual history of humanity, and their tracing of an alternative genealogy. So Carol Christ writes:

> The spiritual quest of a modern woman begins in the experience of nothingness, the experience of being without an adequate image of self. Her drive to pursue her quest beyond the experiences of nothingness, without being trapped in a compromise with a prevailing mythology is rooted in a vision, and an experience, however fleeting, of *transcendence* which she identifies with the vision.[19]

To restore woman to herself requires a quite physical experience of becoming attuned to her body, and through this awareness, to come to a sense of wider attachment to those movements of life, those powers of nature herself in whose arms we are upheld and carried along. This is the broad current of "erotic power," as Carter Heyward calls it, which keeps us appearing in the face of the nothingness that threatens.[20] Here women are to find themselves universally grounded within the nature that belongs to us as earthly creatures, and it is within this nature, this body, that a transcendence is located. To return to the natural, to physics, is to rediscover the feminine root of every living being and to redraw the genealogy of humanity in a line back to Eve rather than to Adam. In this kind of deliberation, there is a rejection of metaphysics in favour of physics, a feminist reading which Adriana Cavarero undertakes "in spite of Plato,"[21] and which is to turn the symbolics of the ethical tradition upside down.

---

[18]   Mary Grey: *The Wisdom of Fools? Seeking Revelation for Today* (London: SPCK, 1993), chapters 2, 10.
[19]   Carol Christ: *Diving Deep and Surfacing: Women Writers on Spiritual Quest* (Boston: Beacon Press, 1980), pp. 11–12.
[20]   See Isabel Carter Heyward: "Undying Erotic Friendship: Foundations for Sexual Ethics," in *Touching our Strength: The Erotic as Power and the Love of God* (New York: HarperCollins, 1989).
[21]   Adriana Cavarero: *In Spite of Plato: A Feminist Rewriting of Ancient Philosophy*, trans. Serena Anderlini-D'Onofrio and Áine O'Healy (Cambridge: Polity Press, 1995).

There is some resistance within an ethic of difference to the notion that the nature of woman and of man is a matter of interpretation. Partly this is due to the suspicion that acts of interpretation come carrying all of the baggage of Cartesian dualism, in which one stands apart from the body to determine its values as if from a distant place. The overcoming of such separation within the self is given with the notion of being participant in a larger flowing of life that bears me into being and in which I find myself to be fulfilled. Partly this is due to a feminist interest in making women visible, and undertaking the rejection of a rejection requires a measure of unanimity and some broad claims of a general common identity. Yet exactly the same question which women ask of the patriarchal tradition, "Am I that name?" can be turned here upon this feminist ethic of difference, by women who do not see or find themselves in its terms.[22] If this identity is not taken on by a process of thinking then, it is argued, it must be a given one which determines the life of any individual woman, as the tradition had done. Indeed, if the medium for the change from one valuation to another is not personal free decision, then women continue to be the helpless victims of forces beyond their control which shape them into the beings they are, fitting them up for their appropriate roles in society regardless of their feelings or attitudes. These questions trouble an ethic of difference, bringing with them dilemmas regarding the identity of woman. For it seems to rely upon some notion of an essence of woman and of man, an essential genderedness, established within "a biology of incommensurability."[23] Is this merely a feminist way of saying that biology determines destiny? One of the outcomes of this feminism of difference has been the ethics of care, prefigured to some extent in the approach to ethical deliberation of David Hume.[24] Hume's recognition that love is not an abstract affair, but a matter of proximity and involvement in personal relationships, is given new impetus in Carol Gilligan's discoveries of the different voice with which women speak morally.[25] Her claims that women engage in moral reasoning as beings in relation to others is a critique of the isolated thinker of liberalism, and points to a relational emphasis in ethics that is concerned for the nurture and sustenance of right relationship. Here

[22] Denise Riley: *Am I That Name?: Feminism and the Category of "Women" in History* (New York: Macmillan, 1988).

[23] Thomas Laqueur: *Making Sex: Body and Sex from the Greeks to Frend* (Cambridge, MA: Harvard University Press, 1992), p. 154.

[24] See Joan C. Tronto: *Moral Boundaries: A Political Argument for an Ethic of Care* (London: Routledge, 1993).

[25] Carol Gilligan: *In a Different Voice: Psychological Theory and Women's Development* (Cambridge, MA: Harvard University Press, 1988). See also Tronto's discussion of Hume in *Moral Boundaries*, chapter 2.

Gilligan notes the ambivalence of women toward language of rights, which may require of them a tear in the fabric of interconnected relationships into which her life is embedded. The possibility of valuing this different voice has led to reconsiderations of what it is to be a self, and of what is meant by such ethical notions as sacrifice and love. Likewise this ethic challenges the ways in which public life reflects the male emphasis on autonomous individualism. The benefits to society in the encouragement of communities of care, and in the nurturing of right relationships of respect between people have been positive outcomes of its emphases on behalf of women. Indeed, the reordering of the public realm to allow the emergence of what had been separated out as private virtues, may be a most encouraging sign of the humanization of social life that will encourage peace and harmony to flourish. In a time of outbreaks of violence around the globe, of major devastations of the natural world, and of increasing regulation in personal and social life, this ethic of women's distinctiveness emerges to call us back into a wholeness of our human qualities to live in balance and in complementarity, women and men together.

An Ethic of Liberation

Yet a third kind of feminist ethic of gender is to be found within a framework of liberation thinking and ethics. The more recent of the three forms of feminist ethic, this one derives from nineteenth-century challenges to the politics of liberalism and the economics of capitalism, particularly as found within Marxism. Here, what is important in understanding our humanness is a recognition of the determinations of ourselves by institutions that shape the material conditions in which we are born and come to live. This form of ethical thinking with gender is drawn to consider, therefore, how it is that we are constructed as women and as men within the actual and practical social context of our daily lives, and thereby to expose the common forms of human enslavement. Its presumption is that gender is a social construction which we as individual persons are made to fit, or are shaped into, by means of the language, the practices, and the norms characteristic of the society in which we live. Here there is no reference to a human nature, but a concern for future reconstructions of gender beyond the inheritance of dualism.

The discourse concerning good within this ethic is characterized by a conviction that beliefs about what is true and good are products of the particular historical situations, material circumstances and social conditions out of which they arise. Thus, it is claimed, there is no such thing as a purely metaphysical truth discovered by or derived from the exercise of our minds, nor is there a timeless human nature which appears in various guises throughout history and across cultures. These things are beyond our knowing. Rather what we believe to be good is something that we receive from our culture. We pick it up from the practices that are customary amongst the people with whom we live, and so it is inculcated as a set of values that are characteristic of our social location and historical period. What this form of ethics requires of us is observation and analysis of how these notions of what is good are constructed, and then insights into processes of social change that would be more humanly fulfilling. So Harriet Martineau, perhaps the first sociologist in the nineteenth century, observed how women and men's lives were being molded into the roles and activities required for maintenance of the good required in the socio-economic conditions of Britain and North America.[26] While men were learning how to work within the institutions of production and exchange, women were being trained for their social function within the institutions of marriage and family, and the practices of reproduction. So we are constructed into two different ways of living, making our decisions within an overall framework of social roles and expectations. Different circumstances will make different demands upon us as human beings. Thus there is nothing fixed or permanent in the gendered roles that we take on. As de Beauvoir would later claim, "one is not born, but rather becomes, a woman."[27]

Another kind of critical reading of the textual field of ethics is here required. The first task is one of demonstration of the constructions of gender in different historical situations and in patterns of language. A predominant assumption that guides these readings is that ethical texts are historic documents, reflecting and reinforcing common cultural assumptions, and thus do not bear authority across time or place. To find in the texts of ethics, not the exercise of a transcendent reasoning so much as a rather more mundane expression of prevailing beliefs and unquestioned values regarding gender, is to debunk the purported timelessness and universality, disinterestedness, and inclusiveness of ethical writings. The hermeneutic of suspicion operative here asks a basic question regarding each text, namely – for whose benefit has it been written? Descriptions of

---

[26] Harriet Martineau: "Women," in Alice S. Rossi: *The Feminist Papers*, extracted from Martineau's *Society in America*, ed. Seymour Martin Lipset (Garden City, NY: Anchor Doubleday, 1962).

[27] Simone de Beauvoir: *The Second Sex*, trans. H. M. Parshley (New York: Bantam Books, 1961), p. 249.

the place of women help us to see that, as Martineau claimed, "the mischief lies in the system."[28] By bringing systems of power relations to our attention, we can begin to question them as underlying causes for the formation of different gender identities. So feminists of liberation have questioned the patterns of gender identity and role that are produced out of changing circumstances of scarcity, conflict, settlement, or colonization. It has on the whole been man's socially constructed position to be among the powerful, while it has on the whole been woman's socially constructed position to be the excluded, powerless outsider to the system. That descriptions of what is good for women and for men, and recommendations for their behaviour and attitudes, virtues and character, are formed out of these systemic power relationships is an important step in the critical demonstration of constructions of gender at work in ethical texts.

The point of this demonstration is to expose ideology, and in particular to debunk the myth of "the natural" by which systems sustain themselves in power. The notion that what we are as women and men is somehow fixed by nature outside of the realities in which we live is used by the powerful to maintain order and to keep people in their places. Thus, it is claimed, what we find in ethical texts is a set of ruling ideas that come to appear before us as somehow essential features of the world. So Gerda Lerner sets out in *The Creation of Patriarchy* to trace "the development of leading ideas, symbols, and metaphors by which patriarchal gender relations were incorporated into Western civilization," and within this drama, "to deduce the social reality which gave rise to the idea or to the metaphor."[29] Deducing this underlying social reality gives us the critical leverage by which we can rise to challenge the power of the status quo and overthrow the identity and role we have been given. These social realities are, of course, also operative in religion, and the ideologies in which they are sustained come to operate as theological truth. As a liberation theologian, Dorothee Sölle expresses this with characteristic sharpness in her claim that all theology is partisan. By turning the interest of theology away from questions of timeless truth, away from abstract theories of God, and into questions of collusion in the pretexts of power, into recognition of the presence of God among the powerless, she points us toward a critical reading of our beliefs. Calling us to recognize the ways in which beliefs about God may reinforce gender injustices may open our eyes and ears to the good news proclaimed in the Magnificat, that God

---

[28]　Martineau: "Women", p. 141.
[29]　Gerda Lerner: *The Creation of Patriarchy* (Oxford: Oxford University Press, 1986), pp. 10–11.

now is "with the lowly, the disinherited and the offended and . . . speaks through them."[30]

Taking seriously the Marxist dictum that the point of philosophy is not to understand the world but to change it, an ethic of liberation engages in strategic considerations of effective action for change. What it is that might be done in order to unsettle dualistic gender constructions involves consideration of a wide range of possible courses of action. Changing the ways we do things in our communal life may bring new dimensions of the human person to light that do not fit neatly into the prevailing definitions of woman and man, and may furnish a continuing source of discontent with the pretensions of settled patterns. Again, this ethic trawls the textual field to discover the moments of creative change and the ways of acting, speakings, and thinking by which a given gender identity has been effectively challenged and overturned. Grace Jantzen's studies of the Christian mystical tradition demonstrate this method, in her interpretation of those voices of women that do not collude in the privatized spiritual virtues of humility and submission which "have been used to keep women 'in their place' in church and society."[31] Rather she finds that "while oppression runs deep, it is also true that from within the mystical tradition, especially (but not only) from some of the women mystics, come creative and courageous efforts at pushing back the boundaries of thought and action so that liberation could be achieved."[32] Finding these places of protest against and within "the technologies of patriarchy"[33] opens up for present-day women the possibility of reconstructing, out of these "dangerous memories," new communities of resistance and solidarity that enact and bespeak gender justice in our time.[34]

This reading of the textual field reveals already the kind of deliberative practice that is involved in this ethic. Ethical reasoning is a matter, first of recognizing and exposing constructions of gender, secondly of dismantling these as fabrications of human power, and thirdly of locating the places of effective spoken and acted protest out of which new social realities may come to be formed. This practice involves the exercise of the human

---

[30] Dorothee Sölle: *Thinking about God: An Introduction to Theology* (London: SCM Press, 1990), p. 70.

[31] Grace M. Jantzen: *Power, Gender and Christian Mysticism* (Cambridge: Cambridge University Press, 1995), p. 20.

[32] Jantzen: *Power*, p. 23.

[33] Jantzen: *Power*, p. 24.

[34] Sharon Welch: *Communities of Resistance and Solidarity: A Feminist Theology of Liberation* (New York: Orbis Books, 1985) and *A Feminist Ethic of Risk* (Minneapolis, MN: Fortress Press, 1990).

capacity for reasoned judgment and for interpretation of the circumstances of one's life, in much the same way as did the first ethic of equality. There still needs to be some kind of an Archimedean point on which I can stand to judge the pattern of things, but which itself is not determined by this pattern. This is a vulnerable place, and the weakness in this ethic of gender begins to appear in its reliance upon an unconstructed location in the midst of the vast and unyielding structures of power that make up human history. An ethic of liberation relies upon an appeal to what is beyond gender dualisms, understood to be a dimension of our humanness that is outside the reach of social constructions. It is this dimension of ourselves which this ethic seeks to liberate so that we may strive for the life that is most authentic to ourselves, and that means a life which may not conform to the pattern of two genders imposed upon us by social convention and tradition.[35] The point of this ethic as a critique of gender therefore is to enable us to recover the commonness of our humanity beyond the constraints and categories we inherit through history, language, and culture. It brings us as women and men before the same problematic that determines our gendered selves, and asks us to reconsider and reshape together how things might go on from here.

This ethic of gender expresses a longing for positive changes in the lived situations of women's lives, and for social reconstructions that are more just. Its concern for economic and social structures that disempower women has contributed to many movements for liberation around the world, in which women seek freedom to reorder their lives. Such movements challenge entrenched cultural ideals of the role and function of women, and represent a threat to patterns of local economic relations that are now seen to be oppressive and unjust to the full humanity of women. Women's belief in the possibility of liberation from these ideals and structures brings already a sense of responsibility for the shape of their own lives, and a determined involvement to change the conditions in which they are living. That such changes will bring about more humane social relations for women and men is the expectation in which this ethic is held. For its conviction is that human beings are more richly complex and more positively creative than the structures of patriarchy have allowed, and in that vast potential for what has been undeveloped and unexpressed in our humanity lies its motivating force. In this is also a theological expression that the potential for transformation of life is already given us in the promise of the kingdom to come. This ethic thus comes to embody one

---

[35] Rosemary Radford Ruether: "Dualism and the Nature of Evil in Feminist Theology," *Studies in Christian Ethics*, 5:1 (1992), p. 39.

form of faith in a liberating deity, who acts in history on behalf of those who are non-persons, who challenges and overthrows systems of power, and who brings all things to fulfilment in a community of justice and harmony.

These differing forms of feminist ethics reveal some of the issues that emerge when one engages in thinking of our humanity with gender. Feminists have been eager to take up the challenge of Enlightenment humanism, both to consider what it means that there are women and men, and how it is that the development and completion of our basic humanness might be accomplished. For feminists of equality, the ethic that will guide this realization is one in which distinctions of gender have only a temporary pragmatic, rather than a fundamental, role to play. Our human capacity for reasoned judgment and the basic freedom of will that defines us as uniquely human are both shared equally by women and men. Differences of gender therefore need only be attended to until they become socially and politically insignificant, and no one notices the difference any longer. Feminists of difference promote an ethic in which we are understood to be thoroughly gendered as human beings, so that the issue becomes one of allowing for the full recognition and expression of each in their differences. Here the valuations of genderedness are significant either as denials or affirmations of these two essential natures. To speak and to act out of one's gender becomes here a personal and a political work of revaluation of values in which difference matters very much. Feminists of liberation reflect upon the social construction of gender which situates women and men in different places of power. An appropriate ethic will seek to overthrow the structures in which these differences are constituted, so that the fuller relational possibilities of our humanity may be empowered and released. What kind of genderedness may lie ahead in new configurations of relationship is awaited with interest.[36]

Running through these forms of feminist ethics of gender is an ambivalent relationship to modern humanism, upon which they are dependent and of which they are at the same time deeply critical. These feminisms have troubled such humanism by raising the question of gender and we have begun to see what some of the deeper issues might be that require our further consideration. In this task, it will be helpful to take up directly

---

[36] Efforts by feminists to bring together these different strands of thinking are published as discussions between Seyla Benhabib, Judith Butler, Drucilla Cornell, Nancy Fraser, and Linda Nicholson in *Feminist Contentions: A Philosophical Exchange* (London: Routledge, 1995); and in a collection edited by Alison M. Jaggar: *Living with Contradictions: Controversies in Feminist Social Ethics* (Boulder, CO: Westview Press, 1994).

some of the accusations that emerge from feminisms about ethics as a discourse concerning good, as a textual field, and as a deliberative practice. For the same ambivalence is here, the same dependence and critique, which is brought to light in the persistent question – what about women? We turn to consider this challenge in the next chapter by taking up the further question – is ethics a man's subject? This will point us towards some of the deeper troubling of ethics which presents itself in a thinking with gender.

3

Is Ethics a Man's Subject?

In the discipline that is ethics, the human self figures. The human self is understood to be the one who engages in the various discourses concerning good that are gathered into the textual field of ethics. It is the self who carries out the work of discovering the truths about our human nature that lie on the distant horizon towards which we are journeying in this life. So too it is the self who provides ethical guidance for the doing of what is good. This work draws the human self into the distinctive deliberative practice which is ethics, moving between the two poles of what is true and what ought to become so. This self, who comes to be the subject of ethics, becomes a kind of mediating figure. It mediates an ethical vision for the rest of humanity who may be caught by the same insights and carried along into a better life as a result of following the advice given. So it is a kind of mediator of humanity to itself, representing us to ourselves for the betterment of our lives. It mediates on our behalf between a vision of ultimate goodness and the ordinary behavior of our lives which might be effected in some way by this vision. In these ways, the human self comes to figure in the formation of the ethical tradition that modernism comes to claim as its own.

A critique of modernism is already at work, however, in feminism as an ethics of gender. For feminism in its different ways has been indicating that the modern self is a man, and thus that the subject of ethics is modelled after man's self-understanding and self-determinations. Such critique begins in that form of feminist ethics which most assumes the role of this ethical subject, namely the ethics of equality. For as women ask the question about their own presence as women, they challenge the hidden boundaries drawn up by this subject in the exercise of his own reasoning. Their claim to be included as equals within this figure is at once both redundant, since the mind supposedly "has no sex,"[1] and yet required if the subject is to be all that it claims to be. The inconsistency of this subject precisely at the point of its uniqueness as a rational being, as a thinking substance, is what thinking with gender equality begins to reveal. To think with gender difference is to unsettle the operation of this subject by proposing another way of ethical reflection. Refusing the mediation provided through this subject's falsely inclusive reasoning, feminists of difference claim to present another subject of ethics whose deliberations are to be exclusively figured. To put the human subject firmly in its place as a man is to clear a space for the subject as woman to come into her own. Feminists of liberation open up another kind of challenge to this subject by emphasizing its uniqueness, less as a core substance within, than as a centre of relationality. Here what is important is the practical dimension of reforming structures and relationships in ways that can be known in experience to be right and fitting. That this would constitute freedom for both genders is the promise of this form of feminist ethics in its changing of the subject. In each of these, the subject of ethics, the self as man, has been challenged and unsettled from its place as a primary figure in the ethical thinking of modernism.

This issue is, however, unsettling for feminism too, insofar as it too is a product of modern thinking. The forms of feminist ethics of gender also presume the existence of and rely upon the deliberative practices of this subject, albeit construed in different ways. The critical thinking brought into play with feminisms shows up the subject of modern humanism for what it is, and in that sense undermines its pretensions. Yet in the ethical analyses and recommendations of feminisms, there seems still to be a subject who figures in the same kind of way, performing the same mediating role between what is and what ought to be, and offering to represent our humanity to us through its construal of the truth that belongs there. Thus while the specific gendered nature of this subject is called to account for itself, the work that it carries out in the ethics of humanism is still to be borne by a subject of some kind. So the question arises as to whether feminisms have displaced this subject, or have rather sought to occupy its place as women. This chapter begins to investigate this question more closely. By considering firstly whether ethics is a man's subject, we take up the feminist challenge. That ethics expresses male subjectivity in its embodied

---

[1] Genevieve Lloyd: *The Man of Reason: "Male" and "Female" in Western Philosophy* (London: Methuen, 1984): "Reason is taken to express the real nature of the mind, in which, as Augustine put it, there is no sex," p. ix. See also Londa Schiebinger: *The Mind has no Sex? Women in the Origins of Modern Science* (Cambridge, MA: Harvard University Press, 1989).

experience of the world is a modern criticism, while its more postmodern form is that ethics itself is a construction and regulation of men as subjects. These challenges bring us secondly into a consideration of some of the theories of masculinity which have sought to reaffirm men as subjects of ethics. Finally we turn to two possibilities for changing the subject of ethics which have been suggested by Seyla Benhabib and by Anthony Giddens, both of whom seek to be responsive to feminist challenges to the subject of ethics.

Man-made Ethics / Ethically-made Man

That ethics is a product of man's experience of the world and his ways of thinking is a common charge within feminist writings. In her book, *The Man of Reason*, Genevieve Lloyd examines "the claim that Reason is 'male'."[2] Her investigation traces the course of the notions of maleness and femaleness as these present themselves in philosophical texts of the western tradition. Central to this task is Lloyd's conviction that in examining ideas of Reason, there is "more at stake" than mere description of an intellectual activity. For she claims:

> Reason has figured in western culture not only in the assessment of beliefs, but also in the assessment of character. It is incorporated not just into our criteria of truth, but also into our understanding of what it is to be a person at all, of the requirements that must be met to be a good person, and of the proper relations between our status as knowers and the rest of our lives.[3]

So her work seeks to examine how it has happened that "character ideals" in the western tradition have come to centre on the idea of Reason, and further to demonstrate that there is an "implicit maleness" of this idea of Reason which operates to construct gender differences. This "male–female distinction itself has operated not as a straightforwardly descriptive principle of classification, but as an expression of values,"[4] and by exposing the values that manifest themselves in man's reasoning, she hopes to be able to "make available a diversity of intellectual styles and characters to men and women alike."[5] For the past does not have to be our norm, but can be a resource from which we draw new possibilities for our living today.

[2] Lloyd: *Reason*, p. viii.
[3] Lloyd: *Reason*, p. ix.
[4] Lloyd: *Reason*, p. 103.
[5] Lloyd: *Reason*, p. 107.

Lloyd is here taking up a claim that has become important to feminist readings of gender difference, namely that the western tradition of thought expresses the man at work, thinking and becoming himself fully human. Feminists seek to expose the male subject who sends forth these representatives of his understanding of himself, masquerading as objective disinterested claimants to truth. In her argument that the sex of the knower is epistemologically significant, Lorraine Code presents the ways in which this knowing man dismisses subjectivity, relationships, and situatedness in the promotion of an ideal rationality. Accordingly what women know is rendered insignificant or troublesome, in favour of the truer account of reality derived from man's detached position.[6] So it is assumed that moral knowledge, knowledge of what is good and right, will be derived from such work of reasoning, in which one moves away from experience toward objectivity, away from particulars toward universal truths. To notice this androcentrism of the philosophic tradition is to turn the tables on this pretension, exposing the particular behind the universal, the specific perspective behind the universalized claims. Debunking the universal man of reason as a particular phenomenon of time and place is a challenge to the kind of reason that permeates the western ethical tradition.

The form which this thinking takes is also claimed to reflect the male subject. Man's imagination is oppositional,[7] his pattern of thinking dualistic, to such an extent that the imposition of this form of understanding brings about the polarization it thinks. Oppositions abound, from the separation of man and nature such that it becomes the realm subject to his dominating intellectual curiosity and technical management, to the division within man himself as he subdues his emotions and his body's impulses by a moral sense of obedience to higher ideals. From the ancient Pythagorean table of contrasting principles to contemporary insistence upon the binary form of the imagination among structuralists, such distinctions come value-laden with a superior and an inferior, a more perfect and a less perfect, a self and the other. These oppositions are reflected in the discourse concerning good, bearing the inheritance of its roots in Platonism, in a way of thinking metaphysically of ethics that the western tradition has found hard to break. It is this oppositional thinking which feminist theologians have located too

---

[6] Lorraine Code: *What Can She Know? Feminist Theory and the Construction of Knowledge* (Ithaca, NY: Cornell University Press, 1991). This is a fruitful question, in that shifting the emphasis from one word to the next opens out new dimensions of the problem at stake here.

[7] See, e.g., Joan Cocks: *The Oppositional Imagination: Feminism, Critique and Political Theory* (New York: Routledge, 1989).

within Christian theology. As Daphne Hampson argues, "the religious forms which we have known have been a male creation. They have corresponded to the self-understanding of men living within patriarchy."[8] Conceiving himself to live within a finite temporal world separated from the divine, man looks for ways of self-transcendence through acts of self-giving or self-emptying, using paradigms of ethical action from which women are excluded, but which are "deeply satisfying to men."[9] Understanding the task of ethics as the overcoming of this opposition begins here as man's project of becoming good.

This suggests to many feminists that ethics reveals man's values, woven throughout its texts as a consistent elevation of his own qualities and capacities, and as a persistent addressing of the problematics of his life. Frequently feminists argue that separation anxiety bothers all of these accounts, indicative either of a loss of the mother at being thrust out of the womb into a vale of lonely self-making, a loss that is turned into a bravado "flight from the feminine,"[10] or on the other hand of a fear of the father registered early on as a sense of inadequacy overcome by making himself worthy according to his father's high standards.[11] This engendering of values reveals an ethical deliberation understood to be for a production, for a self-creation, and in this work the ruling of one's desires and the disciplining of one's thoughts and feelings becomes important. Gilligan's findings regarding moral development reveal the thinking by which this man learns to behave himself in the formation of his identity, the central metaphor of which, she claims, is mirroring. The autonomous self of ethical reasoning learns to be as a reflection of detachment from feelings and commitment to obligations which are its necessary characteristics.[12] Being able to stand his ground in the midst of adversity, and being found to be competent in his accomplishments, become the practices by which his life is to be judged. That this identity requires that "men situate themselves in the centre of the picture, seeing the world in relation to them" is the figure within the whole cultural production of ethics, and of theology, which feminism interrogates.[13] So Hampson calls attention to

[8]   Daphne Hampson: *After Christianity* (London: SCM Press, 1996), p. 165.
[9]   Hampson: *After*, p. 166.
[10]   Susan Bordo: *The Flight to Objectivity: Essays on Cartesianism and Culture* (Albany, NY: State University of New York Press, 1987).
[11]   Hampson: *After*, p. 166.
[12]   Carol Gilligan: "New Images of Self in Relationship," in Carol Gilligan, Janie Victoria Ward, Jill McLean Taylor, and Betty Bardige, eds.: *Mapping the Moral Domain* (Cambridge, MA: Harvard University Press, 1988).
[13]   Hampson: *After*, p. 94.

the male egoism at work "in constructing a discourse about assertiveness, rights and autonomy" which "feminist women have come to find so impossible."[14] Such self-assertion becomes the central theme of feminist accusations of an idolatry of the male, that Hampson is not alone in finding so rife within Christian ethics and theology as to seek to jettison its myth and system altogether.

That the master discourse of ethics becomes a hegemonic assertion of the powerful, of the ruling ones, over the powerless, the subjugated others, leaves women without an ethical voice or subject. If the discipline is already gendered, the differences noted by someone like Freud, that "for women the level of what is ethical normal is different from what it is in men," reproduce women in a derivative position, defined as the ones who lack what men develop.[15] This lies in the middle of so many disagreements and misunderstandings that occur between women and men who seek to work together or to resolve dilemmas of their common life. That we see things differently as women and men, that men are from Mars and women from Venus,[16] is the surface beneath which lies the construction of ethics by the male subject. So feminists like Hampson and Gilligan would argue that until women also can set up the distinctions important to themselves within which a discourse concerning good is conducted, and can express their needs and hopes in the written texts of ethics, and can engage in their own collaborative forms of deliberative practice, then ethics will be an exclusive subject, writing them outside its domain. Reclaiming this outside position, remapping the moral domain, revaluing the devalued other, reconceptualizing the self, refashioning concepts – these are all phrases used by feminists in response to the disclosure of ethics as a male subject. However, there is more to be said.

Figured within our language is another way of speaking about ethics as a man's subject. For while this section has emphasized the way in which feminists expose the active deliberate subject of ethics as man, there is also a sense in which the subject of ethics is understood as a receiving constructed subject, made into man through the operations of this discipline. That ethics makes man is a claim indicative of a change in thinking about our humanness. Already such a possibility begins to be sketched in the

---

[14]   Hampson: *After*, p. 114.
[15]   Carol Gilligan: *In a Different Voice: Psychological Theory and Women's Development* (Cambridge, MA: Harvard University Press, 1988), p. 7.
[16]   Gray, John: *Men are from Mars, Women are from Venus: A Practical Guide for Improving Communication and Getting What You Want in Your Relationships* (London: Thorsons, 1993).

frame of a feminist ethics of liberation, for its emphasis on the structures that shape human life suggests that gender too is such a social and linguistic category into which individual people are fitted. There is resistance here to any form of naturalism that would assume a bodily or biological reality apart from social structuring, and with this challenge, the expressive view of ethics is unsettled. The notion that we express our preexisting natures by means of our ethical values and decision-making, which these latter are then intended to allow to fulfilment, is turned on its head in the strong assertion of a social constructionism. For, as liberationists were already beginning to suggest, beliefs about what is natural do not precede or underlie practices and institutions, but rather are their accompanying justification and rationale. Notions of expressing our natures through our ethics are a significant feature of an ideology of humanistic authenticity which actually serves to inhibit any full critique and consideration of change. So whether ethics has always throughout history expressed the man, and whether it should, from now on, change to express the woman, is for the constructionist not the important matter here.

Rather what a critique of Reason reveals is the way in which particular forms of ethics are embedded in the ideologies of their own time, and as such, serve the function of making gendered beings of us all. This form of argument that ethics is a man's subject is indicative of the problematic of philosophy as it turns into critical cultural theory. This change is the outcome of coming to terms with the death of the human being as autonomous rational subject, that masculine figure which feminisms have been so concerned to displace and to discredit. It becomes possible to investigate "configurations of masculinity" by which "the specifically gendered modern masculine subject . . . man . . . has been invoked, insinuated, constructed, and reproduced. . . ." within our modern theories.[17] To speak of being made a subject is to bring to our attention the cultural myths which are knitted together in a fabric of representations and linguistic practices that shape our behaviour and thinking. As our appreciation of the ways in which human beings are formed out of the material of the cultures they inhabit becomes more secure in its analysis, the less plausible becomes the retention of any kernel of freedom of consciousness, however small, that is supposedly carried around inside each one of these cultural productions. Continuing to place our faith in this private space may give an illusion of power to the powerless. However, it is argued, what has power over our lives is the sex-gender system itself that produces human

---

[17] Christine Di Stefano: *Configurations of Masculinity: A Feminist Perspective on Modern Political Theory* (Ithaca, NY: Cornell University Press, 1991), p. x.

subjects, without intention and without purpose, and ethics is an integral part of this system. Noticeable in this critique is that ethics still serves to make man into the particular gendered subject that he is. Accordingly, man is made into a subject of surveillance by the watchful eye of the power/knowledge regime, a subject of the *polis* under rule of law, and a subject of loss in his speculative reasoning. To take up these arguments is to move our discussion of the ethics of gender into an explicitly postmodern milieu, which the next three chapters will investigate more closely.

Reaffirming Male Subjects

Responding to the challenges and analyses of feminisms have appeared a variety of perspectives on masculinity that attempt to reassert the identity of man, in some cases in answer to criticisms that were recognized to be justifiable, but predominately to affirm men and masculinity in themselves. Like feminisms, these perspectives can be located across a range of philosophical positions, and offer both divergent analyses of the situation of men and distinctive recommendations for positive social and personal change. Already in opening up this kind of investigation, perspectives on masculinity face a question regarding both the substance and the method of their interest. In one sense, to investigate the subject of man is to engage in a familiar task that has already shaped the western intellectual and cultural tradition, so that it is difficult to understand what would be new in such work. Yet because the male subject has become a problem in and for modern humanism, to engage in its closer examination is to acknowledge an awareness that the man is no longer normative, that he no longer speaks for all, and that his perspective on his humanity is a standpoint which can be taken up. The subject he looks to affirm is already one that has been shaken off its perch above it all. Methodologically this presents some interesting dilemmas regarding the politics of the investigation. To demonstrate that man also is a subject constructed by a hegemonic gender system is to claim some equal share in oppression alongside women, and yet the system under investigation is itself understood to be one that operates for the benefit of man. How such a study can proceed without implicitly reinforcing that system and reinstalling man into it, humbled and reformed, is a question that disturbs these perspectives. What it is to claim a masculine identity in the presence of feminist critiques becomes itself a most sensitive ethical issue.

Masculinity, like femininity, is disputed territory. In providing "a map of this territory," Kenneth Clatterbaugh notes the diverse perspectives on masculinity, each of which offers "a theory about the forces that are acting on them and about the changes they would like to make."[18] Within these theories, as within feminisms, can be noted several tensions that shape the field and the methods of its investigation. So there is a tension between a biological determinism that makes for "The Inevitability of Patriarchy"[19] on the one hand, and a social constructionism that finds masculinity to be defined by the patterns of culture and historical processes on the other. As for the former, bringing recent work of sociobiologists to bear on their studies, determinists of both the hard and soft varieties, seek to recover the natural foundations for the superiority of the male sex over the female. Deriving personal and social moral codes from these natural differences results in a strong and well-ordered society in which gender roles are clearly separated and complementary. For this to happen, men will need also to assert their rights, in the face of has been called "the myth of masculine privilege"[20] and the sexism of feminism. The return to the real biological essence of man is here recommended. Counter to this perspective, is an understanding of masculinity as a form of alienation from the full humanity of man, insofar as the material lives of men are shaped and controlled by relations of production. Here theorists seek to understand how such dehumanization of men is deepened by that of women, whom men are rendered powerless to assist, and whose alienation they may unwittingly reinforce by what they are made to do.[21] To seek change in the interlocking structures of oppression, through a politics of resistance, is a task in the mutual interests of both women and men.

Likewise, there is tension in theories of masculinity between a notion of gender as a social role which itself makes the difference, and gender as the bearing of deep psycho-spiritual patterns in unconscious archetypes. The former view seeks the liberation of men from expectations for their lives and stereotypes of their behaviour and feelings, or lack of them. Men too have become subject to patriarchy, being trained to carry out the violence and aggression against women which it requires for its sustenance, a role which also damages their emotional and psychic lives. To become a new man is to reject this role and to affirm the possibilities for being human beyond gender stereotypes in ways that may give new direction to men's

[18]   Kenneth Clatterbaugh: *Contemporary Perspectives on Masculinity: Men, Women, and Politics in Modern Society* (Bonlder, CO: Westview Press, 1990), p. 151.
[19]   Steven Goldberg: *The Inevitability of Patriarchy* (New York: William Morrow, 1974).
[20]   Herb Goldberg: *The Hazards of Being Male: Surviving the Myth of Masculine Privilege* (New York: Signet Books, 1976).
[21]   Andrew Tolson: *The Limits of Masculinity* (New York: Harper & Row, 1977).

lives.[22] Here an economic critique has been broadened, as it has in feminism, into a general cultural critique. Its emphasis on the cultural construction of masculinities allows men too to be self-reflective about the making of their own identities, and the scripts that have been written for their lives, and indeed to recognize that there may also be a plurality of masculinities.[23] The latter view seeks the return of men to their own deeply hidden selves. That this will take us into the land of "wild men and horned gods" is the project of Robert Bly's recovery of the spirituality of masculinity.[24] Here is an affirmation of the difference that men are, by means of a deep descent into the archetypal patterns that lie in the collective unconscious. These patterns are expressed in enduring myths and symbols that form perennial narratives of gender played out in cultural variations throughout history. What one needs is the key to their interpretation, for in reading these appropriately, a man may be initiated into his true manhood.

Theories of masculinity also find their way into theological work. There are attempts to treat the subject of masculinity in biblical studies, as men work alongside their feminist colleagues, seeking to rethink gender through encounter with these texts. So David Clines asks three questions for his investigation of the figure of David: "What does it mean to be a man in our own culture? And what was it like in the world of the Bible? How do our answers to the first set of questions determine or influence our answers to the second set?"[25] His work, part of a larger project of ideological criticism, demonstrates a way for scholars to take a step back "from their own culture and their personal scripts, to bring back into the foreground the otherness of the familiarized."[26] In contrast is the work of those who

---

[22]   Jon Snodgrass, ed.: *A Book of Readings for Men Against Sexism* (Albion, CA: Times Change Press, 1977).
[23]   See Harry Brod, ed.: *The Making of Masculinities: The New Men's Studies* (London: Routledge, 1987); Julia T. Wood: *Gendered Lives: Communication, Gender and Culture* (Belmont, CA: Wadsworth, 1994).
[24]   Robert Bly: *The Pillow and the Key: Commentary on the Fairy Tale of Iron John, Part One* (St. Paul, MN: Ally Press, 1987) and *When a Hair Turns Gold: Commentary on the Fairy Tale of Iron John, Part Two* (St. Paul, MN: Ally Press, 1988).
[25]   David J. A. Clines: "David the Man: The Construction of Masculinity in the Hebrew Bible," in *Interested Parties: The Ideology of Writers and Readers of the Hebrew Bible* (Sheffield: Sheffield Academic Press, 1995), p. 212. See also Clines, David J. A., *Ecce Vir, or, Gendering the Son of Man*, in J. Cheryl Exum and Stephen D. Moore, *Biblical Studies/Cultural Studies, The Third Sheffield Colloquium*, Journal for the Study of the Old Testament Supplement Series 266, Gender, Culture, Theory 7 (Sheffield: Sheffield Academic Press), 1998, pp. 352–75.
[26]   Clines: "David", p. 243.

seek to "recover" notions of "manhood and womanhood" as these are believed to be essentially established in biblical texts. Understanding the Bible to be revealed word of God for human life directs us to conformity with its ideals for gender, and thus to a critical relationship with contemporary cultural ideals.[27] So too there are those theologians who seek to be responsive to the gender critique in their systematic work. Such, for example, would be Jürgen Moltmann, who chooses to make "contributions to theology" which recognize "the conditions and limitations of his own position," such that "theology no longer has to be andro*centric*."[28] In the modesty of this proposal which does not pretend to speak for all humanity, is one kind of response to the charge that theology is a man's subject. Whether these responses will ameliorate the critique of Mary Daly, "if God is male, the male is God,"[29] or the question of salvation posed by Rosemary Ruether, "Can a male savior save women?"[30] highlights the dilemma of these affirmations of masculinity in the context of a patriarchal tradition of theology.

Clatterbaugh's hope is that improvements in "our conceptual clarity regarding masculinity" and in empirical research will direct us towards an effective ethical agenda for a better life.[31] His analysis reveals the dilemma of the ethical subject, able to develop perspectives through a reflective process, yet subject constantly to challenges from other views from outside their scope, and thus also to confrontational relations with other perspectives. This is a vulnerable subject, who recognizes that power is on the agenda already within each of the various perspectives, since it is "the power relations that are built into the social roles of masculinity that most perspectives find problematic,"[32] a subject who then must chart his course between cynicism or skepticism, since there is no completely objective perspective or dogma possible or even desirable.[33] Yet the lack of any defining framework in which these masculinities may find theoretical or political purpose eventually results in their waning influence. Diversities

[27] John Piper and Wayne Grudem, eds.: *Recovering Biblical Manhood and Womanhood: A Response to Evangelical Feminism* (Wheaton, IL: Crossway Books, 1991).
[28] Jürgen Moltmann: *The Trinity and the Kingdom of God: The Doctrine of God* (London: SCM Press, 1981), p. xii.
[29] Mary Daly: *Beyond God the Father: Toward a Philosophy of Women's Liberation* (Boston: Beacon Press, 1973), p. 19.
[30] Rosemary Radford Ruether: *Sexism and God-Talk: Towards a Feminist Theology* (London: SCM Press, 1983), p. 116.
[31] Clatterbaugh: *Masculinity*, p. 158.
[32] Clatterbaugh: *Masculinity*, p. 159.
[33] Clatterbaugh: *Masculinity*, pp. 158, 160.

among men, being just as pronounced as those amongst women, take their toll on identity politics and, lacking a clear theoretical focus for further investigations, the end of masculinities has already been announced, its work of counter-valuations no longer significant in altered ways of thinking.[34] Nevertheless, there has perhaps been a helpful corrective in recognizing that thinking with gender and entering into an ethics of gender is a task of interpretation of our humanity which involves men too. Gender issues then do not only have to do with women, nor is she to be made to be the only one who is gendered, in a way that leaves man's self-understanding intact and untroubled. If perspectives on masculinity have performed this inclusive work, then something of its helpfulness to an ethics of gender may be affirmed there.

Changing the Subject of Ethics

The subject of ethics has been called forth to bear the human being over from exclusion, from silence and invisibility, from disempowerment, and from alienation, into the light of freedom and goodness and truth in which its life may flourish. That the subject of modern ethics may not be able to carry the weight of this emancipatory project for women, bringing her into public and private life as a significant human being in her own right, is the challenge that feminists come to make against man-made ethics. In some cases, alliances may be forged between this critique and the perspectives on masculinity which are pro-feminist or sensitive to the gender critique. Whether these work to obscure the matter of gender further, or to diffuse the momentum for change by a reinstatement of the male subject, is a continuing worry about them.

Yet there are possibilities for changing the subject of ethics within the logic of modernism, which reconstrue our understanding of this subject who carries out its methods of ethical reasoning. Here the work of Seyla Benhabib is important. Her adaptations of the notion of communicative action and of the dialogical self from Jürgen Habermas present a further stage in the development of Enlightenment critical and emancipatory thinking. She recognizes that the gender critique has called into question the universalist tradition of ethical thinking, centred on its disembodied and timeless reasoning self. In this kind of ethics, women become the other, representing body and relationships and historical situations. Constructing

---

[34] John MacInnes: *The End of Masculinity: The Confusion of Sexual Genesis and Sexual Difference in Modern Society* (Milton Keynes: Open University Press, 1998).

her identity out of this otherness may be a corrective to ethical reasoning, so that it becomes more sensitive to the perspective and the situatedness of the ethical subject. However, this living opposition does not adequately address the need for a reformulation of our understanding of ethical reasoning, and of what constitutes the moral point of view, which the gender critique ultimately challenges. The "feminization of practical discourse will mean challenging unexamined normative dualisms as between justice and the good life, norms and values, interests and needs, from the standpoint of their gender context and subtext."[35] This, Benhabib believes, can be accomplished by rethinking the identity of the moral self, and by "situating the self" within communities of discourse in which the art of "enlarged thinking" may be learned and practiced. With these two projects, she seeks to change the subject of ethics and to argue that "the universalist tradition in practical philosophy can be reformulated today without committing oneself to the metaphysical illusions of the Enlightenment."[36]

For Benhabib, the moral self is very much a discrete unique individual, "with a concrete history, identity and affective-emotional constitution."[37] Such a self is not "the generalized self" of early modern moral and political theory, which "requires us to view each and every individual as a rational being entitled to the same rights and duties we would want to ascribe to ourselves."[38] This being is an abstraction, identified by its capacity for agency or by its pure freedom to choose, and thus Benhabib argues it cannot be "individuated" in the real world of bodies, emotions, memory, history, experiences, and relations with others. Rather the moral self is one who reasons in the midst of such situations by attending to the unique individuals with whom she exists in relationships and to the interwoven narratives of their lives. The correction to the gender blindness of man-made ethics is the readmittance of women, not as different moral subjects to be set alongside men, but as ones whose sphere of activity comes to define what the moral subject is in itself. This means acknowledging the centrality of care to human life, as the mode of activity that nurtures and sustains good communication between human beings. For not only do we become the individuals we are through dialogue with the other selves with whom we share our lives, we also learn the enlargement of consciousness associated with moral thinking when we hear and respect, attend to and

---

[35] Seyla Benhabib: *Situating the Self: Gender, Community and Postmodernism in Contemporary Ethics* (Cambridge: Polity Press, 1992), p. 113.
[36] Benhabib: *Situating*, p. 4 and passim.
[37] Benhabib: *Situating*, p. 159.
[38] Benhabib: *Situating*, p. 158.

honour the needs, desire and intentions of others. Thus communicative ethics "attributes to individuals the *ability* and the *willingness* to assume reflexive role distance and the ability and the willingness to take the standpoint of others involved in a controversy into account and reason from their point of view."[39] Beginning with this embedded, encumbered, concrete self, we may develop a new conception of universalism as those norms which set the boundaries within which such individuals may flourish, converse peaceably about the things that matter to their lives, and come to a practicable consensus.

Benhabib's reaffirmation of the ethical subject is an attempt to hold on to the possibility of normative criticism, without which, she argues, feminist theory risks "incoherence and self-contradictoriness."[40] She believes this appropriate ethical universalism may be accomplished without surreptitiously reintroducing the man of reason. The significance of her conception of justice lies here, as she seeks to remove the limitation of its rule to the public sphere and to reconstrue its ideal of impartiality. Some conception of justice is necessary as a framework within which to uphold the proliferation of diversities and to sustain "the rationality of democratic procedures."[41] Yet it is a conception of justice that is not imposed upon, but rather emerges as normative out of real encounters with others, for it is the condition of their fruitful continuation. Thus taking real account of differences is sustained rather than obscured by appeals to justice in our ethical reasoning. What cannot be abandoned, and what she herself cautions against, is some remainder of "the specifically *modern* achievement of being able to criticize, challenge and question . . ."[42] with which women especially may still question the conventions of society. For this, some culturally transcendent principles may be necessary, and some access to them left open. A reasonable defence of the best of the Enlightenment inheritance of ethical thinking with a reconstrued subject is for Benhabib the appropriate response to counter a widespread disillusionment with the project of modernity.

A different kind of changing the subject of ethics is offered by Anthony Giddens, whose book on the transformation of intimacy reintroduces sex to an ethics of gender. Finding that what used to be a private concern now features in the public domain, it is sex, he says, that now "speaks the language of revolution."[43] His interest in this work is not so much in the

---

[39]   Benhabib: *Situating*, p. 74.
[40]   Benhabib: *Situating*, p. 213.
[41]   Benhabib: *Situating*, p. 16.
[42]   Benhabib: *Situating*, p. 74.
[43]   Anthony Giddens: *The Transformation of Intimacy: Sexuality, Love and Eroticism in Modern Societies* (Cambridge: Polity Press, 1992), p. 1.

economic and political dimensions of society, as in the qualitative changes noticeable in the "emotional order," that is, in the personal relationships of women and men as women claim their equality.[44] Something new is happening here through the emergence of a "plastic sexuality" that is no longer tied to the requirements of reproduction, nor to the provision of a necessary biological foundation for the identification of gender.[45] The malleability of sex, and the possibility of a radical pluralism of sexual choices, means that its potential for emancipating and democratizing relations of women and men is profound. Indeed, while emancipatory politics concerns itself with "the internally referential systems of modernity" being oriented to the "control of distributive power," it is sexuality which confronts power "in its generative aspect," and thus holds a different key to changing the subject of ethics.[46] It is to interpret some of the signs of this transformation, and some of its ethical ramifications that he writes the book.

Giddens recognizes that in modern societies, control of the social and natural worlds, which has been the male domain, has been facilitated through the development of reason as something set apart from emotion. This, he argues, is personally experienced as "a massive psychological process of repression," but more importantly it has become an institutional division along gender lines. The more reason has exercised its social control, the more deeply entrenched became the binary code of gender divisions that shaped individual self-identity. Accordingly, "Reason cuts away at ethics . . . because moral judgements and emotional sentiments come to be regarded as antithetical."[47] So long as emotion is deemed "wholly resistant to rational assessment and ethical judgement," the democratisation of the social order is impaired.[48] While he suggests that "the fostering of democracy in the public domain was at first largely a male project," it is now the democratization of the personal life "in which women have thus far played the prime role," that beckons us to revalue emotions.[49] Essential to this revaluation is "refusing maleness," that is, "a task of ethical construction, which relates, not only sexual identity, but self-identity more broadly, to the moral concern of care for others."[50] For Giddens changing

---

[44] Giddens: *Transformation*, p. 1.
[45] Giddens: *Transformation*, p. 2 and passim.
[46] Giddens: *Transformation*, p. 197.
[47] Giddens: *Transformation*, p. 200.
[48] Giddens: *Transformation*, p. 201.
[49] Giddens: *Transformation*, p. 184.
[50] Giddens: *Transformation*, p. 200.

the subject of ethics reflects a process of the transformation of intimacy in a way that calls for us to "remoralise" the moral and existential issues that have been "pushed away from everyday life."[51] In this development of "life politics" lies the potentially subversive influence of an emphasis on emotional fulfillment, which has "democratic possibilities in the global political order at the most extensive level."[52]

Giddens's work may be said to be representative of those writings by men for whom the inclusion of intimacy within the concept of what it is to be a man is a significant outcome of feminist questions regarding the gender of the ethical subject. For some, this recovery of a relational dynamic of the personal, social, and spiritual life is the most significant factor in the redeeming of masculinity from the crises and fears that have become central to masculine identity formation.[53] To become a man who is not afraid of emotion, or helpless in friendships especially with other men, or cocooned in a "shell of manliness,"[54] is to embark on a journey of personal authenticity that is considered both more natural to the wholeness of man, and more true to the persons God made for relationship. The context for this change from gender dualism that so badly affects both women and men is the emancipation of sexuality, as "anatomy stops being destiny"[55] and as sexuality through eroticism becomes a quality "in social relations formed through mutuality rather than through unequal power."[56] Our ethical work, he suggests, is in providing the framework for this new "democratic personal order," which "provides for the elaboration of individuality"[57] and for the protection of personal autonomy in being self-reflective and self-determining. The return of sex to gender, it seems, corresponds to the return of the personal from the political.

In this chapter, we have examined some of the different ways in which the human subject figures in ethics. From feminisms comes the challenge that the subject of ethics is man, whose rational speculations take him from the world of emotions and relationships in which he is embedded, and whose decisions thereby both imply and manifest a gender dualism

---

[51]   Giddens: *Transformation*, p. 197.
[52]   Giddens: *Transformation*, pp. 3, 195–6.
[53]   J. Michael Hester: "Men in Relationships: Redeeming Masculinity," in Adrian Thatcher and Elizabeth Stuart, eds.: *Christian Perspectives on Sexuality and Gender* (Leominster: Gracewing, 1996), pp. 84–97.
[54]   Hester: "Men," p. 87.
[55]   Giddens: *Transformation*, p. 199.
[56]   Giddens: *Transformation*, p. 202.
[57]   Giddens: *Transformation*, p. 188.

masquerading as inclusively human. The critique of this subject questions the mediation of the ethical undertaken by man on behalf of all human beings, accusing it of a pretentious universality that is constructed on an exclusion of women. To bring this mediation into question is to expose a dynamic of human subjection which it has been the particular contribution of postmodern theories to investigate. In response to this critique, theories of masculinity have attempted a restoration of man as woman's complementary other, therein reproducing the traditional problematic of gender difference. Another response has been for an ethics of gender to consider whether and how the subject of ethics may be changed, so that the human subject may live on to found an other mediation. The meeting of woman and man in a democracy of concrete selves is the hope of Benhabib and Giddens, who seek to keep the project of modernity alive. For them, it is possible for ethical thinking to survive this change of subject, and thus in some way for them both, the subject lives on to perform its deliberative practice for a new humanity. This is the issue that must still be pressed, for thinking with gender in postmodernity brings us more vulnerably before the matters of what it is to be as human being, of what it is to engage in ethical thinking, and of what it might be to speak of a transfiguration of the human, and it does so by problematizing the body, subjectivity, and agency. That these matters have now come to the surface out of thinking with gender means that the survival of ethics as we know it may be more deeply thrown into question than this change of subject may suggest. We pursue this problematic more closely through the next three chapters.

4

The Matter of Bodies

One of the areas opened up by enquiries into gender is the matter of bodies. Bodies have been rendered problematic by thinking with gender. Because thinking with gender emerged as a critique of biology, it brings with it a number of troubled questions – about what it is to be in the body, what it is to live as embodied, what it signifies to be humanly bodied, in what ways the body is valued, and in what ways individual and social bodies are interrelated. Judith Butler poses the relevant questions that have appeared by asking whether the body is "a passive medium" on the surface of which cultural meanings of gender are inscribed, or whether the body is itself a construction that may "*come into being* in and through the mark(s) of gender."[1] Is the matter of bodies some preexisting stuff onto which cultural definitions and categories write, or do bodies themselves come to matter through our knowing and understanding of them? This matter of understanding the body, this understanding the matter of bodies lies within the thinking of gender and, in this chapter, is given its own attention. Two sections will provide a framework for this consideration. First, we will examine the conflicting views of gender as that which is determined by the body or as that in which the body is transcended. This is a conflict which features throughout the history of feminist investigations of the embodiment of women, and now finds a place also in the discourse regarding men and masculinity. It will be helpful to begin with the dialectic which these opposing positions set in motion and in which the Enlightenment inheritance of thinking is manifest. Secondly, then, we will turn to those postmodern writings which open out other ways of theorizing bodies. Postmodern theorists have made use of notions of

---

[1] Judith Butler: *Gender Trouble: Feminism and the Subversion of Identity* (London: Routledge, 1990), p. 8.

textuality, of trajectories of power, of cultural practices, and of symbolics, in order to think again the matter of bodies. Some of this thinking will be examined here as, with it, is a distancing from the inheritance of modernist thinking which may help us to understand anew the place of body in an ethics of gender.

Modern Bodies

The critical thinking with gender which has appeared during the modern period has shared, not surprisingly, in one of the philosophical conundrums of the time, and this has to do with how we are to understand minds and bodies and their relations with one another. It is conventional in histories of modern philosophy to lay some of the responsibility for the shape of this problem upon Descartes, whose particularly sharp form of dualistic thinking about human being set a pattern that subsequent thinkers are still discussing. So large does his figure loom in the writings of many feminists that it has often been difficult for them to read the history of thought that preceded him without, so to speak, wearing his spectacles. Typically, feminist writings have assumed that the representation of woman as associated with the body, the emotions and passions has enabled and sustained the representation of the man of reason, associated with transcendence of the bodily. Whether the dividing of mind and body into two separate and metaphysically distinct entities is a consistent pattern of dualism that can be read into the whole of the western tradition, or whether Cartesianism is an episode of modern thinking which we can now see our way around, has been a contentious issue within the writings of those concerned with gender questions. In this section, we examine two positions on gender which are possible, given this modern inheritance of dualism, to begin to see what some of the ethical issues are that appear there. Thus, there are those for whom gender is a matter of the reasonable exercise of thought and decision as we assume an identity for the body, and there are those for whom gender is a matter of physical givenness as the body provides the limiting conditions for this identity. The conflict between these positions provides the setting and the impetus for the emergence of postmodern gender thinking.

To consider the first position, the writings of Simone de Beauvoir and Jean-Paul Sartre can provide insight, for they both explore how it is that the body is entered into and lived in by human freedom. Sartre's important philosophical work, *Being and Nothingness*, suggests already in its title an approach to human life cast within and between two quite different kinds of being.[2] On the one hand, there is being-in-itself, *l'être-en-soi*, the being of the phenomenal world, that is, the stuff of which the world outside of ourselves is made. Being-in-itself as the matter of the world is passive and docile, viscous, slimy, a gelatinous stuff that merely waits, that is simply there, and thus our encounter with it in its raw state makes us feel nauseous. We seem to be in the presence of something that is wholly other to ourselves. Being-for-itself, *l'être-pour-soi*, on the other hand, is that nothingness which is pure freedom, and this is the being which is human consciousness. Freedom appears therefore as a tear, a rift, a hole, in being-in-itself, as consciousness erupts, to draw matter to itself, to make sense of it, to shape it into distinct objects by its definitions, to form it into patterns for the fulfillment of freedom's purposes, to order its messiness by means of schemes and maps, to determine what is its essence. The for-itself is the ultimate principle of human being according to which I am utterly free to choose, indeed, I am condemned to be free to choose at each moment of my life how I am to exist in the midst of the in-itself. I am free, I am freedom, and for human freedom, that I exist is prior to any description or determination of my life; human existence precedes essence.

Given such an ontology, the body requires particular attention. It is all very well to claim that we are completely free, as being-for-itself, to make and define and shape the world around us, but in what way do we live in and with our bodies, which would seem to share in the essence of being-in-itself? Here we discover that, for Sartre, the body is being-for-itself, since the body is the necessary form that human freedom takes to exist in the world. The body is "the contingent form which is assumed,"[3] and thus it can be said that "I exist my body"[4] insofar as it provides the nothingness which I am with its situation, its orientation, its engagement with being-in-itself. The body therefore lies on the dividing line of two kinds of being. It is the location of the meeting between the for-itself as freedom and the in-itself as matter. There are, however, other dimensions of the being of the body, and these are discovered in the encounter with other people. For in the look of others, I become an object through my body, so that my body becomes known by others, used by them, studied and examined, looked upon, and insofar as I exist my body, I become frozen, stuck, fixed by this objectification. This knowledge of myself through the eyes of others begins for me a most difficult and tortuous journey of relationships with

---

[2]   Jean-Paul Sartre: *Being and Nothingness: An Essay in Phenomenological Ontology*, trans. Hazel E. Barnes (New York: Citadel Press, 1965).
[3]   Sartre: *Being*, p. 285.
[4]   Sartre: *Being*, p. 327.

them, in which I face continual choices about how I am to be known in my body. Shall I refuse the picture others have of me or shall I agree to accept it? And all the while, I cannot escape the fact that what others know or think of me already entirely evades my control, so that I in my body somehow experience being *made* responsible for things that I cannot possibly *be* responsible for, and in this I experience an alienation in the body, an alienation which is all the keener because I know myself to be a freedom.

Such an account would seem to suggest that the embodiment of women and of men is a purely contingent matter, which has no significance in itself, but simply constitutes the mode of our engagement with the world as we happen to be born into it. Further, it would seem to suggest that the significance of my being woman or man appears with the look of others, who read me, who tell me what I am, and so it is in the mode of being-for-others that I come to be as gendered, with all that that means among the people with whom I have to deal. The ethical question becomes a matter of continual decision about whether and in what ways to accept or to cast aside what others make of me, so that relationships with others are always tense, unresolved battles of images, which are unavoidable, but at the same time incapable of depriving me of the existence in the body which is authentically my freedom. This is the dilemma which de Beauvoir traces for women in *The Second Sex*. Taking up the forms of bad faith that manifest themselves in women's thinking through the body, she argues that women let themselves be called the second sex, allowing that they can and should be treated as "other" to men, and in this handing over of responsibility for themselves, their own bodies bear the consequences. Woman's bodied life becomes a passivity, a giving over, for she makes of herself what she thinks men want her to be, and thus abandons her freedom. "In a sense her whole existence is waiting . . . since her justification is always in the hands of others."[5] Thus in de Beauvoir's claim that "One is not born, but rather becomes, a woman,"[6] lies a challenge to the interpretations of woman's embodiment, to the perspectives in which her body has been viewed in the look of others from within the cultural tradition, for it is clear that these cannot finally determine woman as she is in herself. Therefore the "body is not enough to define her as woman; there is no true living reality, except as manifested by the conscious individual through activities and in the bosom of a society."[7] The ethics of

[5] Simone de Beauvoir: *The Second Sex*, trans. H. M. Parshley (New York: Bantam Books, 1961), p. 575.
[6] De Beauvoir: *Second*, p. 249.
[7] De Beauvoir: *Second*, p. 33.

gender arises here in the social context of entangled freedoms and becomes a question of how I will sustain my own freedom to weave my way through its impositions on me. My freedom in the body is always a choosing and is always therefore at risk of giving itself up to others' determination.

In these writers, we find one kind of approach to body which suggests that, in the end, it is human freedom that is responsible for the shaping of the body's matter into its significance, and that even the determination of the body by the look of others and by cultural valuations, cannot deprive freedom of its authority over bodily matters. There is, however, a lingering question which appears explicitly in both of their works, and that has to do with sexual differentiation. While wanting to say that "man and woman equally exist," and that it is purely "contingent for 'human reality' to be specified as 'masculine' or 'feminine',"[8] nevertheless there remains a question about whether sexuality is "a necessary structure of being-for-itself-for-others."[9] The matter of the body as sexed appears here, and in this question lies the concern which is taken up by the opposing position. This places emphasis upon what is given to us prior to the emergence of individual freedom, and thus upon that which forms the reality or the nature that any particular existence is born into. The writings of sociobiologists have been influential in promoting this approach to the body, for they have sought to ground human freedom and reason in the natural bodily world of which these are an outcome. Saying that we are animals who think and feel, speak and develop culture, becomes a way of drawing our attention to the context of natural inheritance that precedes our particular lives and histories. The work of Mary Midgley is interesting in this regard, for she shares what has been a widespread concern among many feminists for an affirmation of bodiliness as something which is of value in itself, not something to be manipulated or directed by a finally detachable freedom, but something which gives to us, which carries for us, its own meanings. She presents a reasonable naturalism in which the body comes, earthed and sexed, into being ahead of us.

For Midgley, as a philosopher who is both sensitive to the interests but critical of the doctrinaire claims of sociobiology, the roots of human nature lie in the complex set of inborn active and social tendencies with which we are endowed as animals and which bestow upon us a framework within which values can develop and make sense.[10] She is drawn to this

[8]   Sartre: *Being*, p. 359.
[9]   Sartre: *Being*, p. 360.
[10]   Mary Midgley: *Beast and Man: The Roots of Human Nature* (London: Methuen, 1979).

approach for its potential to overcome the Cartesian inheritance of a separation of mind from body, and for its insights into the accompanying muddle in ethical theory over facts and values. Such an understanding of the body seeks therefore to be holistic, to give attention to all of those interactive moments in which instinct and purpose, feeling and thinking, impulse and decision, limitation and imagination, contingency and possibility, come together and overlap and work cooperatively for the good of the whole human being. These things, she argues, are not so unusual in our daily lives, nor are they so extraordinary that we cannot find similarities between our human bodies and those of other species of animal. Indeed, it is in the body that all of these become possible to us, for it provides us with occasions and with matters, with needs and with appetites, that require concentration of our energy into reasoning and deciding, into organizing and developing, which our bodied lives are most capable of undertaking well. So she argues that our practical reasoning sets about its work of determining "what would be best 'for such a creature as man'," understanding that "the range and pattern of possible aims is given with the species."[11] Embodied moral decisions are thus not a matter of choosing anything at all, but of knowing that "once the nature of a species . . . is given, there are limits to the ways in which you can hope to make sense of it."[12]

Thus Midgley seeks "to get away from the essentially *colonial* picture . . . in which an imported governor, named Reason, imposes order on a chaotic alien tribe of Passions or Instincts."[13] Such an image honored Thought, but could not, she claims, "establish values," and it is for the bringing together of these again that she seeks to develop her picture of "continuity." Her argument that "what matters" comes already with the body to be discerned and fitted out by the mind, is an attempt to recover the Aristotelian sense of matter fitting its form.[14] This way of thinking the body guides Midgley's reflections upon the concerns that gender raises, for she seeks to discover within human culture, those roots in nature that social structures and roles are developed to complete. "Culture is natural,"[15] she argues, in the sense of being an accomplishment of which the human species is capable, and so it is a compliment to its institutions to say that they meet human needs.[16] Thus sexual behaviour emerges at a certain

[11] Midgley: *Beast*, p. 281.
[12] Midgley: *Beast*, p. 281.
[13] Midgley: *Beast*, p. 260.
[14] Midgley: *Beast*, p. 280.
[15] Midgley: *Beast*, p. 285.
[16] Midgley: *Beast*, p. 303.

stage of personal development out of "an inherent disposition,"[17] to find its form in institutions of marriage, varied across cultures, which cater for its real demands by providing a structure of long-term commitment.[18] At the same time, Midgley has little time for "sex-linked moralities" which, she argues, "cannot really be of much use," since "we all have the emotions of both sexes within us – not enough to realize them fully, but enough to need more, enough to make a single-sex world a poor one for anybody."[19] This kind of thinking "establishes values" for her, such that she goes on to be critical of those who think that sexually different means inferior, a splitting of the human race "that is not rational at all," and of those cultures in which the two sexes operate entirely separately, which "waste a great part of human potential."[20] Holism emerges here as that which is of most value to natural bodies, so that to think the pattern of the whole as the form in which the particularities of matter may come into their own, provides a framework for the ethical questions that gender raises.

Most writers who find themselves in this second position would argue that the matter of bodies is to do with sexual difference, and that it is this which shapes what becomes gender, which precedes, or even underlies, gender. As Moira Gatens has put it succinctly: "Concerning the neutrality of the body, let me be explicit, there is no neutral body; there are at least two kinds of bodies: the male body and the female body. . . ."[21] Thus, in contrast to the existentialism of Sartre and de Beauvoir for whom the human being is fundamentally a nothingness, here the human being is a sexually specific subject grounded in nature and this, it is argued, can be no bad thing. What is impressive about Midgley's work is that she seeks so carefully both to avoid the overeager claims of biologists to have identified gendered genes that rigidly determine patterns of behavior and values, and to urge a commonality of concern for the whole of nature, on whose behalf the highest sympathies and reasonings of women and men are adapted.[22] Yet in her approach, there are still questions that thinking with gender raises, for who is it who thinks what it is that is natural, and who is it who posits something like a real world into which we then understand ourselves to be placed? This is surely a human thinking, and once we have thought it, what does it mean that we turn those thoughts back upon

[17] Midgley: *Beast*, p. 55.
[18] Midgley: *Beast*, pp. 302–5.
[19] Midgley: *Beast*, p. 353.
[20] Midgley: *Beast*, p. 353.
[21] Moira Gatens: *Imaginary Bodies: Ethics, Power and Corporeality* (London: Routledge, 1996), p. 8.
[22] Midgley: *Beast*, p. 361.

ourselves to shape our behaviour and our decisions? A naturalism of the body is engaging in just this work of self-reflection, which it then claims to be grounded, rooted, earthed in some greater whole or more funda- mental reality that lies outside its reflection. This is precisely a way of thinking which Sartre claimed to be the work of a freedom, which draws maps of the world and devises systems of classification for the things that are found there. It is I who then freely decides to place the body within one of these systems or maps.

The opposition that runs between these two ways of thinking the body reflects the modern inheritance of dualism, and the unresolvable concerns that lie along its fault line have been the focus of much attention in feminist and in gender theory. These interpretations of body carry implica- tions too for understanding ethics. If, on the one hand, thinking the body and existing the body as freedom is ultimately in our own individual hands, is there any moral to our thinking? Sartre suggests that the moral lies in authenticity, and thus that my being authentic in my body is what matters. Authenticity is a matter of my choosing, so that it is conferred on my body by freedom. The moral "ought" of my free decision directs the "is" of the body. If, on the other hand, the body comes already envalued to us, then reasonable interpretations of it always remain within the scope of its unfolding, and ethical thinking turns back to affirm what is there. What, then, is distinctive about ethics as a form of deliberation, and in what sense may its thinking be considered to effect anything? Midgley's account suggests that the moral lies in the realization of what is given, and thus that what is authentically human is conferred by my body upon my freedom as the realm within which my choices make any sense. The "ought" lies in the body's "is." This dilemma of the "is" and the "ought" haunts modern thinking, and through the questions raised by gender, it may be seen to come to reside in the body. For it seems that the body has become problematic to us, or rather that the body has become the bearer of the problematization of our thinking, and so our existence as bodied human beings bears these troubles forth into the world. Much that is clustered under the heading of postmodernity is an expression of these difficulties, as bodies reveal something of what is the matter with them.

Postmodern Bodies

These dilemmas of modernism become the kinds of concerns taken up by those cultural theorists and philosophers who seek specifically to address its problematic. In general, we may say that postmodern thinking is not so much an attempt to overcome the problems of modernism by providing a more compelling or comprehensive overall vision of understanding, as it is an entering more deeply into the troubled areas of modern thinking to attend to the anguish that lies there. The aim is not to provide a solution, so much as to lay open the difficulties in another way. So here, there is not a better theory of the body suggested, that may resolve the mind–body problem or provide definitive answers in the sex–gender debate. Rather, there is an effort to think the matter of bodies differently, and in that difference perhaps to find an other way through the problematic inherited with modernity. So it is not a new theory, or set of theories that we examine, but a way of thinking through, a theorizing the body, by which we may come to some new insights for an ethics of gender. In general again, it may be said that postmodern thinking undermines the possessive individualism that disturbs modern thinking with its anxiety about control of the body's matter. Rather, there is a thinking of the givenness of the body as a process of mattering, in which I come to be as embodied. The body's coming to matter opens another way of speaking into the problematic of modern thinking.

One of the ways in which postmodern thinking speaks of the body coming to matter is through an investigation of its formation in the social world. What proves interesting here is the way in which bodies come to be members of a social body, bearing the marks of social codes and carrying out the work of this social body in their various activities. So Michel Foucault speaks of docile bodies, and Pierre Bourdieu, of inhabited bodies, both as forms of theorizing this social formation of the matter of bodies. The making of the substance of bodies, the making of their matter, came to be the central concern in much of Foucault's study of the regulatory practices of social institutions and discursive systems. There is indeed something substantial about the body, but for Foucault this is not unformed matter, being-in-itself, nor is it an innate biological nature. What makes the body substantial is not its raw material. Rather, the body receives its matter as a kind of ethical substance, which it bears on behalf of the society in which it is formed. The body becomes substantial as a construct of the institutions and fields of discourse in the midst of which it appears, so that it becomes the embodied appearance of the particular needs and interests of any given society. He asked, for example, "What mode of investment of the body is necessary and adequate for the functioning of a capitalist society such as ours? . . . One needs to study what kind of body the current society needs."[23] Asking what is required by the social body

---

[23]   Michel Foucault: *Power/Knowledge: Selected Interviews and Other Writings 1972–1977*, ed. Colin Gordon (Brighton: Harvester, 1980), p. 58.

leads us to interpret individual bodies as the particular locations of society's investment. A body comes to matter as that in which society has deposited its value and from which it expects a return. Thus there is always a "political anatomy" that substantiates the matter of bodies.[24] In this is an overturning of the metaphysics of substance that purports to be the foundation for the political.[25]

Bodies come to matter by means of techniques of social power, exercised as power/knowledge systems. The docile body is "directly involved in a political field" in which "power relations . . . invest it, mark it, train it, torture it, force it to carry out tasks, to perform ceremonies, to emit signs."[26] This is not so much a matter of my already-existing body being taken over, or being put upon by an external power, as it is a matter of my being made into a body in the first instance, constructed by the exercises of power in which I am already intimately involved, to be both "a productive body and a subjected body."[27] My body becomes useful in being made to produce for social needs, and so it comes to be recognizable as it is trained for the part it is to play. Important to this process is the receiving of knowledge, for it is knowledge that embodies and distributes social interests, and produces acceptable ways of thinking. The mode of becoming productive is also the mode of the body's subjection to disciplines that render me useful and of service. This comes about through processes of confession to teachers, doctors, priests, counsellors, agony aunts, and consultants, in which I come to see things, to know things, the way these professionals know them. My body comes to be adapted to the shape of this knowledge, disciplined by its requirements, subjected to its routines. Through this formation in the power/knowledge system, the body becomes an ethos, by which Foucault means, a manner of being. The body becomes a manner of being, formed within the political economy of its society, and shaped by its moral codes.[28] The moral codes of a society articulate its investment and expectation, its accounting of bodies, and these then take up residence in its members, in a colonization of its docile bodies. Thus it is that Foucault speaks of the soul becoming the prison of

---

24 Michel Foucault: "Docile Bodies," in *The Foucault Reader*, ed. Paul Rabinow (Harmondsworth: Penguin, 1986), p. 182.
25 See Butler: *Gender*, pp. 16–17.
26 Michel Foucault: "The Body of the Condemned," in Rabinow, ed., *The Foucault Reader*, p. 173.
27 Foucault: "Body," p. 173.
28 Michel Foucault: "Politics and Ethics: An Interview," in Rabinow, ed., *The Foucault Reader*, p. 377.

the body,[29] in a way that succinctly undermines the privilege of the soul over the body so prized in western thinking.

In his work, *Outline of a Theory of Practice*, Pierre Bourdieu too analyzes this interface of individual and society which the body is. His is another attempt to move beyond the dualistic thinking the body of modernism, this time by focusing on processes of incorporation, that is, how it is that individual bodies come to be incorporated into the wider society in which they exist, and how it is that the social comes to be incorporated in the thinking and behavior of individuals. The body is the site of this mutual incorporation, one with another, the mechanism for which is the *habitus*. By *habitus*, Bourdieu means "systems of durable, transposable *dispositions*," that is, long-term patterns of thinking and acting by means of which we come to occupy our places in the social order.[30] These dispositions "are objectively organized as strategies without being the product of a genuine strategic intention,"[31] and it is their acquisition by which bodies come to be inhabited. Rather than being a passive or docile body, the body here is the subject of practices which are learned like the way to play a game is learned, and, by being imitated continuously as one grows in expertise, are then ingrained into the body's appearance and activity. At this point the practices become unconscious, since their actions have been internalized by a subject who complies with them. The process of learning social practices is the achievement of *habitus*, and it is both a complex and a subtle one, involving the thoughtfulness of the individual in taking on a role, in being receptive to social conventions, and the durability of bodily expressions which keep reenacting social meanings unconsciously. Thus the body becomes inhabited by the material frameworks of social relations, by being practiced in particular ways, by being trained, by being receptive to the meanings of social relations and thus by coming to be the embodiment of them.

Bourdieu offers in this "reflexive sociology" an analysis of *doxa*, those social conceptions produced by an established order that acquire the force of being thought "natural." In a way that runs parallel to Foucault's description of systems of power/knowledge, Bourdieu writes of "systems of classification" which maintain the symbolic order of society by reproducing it in the bodies of its members. "Schemes of thought and perception,"

---

[29] Michel Foucault: *Discipline and Punish: The Birth of the Prison*, trans. Alan Sheridan (New York: Vintage, 1979), p. 30.
[30] Pierre Bourdieu: *Outline of a Theory of Practice*, trans. Richard Nice (Cambridge: Cambridge University Press, 1977), p. 72.
[31] Bourdieu: *Outline*, p. 73.

he writes, become "political instruments which contribute to the reproduction of the social world," by objectifying "a sense of reality" that provides the context for the *habitus* of individuals.[32] So it is that gender
difference comes to be considered essential, through a "thousand-year
project of socialisation of the biological and of biologising the social,
which reverses the relation between cause and effect," since "the work
aimed at transforming into nature the arbitrary product of history finds its
apparent foundation in the appearance of the body, at the same time as it
creates very real effects on the body and inside the brain. . . ."[33] Here is a
statement of the effectiveness of gender ideology in making bodies, in
bringing about in bodies what it proclaims to be true. Thus the distinction
of male and female is a *doxa* of sexual difference, like all *doxa*, secured by
"the misrecognition, and hence the recognition, of the arbitrariness on
which they are based,"[34] and like all *doxa*, inhabiting the bodies of a given
society as they come to matter within it. It becomes the task of ethics to
close the gap, to bridge the divide between this "natural" and this "social,"
so that the two come into "a quasi-perfect correspondence" in the *habitus*
of bodies.[35]

For both of these sociocultural theorists, the matter of bodies is socially
formed, and the means for that formation is knowledge that inscribes
docile bodies with its text, or *doxa* that come to inhabit bodies. Thus
Bourdieu writes:

> . . . nothing seems more ineffable, more incommunicable, more inimitable,
> and, therefore, more precious, than the values given body, *made* body by
> the transubstantiation achieved by the hidden persuasion of an implicit
> pedagogy, capable of instilling a whole cosmology, an ethic, a metaphysic, a
> political philosophy, through injunctions as insignificant as "stand up straight"
> or "don't hold your knife in your left hand."[36]

Both of these theorists undertake a troubling of humanism, for the matter
of bodies is neither an unformed flesh awaiting human decision, nor the
bearer of biological limitations and potentialities. The body is not presocial,
or precultural. For Foucault, the body is that surface upon which society

---

[32] Bourdieu: *Outline*, pp. 164–5.
[33] Pierre Bourdieu: "La Domination masculine," *Actes de la Recherche en Sciences Sociales* 84 (1990), p. 12. Cited in Bridget Fowler: *Pierre Bourdieu and Cultural Theory: Critical Investigations* (London: Sage, 1997), p. 136.
[34] Bourdieu: *Outline*, p. 164.
[35] Bourdieu: *Outline*, p. 164.
[36] Bourdieu: *Outline*, p. 94.

writes, such that it comes to life as discourses appear on its flesh. Gender is such a writing the body, so that the body comes to matter as an effect of domination by a system of power/knowledge. Because we cannot speak of the body before its social inscription, Foucault finds the possibility of transformation to lie only in playful reinscriptions of the body through aesthetic creativity, body-art or body-as-art. Yet the body is that upon which something is inscribed, and in this is a presumption of its being-there, waiting to come out in our discourses. For Bourdieu, the body is something of a memory system, which learns behavior and demeanor in what he calls its "body *hexus*." In its inculcation of social values, the body comes to matter as the bearer of properties, sexual and physical, which are praised or stigmatized by the social structure and by the body's own position within it.[37] Thus is "history turned into nature,"[38] by the ethical practices of inhabited bodies.

Understanding the body to be as a social formation, or as the site of a transubstantiation of social values into material form, these theorists un-ravel the substantiality of body as some prior natural matter received into the social world, bearing messages or drives that condition its realization within society. To speak of these messages or drives as preexisting is already to speak from the place of social interpretation and need. This point is pressed to its logical conclusion by Jacques Derrida, who speaks of the body itself as discursive. His is a notion of body understood as text. As we have seen, Foucault too emphasized the constitution of the body by discourses, which order all of the dimensions of the body, and thus effect its nature. Discourses, as ways of formulating knowledge, are associated with the social practices that empower us, and so everybody is discursively constructed within the power relations of any institution or set of prac-tices. Sexuality is such a discourse, a way of formulating knowledge about the dimensions of the body, and it is a discourse which is historically specific, embedded within the practices and the institutions of its time. The sexuality of the body thus cannot be abstracted from its actual situ-ation in history, since it has no meaning apart from the ways in which it is defined within particular discursive practices. While this consideration of the docile body seems almost to suggest that the body is some thing, which society then works over for its purposes, or upon which it inscribes, there is in Derrida a stronger sense of the body not being any thing at all, but a name for a site of interactive discourses that leave their traces across its path. So committed is he to a critique of the metaphysics of presence,

---

[37]   Bourdieu: *Outline*, p. 87.
[38]   Bourdieu: *Outline*, p. 78.

that the body becomes utterly dissolved into the language that speaks it forth into the world. The body *is* only as text, and "there is nothing outside the text."[39]

The method for this critique is deconstruction, by which we refuse this "outside," turning whatever is written or spoken about body back into itself. In refusing to think that there is some matter behind, or underneath, or beyond language, Derrida deconstructs texts of the western tradition that repeat a metaphysics of mind over against matter, and thereby seek to control the centre from which meaning is apportioned. He carries out this deconstruction, not by proclaiming the victory of one over the other, nor by seeking a higher synthesis, but by returning us entirely into the language in which we speak of these things. So language "has not fallen from the sky, its differences have been produced, are produced effects, but they are effects which do not find their cause in a subject or a substance, in a thing in general, a being that is somewhere present, thereby eluding the play of *différance*."[40] In this thinking, there is a subversion of dualistic formulations, by reminding us that the differences of which we speak are produced effects, part of an economy of language that eludes the possibility of its death, and of its being transported by a resistance to its economy.[41] To effect this dying and rising is to think without sexual difference, and thereby to displace the binary logic of western thought which has bound the body, as a dead thing fixed in texts that can no longer speak life, and which has privileged freedom and reason as those uniquely human contributions to the material world of nature. Binary logic will reinscribe the unequal polarity of male and female endlessly. This leads Derrida to a strong claim for the potential of language, for "what opens meaning and language is writing as the disappearance of natural presence."[42] Thus do we become responsible for bodies coming to matter in discourse. To think the discursive body is to think in antiessentialist, and antihumanist ways, for it is a thinking which deeply questions the ethics that have been formulated by the metaphysics of presence in its will to truth. To live the body requires new speaking.

In postmodern thinking of the body, a way is sought through the dualism inherited in the modern western tradition of thinking the body.

---

[39]   Jacques Derrida: *Of Grammatology*, trans. Gayatri Chakravorty Spivak (Baltimore, MD: Johns Hopkins University Press, 1976), p. 163.
[40]   Jacques Derrida: "Différance," in *Margins of Philosophy*, trans. Alan Bass (London: Harvester Wheatsheaf, 1982), p. 11.
[41]   Derrida: "Différance," p. 5.
[42]   Derrida: *Grammatology*, p. 159.

Between, on the one hand, the freedom of a nothingness which comes to be situated in a body and so to be embodied by its physicality, yet which is always of another substance to the body, and on the other hand, a bodied evolution out of which human reason and freedom come to be constituted as possibilities for the body's own self-reflection and direction, yet which are bound to a physical reality believed to take precedence, between these two positions of modernity, postmodernity thinks through the body in other ways. The docile body is the one that is enabled by regimes of power/knowledge to take up its place as normal and to enact in its ethos, its manner of living, the discipline into which it has been constructed. The inhabited body is one that bears the unspoken *doxa* of the social order by means of the *habitus*, that is, the learning of practices in which bodies both receive and enact the material reality of their culture. The discursive body is the one that is constructed as we speak, that weaves its way between the stable places of meaning which would secure it against its future, and the openness of language which can bring it to mean and thus to be something quite different, a body constructed in difference.

These ways of thinking the body have opened up new issues for an ethics of gender. Rather than gender understood as a chosen way of being in the body, so that it all comes down to my freedom, or gender as the social development of the sexed body, so that nature takes its course through me – ways of thinking that are given in modernity, postmodern thinking suggests a new possibility regarding the matter of bodies. Interestingly, the notion of "matter" has come to figure in the writings of a moral theologian and a literary theorist in not dissimilar ways, and it is with the suggestions that lie within their work that we bring this chapter to a close. Helen Oppenheimer is one among a number of philosophers who have looked for a way through the split between the "is" and the "ought" that plagues modern moral philosophy. In its different formulations, this division was believed to enhance the exercise of human freedom in choosing what is to be of value, without being bound by material facts. Modern ethics has taken its place within this assertion of its power of valuing on the one hand, and its constructed "other," namely, the realities of natural, physical things as they are. The question of gender appears in this difference. Oppenheimer suggests that mattering is a bridge concept, which is not to be explained in terms of anything else, but carries its moral meaning with it.[43] We learn that we matter in the context of relations with other people who then come to matter to us, and we learn that mattering is a human activity that has substance and that therefore gives substance to our

---

[43]   Helen Oppenheimer: "Mattering," *Studies in Christian Ethics* 8:1 (1995), pp. 60–76.

lives. These forms of mattering, for Oppenheimer, take place within an overall context of a God who matters and in whose mattering, we come to be rooted in love. Such thinking might be considered a positive theology of mattering.

A kind of negative theology of mattering is to be found in the work of Judith Butler, who takes up the subject from within its postmodern troubling, that is, from within a thinking which is concerned for mattering both as human activity, and as what is understood to be taking place in the world of matter, in what is called material reality. Butler recognizes that postmodern thinking has challenged materialism, for to "problematize the matter of bodies may entail an initial loss of epistemological certainty. . . ."[44] Indeed, some of the thinking above seems to suggest that bodies are not real, that they do not exist independently of human thinking them or social ordering of them, and thus to idealize the body further away from any notion of its irreducible materiality. Rather than respond with a renewed realism, Butler seeks in her gender theory "to free [materiality] from its metaphysical lodgings,"[45] and thus to reopen the debates from Greek philosophy regarding what matter is understood to be.

One step in this liberation of matter is to question the notion that matter exists as some kind of permanent exterior to thinking, and further that the body is "posited as prior to the sign, is always *posited* or *signified* as *prior*."[46] What happens in this signification is that the body is produced, it comes to be what its sign has said.

> This signification produces as an *effect* of its own procedure the very body that it nevertheless and simultaneously claims to discover as that which *precedes* its own action. If the body signified as prior to signification is an effect of signification, then the mimetic or representational status of language, which claims that signs follow bodies as their necessary mirrors, is not mimetic at all. On the contrary, it is productive, constitutive, one might even argue *performative*, inasmuch as this signifying act delimits and contours the body that it then claims to find prior to any and all signification.

By raising the question whether language can "simply refer to materiality" or whether it is "the very condition under which materiality may be said to appear,"[47] Butler engages the "empiricist foundationalism" that lies

---

[44] Judith Butler: *Bodies That Matter: On the Discursive Limits of "Sex"* (London: Routledge, 1993), p. 30.
[45] Butler: *Bodies*, p. 30.
[46] Butler: *Bodies*, p. 30.
[47] Butler: *Bodies*, p. 31.

within much modern and feminist thinking the body, with an unmasking of "the genealogy of power relations by which it is constituted."[48] Bodies come to matter in the interface of these relations. Bodies materialize within a field in which they are bound, formed, and deformed by "a set of enforced criteria of intelligibility," as they are given meaning, and as they assume the matter of their significance.[49]

Butler's analysis here greatly sharpens the ethical question that gender raises. For all of these thinkings of the body have been in some way about formation, about the formation of bodies as sexed/gendered, and thus about the ways in which I come to matter in the body, the way in which I come to be formed in the body that matters. What I find Butler asking is that an ethics of gender not reproduce the very metaphysical separations it is intended to overcome, that it not by its own thinking and recommendations repeat the difference of body/mind in which gender has been rendered problematic throughout modernity, and thus bury the questions which come to matter in the body of gender theory. This will happen with each new normative regime in which the bodies of woman and man come to be refigured. It also, she suggests, will happen with each attempt at a positive theology of gender, at a new more "inclusive representability" which seeks to be so expansive as to include, "to bring in every marginal and excluded position within a given discourse," and thus to admit of no "outside" and thus to "domesticate all signs of difference."[50] Rather, she proposes that "The task is to refigure this necessary 'outside' as a future horizon, one in which the violence of exclusion is perpetually in the process of being overcome."[51] That the matter of bodies might bring forth such transformations as a holding open of the future is the hope within a postmodern ethics of gender.

The matter of bodies has been an area of discussion in which gender theory has participated in the change of the times, as western thinking moves from a modern phase of development into a postmodern one. The categories of thinking the body have been troubled by gender questions, within feminisms as the constructing and valuing of women's bodies becomes a moral and political issue of some deep and continuing concern, and within gender theory as the issue opens out into one of theorizing what the body is understood to be. In this new way of philosophy, there has been an unsettling of both normative and theoretical frameworks. This

---

[48]   Butler: *Bodies*, p. 35.
[49]   Butler: *Bodies*, p. 55.
[50]   Butler: *Bodies*, p. 53.
[51]   Butler: *Bodies*, p. 53.

has not happened without a certain ambivalence, since the gender critique has taken shape within the very dilemmas of modern thinking that are now displaced. Nevertheless it is the hope expressed here that such displacement may be the opening for a new thinking what is the matter with bodies, a thinking that unsettles the presumption of some preexisting secure material universe into which human beings are to appear. In questioning how it is that bodies come to matter, thinking with gender turns Christian theology too back its own central affirmations regarding the coming to matter of God and the turning of matter into God, and asks that these be considered anew. So the radical character of much that appears with the postmodern is a turning into inherited ideas with renewed interest.

5

The Subject of Language

The subject of language is a second area of discussion, in which it is possible to trace the ways this subject has been troubled within modern thinking, and in which it is being thought again in postmodern theory. Language has figured already in the discussion of the matter of bodies, for the discursive formation of the body comes to prominence in each of the postmodern theories we examined. There too we could begin to see how the subject of language presents itself. In brief, it may be said that within modernism, disputes about who is the subject of language bring out the problematic of language, understood as a mode either of representation or of the social formation of subjects. With the first, language becomes the medium through which the essence of human life may be presented as an ethical ideal or end, in relation to which subjects come to identify themselves and deliberate about their activities. With the second, language becomes the coordinating grid of social values and meanings, in the intersections of which, subjects come to figure as significant participants in a meaningful interactive world. In both, the assumption of the subject as the speaker or user of language figures as that necessary presence that ultimately legitimates the project of language. It is precisely this presenting subject of language that postmodern theories begin to render problematic, and in this appear new questions for thinking with gender. After considering modern notions of the subject as speaker, especially as these appear within feminist ethical and theological writings, we then consider the decentring and death of the subject in postmodern thinking, whereby language comes to be thought in an other way as that which speaks the subject into world. With this turn of thinking, new ethical questions of gender come to be figured.

Assumptions of the Subject of Language

Feminist theology and ethics during recent decades has been much exercised with issues of language, since women have understood themselves, as subjects, to be the site of the problematic of language within modernism. A significant dimension of feminist critique has been a moral challenge to the representation of women in the western cultural tradition, a philosophical challenge to the adequacy and legitimacy of these representations as images of the human subject, and a theological challenge to the representation of the divine believed to be the grounding principle of these images. These challenges have been encouraged by the development of Enlightenment humanism, in which the human subject as the one who knows and the one who speaks, and thus the human subject as authority, come to the surface in western thinking. The human-centredness of this approach to epistemology and to ethics is one in which women have been seeking to play their own part alongside men. Thus the ethical and pastoral concerns for women have been about the misrepresentation, the devaluation, and the silencing or invisibility of women, all of which are the consequence of inadequate or illegitimate images of the gendered subject propounded throughout centuries of ethical and theological teaching. What has been invoked to challenge these representations has been an other subject, an other author, to come to speak, and for this, feminist writers have called upon women's experience and women's situatedness to speak as a different subject. Here it is not so much the individual subject that is prominent, as it is the social subject, embedded in the particularities of situations and embodied in relationships, who works within the linguistic frameworks of a given culture to promote positive changes. This move from challenging representations to affirming re-presentations will be examined in this section of the chapter.

Rosemary Ruether's book, *Sexism and God-Talk*, may be understood to be a feminist critique of the subject of theological language. Central to this work is the conviction stated early on in the book that "If a symbol does not speak authentically to experience, it becomes dead or must be altered to provide a new meaning."[1] Ruether claims that such is now the case with the western theological tradition, comprising dead symbols in which human beings have become trapped. Her critique of the subject as represented in

---

[1] Rosemary Radford Ruether: *Sexism and God-Talk: Towards a Feminist Theology* (London: SCM Press, 1983), pp. 12–13.

theological language reveals the ways in which subjects have become embedded in language that is no longer authentic to their experience, nor is it justly inclusive of the whole of the humanity it seeks to represent, and thus she questions what the subject of this language is said to be. In the study of human beings which is Christian theological anthropology, "a dual structure" is used to understand our humanity, which "differentiates the essence from the existence of humanity." This ethical language separates what humanity is "potentially and authentically" from what humanity "has been historically." It speaks theologically of this essential human subject as the *imago dei*, the image of God that "represents this authentic humanity united with God," and of the existing human subject as the fallen, sinful descendants of Adam and Eve.[2] The concern that motivates so much of Ruether's theological work is that this "dual structure" is a front for the man, a cover, a mask for the promotion of the interests of the male subject and for the demotion of those of the female subject.

To substantiate this concern takes her through investigation of texts from the tradition to show how this duality, while affirming a fundamental "equivalence of maleness and femaleness in the image of God," nevertheless allows this to be "obscured" by another tendency to identify the sinful, fallen human subject with woman. Femaleness becomes thereby linked "with the lower part of human nature in a hierarchical scheme of mind over body, reason over passions," and thus with "the sin-prone part of the self."[3] The consistency of Ruether's critique of this subject of theology leads her to expose a range of dualisms that the divided self spawns, and that are used to justify mistreatment and devaluation of whatever group is identified as "other."[4] Within these exposures appears the question of redemption, for Ruether has asked what has become a quite decisive question for feminist theology, namely whether a male subject redeems female subjects, "Can a male saviour save women?"[5] Hers is a concern that women will repeat their subjection to false and disabling hierarchical thinking by submitting to the mediations of a man, since to acknowledge their need for him and the sacrifice of their lives for his love is further to render them silent as speaking subjects themselves. The story of this dilemma is told as a historical narrative in Ruether's recent book *Women and Redemption*, in which she repeats the hope that finds expression

[2]   Ruether: *Sexism*, p. 93.
[3]   Ruether: *Sexism*, p. 93.
[4]   Rosemary Radford Ruether: "Dualism and the Nature of Evil in Feminist Theology," *Studies in Christian Ethics* 5:1 (1992).
[5]   Ruether: *Sexism*, p. 116.

in so much she has written, the hope for "a new humanity."[6] For she still holds onto the belief that gender relations have been changed by a definitive redemption, that in Christ there is neither male nor female, and thus that there is a revelatory event according to which all renderings of the subject of theological language should be judged. Thus is it suggested that the true subject of language is beyond the dual structure, beyond the ethical ideals that create hierarchical divisions, and that redemption "becomes transformed gender relations that overcome male domination."[7]

Ruether's work highlights how significant it has become in feminist thinking for women to represent themselves, to present themselves in speaking and writing, and in this changing of the subject lies a paradigm shift for theological language. For now, the subject of the language of redemption is no longer Jesus, but ourselves, for while his is a "root story," redemption "cannot be done by one person for everyone else . . . but it happens only when all of us do it for ourselves and for one another."[8] What women find in this story is a redemptive paradigm of dissent, taking the side of the oppressed, "living a praxis of egalitarian relations," and "pointing toward a new time" which is anticipated in communal celebrations now.[9] Since "No one person can become the 'collective human' whose actions accomplish a salvation that is then passively applied to everyone else,"[10] the subject of language is now understood to be multiple, polyvocal, diverse, particular, multireligious and multicultural, plural, and contextual. This new subject with its greater inclusivity, with its wider concern for liberation "that can meet and converge around the world," with its resistance to all forms of hierarchical domination, this new subject overcomes the old one, bringing new meaning to theological language. That such a change brings feminists to ask whether this does not also mean the end of Christian theology is perhaps not surprising, for Ruether herself acknowledges this to be "a human project, not an exclusively Christian project."[11] So it is that feminist theologians, like Daphne Hampson, pursue the logic of these changes to the conclusion that "No notion of God must be allowed to disrupt the centrality of human beings (understood together, one would hope, with the rest of the creation) to the picture" and to the

---

[6]   Rosemary Radford Ruether: *Women and Redemption: A Theological History* (London: SCM Press, 1998); see Introduction, pp. 1–11.

[7]   Ruether: *Redemption*, p. 273.

[8]   Ruether: *Redemption*, p. 275.

[9]   Ruether: *Redemption*, pp. 276–7.

[10]   Ruether: *Redemption*, p. 275.

[11]   Ruether: *Redemption*, p. 281.

affirmation of the relational subject in its inclusive spirituality as an over-coming of male autonomous individualism.[12]

This thinking about the subject of theological language forms around a cluster of assumptions that appear with Enlightenment humanism which it might be helpful at this point to make explicit. One of these would be the assumption of responsibility, for underlying the critique and the reconstruction of the subject which this kind of feminist thinking presents, is the belief that human beings are responsible for the speaking of themselves, for their own use of language, and thus for the representations of themselves that this language presents as credible. The assuming of responsibility by the subject of language has been important to feminist philosophers who have been arguing for alternative epistemologies, for whom "to know" something has been understood to mean "to put it into words." De Beauvoir already held men responsible for knowledge: "Representation of the world, like the world itself, is the work of men; they describe it from their own point of view, which they confuse with absolute truth."[13] What women must do to challenge male constructions of knowledge is to take responsibility for their own ways of knowing, and thus to posit an altern-ative, to speak in answer to a question that may have been asked derisively, "What Can She Know?" with the construction of a knowledge from their own "specifically positioned subjects."[14] This speaking is a political and moral responsibility, a deliberate refusal of the oppressed position of silent one, of victim, in which one is rendered an "incredible woman." The pastoral implications of this are explored by Riet Bons-Storm, who is persuaded that the transition to becoming a "credible subject" is the key moment for women in taking on the fullness of their humanity, "in thinking of themselves as trustworthy knowing subjects," and thus "as credible subjects of their own authentic stories."[15] This is the sense in which women are to become authoritative, as the authors of their own narratives, and thus as full subjects in their own right. To become a subject of language is to assume responsibility for the narration of one's life and knowledge into speech.

[12]   Daphne Hampson: *After Christianity* (London: SCM Press, 1996), p. 11.
[13]   Simone de Beauvoir: *The Second Sex*, trans. H. M. Parshley (New York: Bantam Books, 1961), p. 161.
[14]   Lorraine Code: *What Can She Know? Feminist Theory and the Construction of Know-ledge* (Ithaca, NY: Cornell University Press, 1991), p. 170. See also Lorraine Code: "Taking Subjectivity into Account," in *Rhetorical Spaces: Essays on Gendered Locations* (London: Routledge, 1995), pp. 23–57.
[15]   Riet Bons-Storm: *The Incredible Woman: Listening to Women's Silences in Pastoral Care and Counseling* (Nashville TN: Abingdon Press, 1996), p. 79.

Within this, there is the assumption of power, by which the resources for and commitment to this overthrowing of the male subject is to proceed. For within language is believed to be a central principle ordering gender relations in politics and subjectivity, a principle which "is exemplified by, and in turn governs from" its place in language.[16] To get hold of this ordering principle within "reigning discourses," to break it open on behalf of women, is to discover the power of language itself to change the language that prevails. The work of feminist theology, which Rebecca Chopp understands to be "an activity of and in language and discourse," seeks to tap into this "vitality" of discourses, and bring it forth as power, in the form of a "proclamation of emancipatory transformation."[17] What is needed for this transformation is a higher ordering principle by which gender relations within language may be challenged, and this is the role of theology. For, "Theology is knowledge and words about God, and linguistically, God is understood as the Word," so that for women now to speak this Word as "speaking of freedom" is to assume God's power as Word into their own lives.[18] This requires more than speaking *about* freedom in some detached, theoretical discourse, for language is "the site where our subjectivity is formed," and thus, for it to be liberating language, it must "birth new meanings, new discourses, new signifying practices"[19] in the midst of the dominant socio-symbolic order.[20] Speaking of freedom must itself therefore be transformative, it must empower women in that Word becoming embodied in their words, and thus it must be upheld by the conditions for this possibility existing in the church, which is itself called to be a proclaiming community.[21] For this work of transformation, strategies are required, and thus women examine "the limits and possibilities of what a human subject is allowed to be and to experience," and then plan the resistance by which "new possibilities and visions" may arise.[22] Thus to become a subject of language is to assume power for the speaking of freedom and the empowering of other subjects to speak.

[16] Rebecca Chopp: *The Power to Speak: Feminism, Language and God* (New York: Crossroad, 1989), p. 1 (citing Hélène Cixous: "Sorties," in Elaine Marks and Isabelle de Courtivron, eds.: *New French Feminisms: An Anthology* (Brighton: Harvester, 1986)).

[17] Chopp: *Power*, p. 3.

[18] Chopp: *Power*, p. 3; cf. pp. 10–15.

[19] Chopp: *Power*, p. 12.

[20] Chopp: *Power*, p. 14.

[21] Chopp: *Power*, p. 124. See also Rebecca Chopp: *Saving Work: Feminist Practices of Theological Education* (Louisville, KY: Westminster John Knox Press, 1995).

[22] Chopp: *Power*, pp. 126–7.

It has been important within feminist writings to emphasize that the assuming of responsibility and of power was to be a new realization of the social subject, and thus not a repetition of the autonomous individuality that finds its way into liberal politics and philosophy. The careful work of Seyla Benhabib sets this out clearly in the form of three steps that are crucial for the formulation of what she calls a "post-metaphysical" language, a language that will free us from the metaphysical illusions of the Enlightenment itself.[23] These illusions have been grounded in the notion of the individual subject as a self-centred being, and in order to free ourselves of their errors, we must uncover their premises and arguments, and proceed with new ones.[24] The first of these new premises is to ground truth in "the discourse of the community of inquirers" rather than in the attributes of an individual consciousness.[25] What I can know, exercising my own reasoning and sensing capacities, relies upon communication with others and is only validated there, not in the privacy of my mind. I cannot claim privileged status as a knowing subject. The second premise is "the recognition that the subjects of reason are finite, embodied and fragile creatures," that they are situated selves who speak from a perspective from within the social body in which they have been formed. It is because the self is a social being that it is "capable of language, interaction and cognition," and thus is able to speak the narrative of its life at all.[26] The third step is an ethical one of starting from the premise that "the moral point of view" emerges from within social interactions, and thus that ethical norms are to be established through a form of "interactive rationality," rather than by means of individual insight or detached knowledge.[27] In these ways, Benhabib seeks to develop new "conceptions of self, reason and society," as ways of proceeding towards a new universalism in ethics.

Benhabib believes this new procedure to be appropriate for an ethics of gender, for she seeks "to 'engender' the subject of moral reasoning, not in order to relativize moral claims to fit gender differences but to make them gender sensitive and cognizant of gender difference."[28] Thus she does not intend to reinstate preexisting gender differences, as if these carried implicit moral meanings and outcomes, but to provide a framework in which these

---

[23]   Seyla Benhabib: *Situating the Self: Gender, Community and Postmodernism in Contemporary Ethics* (Cambridge, Polity Press, 1992), p. 4.
[24]   Benhabib: *Situating*, p. 7.
[25]   Benhabib: *Situating*, p. 5.
[26]   Benhabib: *Situating*, p. 5.
[27]   Benhabib: *Situating*, p. 6.
[28]   Benhabib: *Situating*, p. 8.

differences can come out into open discussion and recognition. This plays a major part in what Benhabib understands to be "post-metaphysical," for "the subject of western philosophical discourses is constituted at the price of repressing difference, excluding otherness and denigrating heterogeneity."[29] Feminisms have facilitated the appearance of the relational subject, as the excluded other, and in bringing it forward have spoken "in a different voice," in an other language of the subject. Benhabib is aware of the danger that this "different voice" might speak a new ideal of woman that all women must come to own and to represent. Such would be a rein- statement of an essentialism in which the subject might again be hidden. Rather, what is needed politically and ethically is a context in which diversities of human subjects may come to be known and to be significant participants in a community of discourse. This can take place in the context of public conversations, of public dialogue, that are not "the mere exchange of information or the mere circulation of images," but discourses which "result in" enlarged thinking, an enlargement of mentality, that takes in differences and seeks their democratic harmonization.[30] The rela- tional subject thus encourages the articulation of differences, for this allows individuals "to comprehend and to come to appreciate the perspective of others," and in this, friendship and solidarity result.[31]

The social and political vision here for an interactive universalism brings forth an other subject of language, who is situated, embedded, embodied, and participant in social intercourse, and it is this fabric of interwoven conversations which is to be the context of ethical life, the source of its motivations, and the goal of its activity. It is a pragmatic vision for im- provements that will make a difference to real people's lives, as subjects come together to articulate their perspectives and needs, and to negotiate their way through to enlarged thinking and concern. It is a vision for a democracy of subjects who can be respected as diverse, within which gender differences can come to matter and to take their place amongst the many other dimensions of human subjectivity that are important. It has been the critique of the subject of language within feminisms that has opened the way for this new conception of the subject as an interactive self, a subject that overcomes both the presumptive universality of the man of reason and the divisiveness of its dual-structured humanity, and that comes to be spoken in the midst of the more encompassing, more com- prehensive setting of open-ended social communication. In this sense,

---

[29] Benhabib: *Situating*, p. 197.
[30] Benhabib: *Situating*, p. 121.
[31] Benhabib: *Situating*, p. 140.

Benhabib's is a further move in Hegelian dialectical thinking toward a higher reason in the context of which all differences are to be valued and to be given place for their articulation. It is on behalf of these subjects that a new understanding of community is needed, one which feminist theologians have been articulating in the theology of the redemptive community. For redeeming, understood as social relation, restores wholeness and heals divisions so that the subject comes to be as an integrated relational self. This vision of redemption is upheld by the affirmation of a relational deity, whose name is now problematic since it carries in its speaking the presumption of a divided humanity. To speak of God, for God to be the subject of language, feminist theologians have looked for that most inclusive of beings in whom the diversities and pluralities of this richly fabricated humanity might be held and nurtured, sustained and encouraged. Elizabeth Johnson writes of this God as *She Who Is*, a formulation which she argues is linguistically possible, theologically legitimate, and "existentially and religiously . . . necessary if speech about God is to shake off the shackles of idolatry and be a blessing for women."[32] Such a speaking of God provides a new "ground of hope" for resistance to the "ontology of inferiority" carried in language, and for a share in her creative power of love.[33] This God sustains human subjects within the renewed language of redemptive dignity and wholeness.

Assumptions of the Language of Subjects

With postmodern thinking, the assuming of the subject is brought into question by notions of its decentring and death. In the context of a quite extensive critique of the metaphysics of presence, even that work which Benhabib speaks of as "post-metaphysical" appears as modernist in outlook and fundamental assumptions. There is a certain sense in which postmodern thinking is a shattering of illusions, and thus an extension of the kind of critique with which the Enlightenment itself began, so that it appears as a critique of a critique, itself therefore a further overcoming. There is another sense, however, in which the thinking that comes to be articulated in postmodernity is dissociated with modernity, so that it comes to be as a break with the past, as an event of thinking in which new things come to be figured in language. Something of this linguistic disruption is explored

[32]   Elizabeth Johnson: *She Who Is: The Mystery of God in Feminist Theological Discourse* (New York: Crossroad, 1997), p. 243.
[33]   Johnson: *She*, p. 245.

here as we consider in what ways thinking with gender undermines the subject of language. Four dimensions of this troubling of the subject can be presented here so that we can uncover the assumptions that lie within the language of subjects, and open up an other way to speak. Within postmodernity, and specifically within the thinking of gender that speaks postmodernity, these dimensions appear as simulations, parodies, unauthorized versions, and absences, all of which speak trouble into the assumptions of the language of subjects.

In his essay on the simulacra, Jean Baudrillard describes the unravelling of the referential theory of language that is happening within "Western faith." This faith has been constituted by a confidence in "the dialectical capacity of representations as a visible and intelligible mediation of the real,"[34] the basic principle of which is that the signs we use, in words and images, refer to what is "the real," according to a principle of equivalent exchange value. In using these signs, we receive the meaning of the real, the words or images mediating the real to us, bringing us its meaning and reflecting to us, re-presenting to us, what is basic reality. Signs were thus believed to be sacramental, bearing meaning into our thinking, the "wager" of this western faith being that there is a final guarantor of this meaning, who is God. It is this "Utopian" faith that there is a standard by which we can distinguish what is certainly true from what is certainly false, sustained by the divine being, with which the human subject is launched into modernity, beginning with Descartes and sustained by the projects of modern science and psychoanalysis. What has happened to this "representational imaginary" is in consequence of the production of simulations that feign to have what they do not have,[35] and postmodernity may here be understood to be an age of simulations. This is a time in which there is a "generation of models of a real without origin or reality."[36] Consider Disneyland, in which there is "No more mirror of being and appearances, of the real and its concept . . ." but rather a "hyperreal" that is "no longer measured against some ideal or negative instance."[37] In the appearances of the hyperreal, simulations can no longer be detected and disciplined, so subverting and "submerging the truth principle."[38] While within modern

---

[34] Jean Baudrillard: "Simulacra and Simulations," trans. Paul Foss, Paul Patton, and Philip Beitchman, in *Selected Writings*, ed. Mark Poster (Cambridge: Polity Press, 1988), p. 170.
[35] Baudrillard: "Simulacra," p. 167.
[36] Baudrillard: "Simulacra," p. 166.
[37] Baudrillard: "Simulacra," p. 167.
[38] Baudrillard: "Simulacra," p. 169.

thinking, there was an effort to draw accurate maps to represent reality in a language the subject could speak, with postmodern simulations, the map is understood to precede the world, the "precession of simulacra" itself "engenders" the world and thereby all referentials are "liquidated."[39]

What are assumptions of the language of subjects in this time in which "simulation envelops the whole edifice of representation as itself a simulacrum"?[40] Characteristic of feminist thinking has been an attempt to bring an other subject to speak, a strategy which may be considered to be "transgressive behaviour," that contests "the *distribution* of the real," challenging the location and the power of the boundaries of reality, and requiring the force of law to reinstate their truth in an other place. However, simulations suggest "that *law and order themselves might really be nothing more than a simulation*,"[41] and thus, Baudrillard suggests, the attempt to reestablish order will prove "practically impossible."[42] Nevertheless there are strategies of the real to reassert its power, and these may be found too within discourses of gender as they strive to keep the meaningful subject of language alive. The "weapon of power" is "to reinject realness and referentiality everywhere, in order to convince us of the reality of the social, of the gravity of the economy and the finalities of production,"[43] and thereby to reinstate the moral and political onto a map with recognizable reference points and distinguishable goals. That this is a failed attempt is obvious for Baudrillard in the "characteristic hysteria of our time: the hysteria of production and reproduction of the real," in the operations of power which "now produces nothing but signs of its resemblance,"[44] and finally in nostalgia in which there is "a proliferation of myths of origin and signs of reality" in a "panic-stricken production of the real and the referential."[45] That "none of our societies know how to manage their mourning for the real," that all of us seek "by an artificial revitalization" to try to escape,[46] are assumptions of the language of subjects within which an

---

[39] Baudrillard: "Simulacra," pp. 166–7. As an example of the manufacture of this hyperreal, one might cite Lorraine Code: "The project I am proposing, then, requires a new *geography* of the epistemic terrain: one that is no longer primarily a physical geography, but a population geography that develops qualitative analyses of subjective positions and identities and of the social-political structures that produce them." Herein a Disneyfication of epistemology? "Taking Subjectivity," p. 52.
[40] Baudrillard: "Simulacra," p. 170.
[41] Baudrillard: "Simulacra," p. 177 (original emphasis).
[42] Baudrillard: "Simulacra," p. 179.
[43] Baudrillard: "Simulacra," p. 179.
[44] Baudrillard: "Simulacra," p. 180.
[45] Baudrillard: "Simulacra," p. 171.
[46] Baudrillard: "Simulacra," p. 181.

ethics of gender becomes allied with power, turning into ideological discourses and discourses on ideology that search for truth "to counter the
mortal blows of simulation."[47]

The work of Judith Butler brings out assumptions of the language of
subjects in another way, through her analysis of the problematic of identity
politics and her celebration of parodies of gender. She is critical of the
ethicopolitical injunction of feminism, that there be a subject, "woman,"
around and on behalf of whom its project is to be carried out. This
requirement reproduces and reinforces a "representational discourse" which,
Butler claims, undermines by its very constraints "the presumed universality
and unity of the subject" it commends. This is so, first, because the construction of the subject is constantly haunted by those it fails to encompass
or to comprehend, a paradoxical exclusivity that accompanies even the
most inclusive of representations, for every establishment of a domain is
bounded by some contestable conception of what is deemed to be common. This is so, secondly, because this subject-making is reliant upon "a
stable notion of gender,"[48] in which the subject "woman" can be made to
appear and upon which an ethics is to be founded, thus both producing
and restraining its subjects. Butler recognizes that there is no position
outside this field constituted by the language and politics of representation,
since there is not a better representation somewhere else. Rather, her
book, *Gender Trouble*, is an extended "critical genealogy of gender categories"[49] within the present structures that "engender, naturalize, and immob-
ilize."[50] Agreeing with de Beauvoir's claim that one *becomes* a woman, she
suggests that "Gender is the repeated stylization of the body, a set of
repeated acts within a highly rigid regulatory frame that congeal over time
to produce the appearance of substance, of a natural sort of being."[51] A
genealogical critique deconstructs this ontology of gender, by locating and
exposing those "contingent acts that create the social appearance and
naturalistic necessity of gender," for it is within these structuring practices
that notions of "identity" or of "subject" become intelligible.[52]

Contesting both sociological and philosophical notions of "the person,"
presumed to have some kind of "ontological priority" over and above
social context, Butler argues that a notion of consistent identity over time

[47] Baudrillard: "Simulacra," p. 182.
[48] Judith Butler: *Gender Trouble: Feminism and the Subversion of Identity* (London:
Routledge, 1990), p. 5.
[49] Butler: *Gender*, p. xi.
[50] Butler: *Gender*, p. 5.
[51] Butler: *Gender*, p. 33.
[52] Butler: *Gender*, p. 33.

"is assured through the stabilizing concepts of sex, gender, and sexuality."[53] It is these "*regulatory practices* of gender formation and division" that constitute the "identity, the internal coherence of the subject,"[54] and thus which are rendered unstable by "the cultural emergence of those 'incoherent' or 'discontinuous' gendered beings who appear to be persons but who fail to conform to the gendered norms of cultural intelligibility by which persons are defined."[55] Such is the place of parody, for "parody is *of* the very notion of an original," and thus gender parody "reveals that the original identity after which gender fashions itself is an imitation without an origin."[56] These imitations continually displace the hegemony of gender by throwing into question the meaning of the original, and in this troubling of gender, a resignification and recontextualization takes the place of stable identities. For Butler, parodies of gender expose "the phantasmatic effect of abiding identity as a politically tenuous construction," thus rendering gender "neither true nor false, neither real nor apparent, neither original nor derived."[57] Such a deconstruction of identity exposes the foundationalism of modern politics which "presumes, fixes and constrains the very 'subjects' that it hopes to represent and liberate"[58] and in so doing, opens the way for "a new configuration of politics," no longer "derived from the alleged interests that belong to a set of ready-made subjects,"[59] but re-signing gender through radical proliferations within the existing "terrain of signification."[60] Assumptions of the language of subjects are thereby displaced.

Simulations and parodies are subversions of the notion of a "real" or an "original" of which each subject is said to be a representation, and to which each subject refers as foundational for its identity. Assuming "the real" is thus exposed as a linguistic necessity for the appearance and regulation of subjects by these fabricated reproductions that impersonate and imitate what is not there. Further disruption of these assumptions is proposed in the work of Luce Irigaray, whose unauthorized versions of sexual identity challenge the language of subjects in yet another way. As far as subjects are concerned, women have not figured in their social or linguistic constructions. Irigaray's argument that the human subject has been conceived out

53 Butler: *Gender*, pp. 16–17.
54 Butler: *Gender*, p. 16 (original emphasis).
55 Butler: *Gender*, p. 17.
56 Butler: *Gender*, p. 138 (original emphasis).
57 Butler: *Gender*, p. 141.
58 Butler: *Gender*, p. 148.
59 Butler: *Gender*, p. 149.
60 Butler: *Gender*, p. 148.

of the embodied experience and imagination of man, bearing "the shape of the male body and the rhythms of male sexuality,"[61] and within a language that is phallogocentric, exposes the absence of woman in the symbolic order. The assumption is that man defines himself as a subject by means of a differentiation from that which is "Other," so that he becomes the one who is universally normative, while woman is understood to be the not-subject who is particularly situated and restrictively embodied. Ensuring his self-understanding by reference to a God who serves as the horizon of his subjectivity, within which this representation can appear, leaves woman "deprived of God,"[62] and made to fulfill a "vocation for collaborating in the redemption of the world through suffering and chastity" within man's religion.[63] In this system of signification, woman cannot appear as herself, for she is outside its domain, effectively hidden by the projection of the "Other" onto her. Woman thus is unrepresentable as a subject, for she is the sex which is not "one" in opposition to that of man, but something entirely different of which the language of subjects within the symbolic order cannot conceive.

Irigaray argues for the presentation of woman by women themselves in their radical difference from the subject and its Other of man's linguistic order. Within the assumptions of this order is a hierarchical relation, which "requires that whatever has been defined – within the domain of sameness – as 'more' (true, right, clear, reasonable, intelligible, paternal, masculine . . .) should progressively win out over *its* 'other,' its 'different' – its differing – . . . ."[64] Woman, by writing in a language that is not one, affirms a plurality which is a subject that is not one, and thus resists the dichotomies founded in an order, a grammar of gender, that privileges oneness. In this way, she will come out from behind the mirror of man's representative subject, disrupting the speculum of the other woman she is made to be, and coming into her own genuine otherness out of which an ethics of true sexual difference may at last be articulated.[65] Irigaray understands that this journey into otherness will require a new formulation of desire and of transcendence, for she assumes these to be the conditions

---

[61]   Margaret Whitford: *Luce Irigaray: Philosophy in the Feminine* (London: Routledge, 1991), p. 150.
[62]   Luce Irigaray: *Sexes and Genealogies*, trans. Gillian C. Gill (New York: Columbia University Press, 1987), p. 64.
[63]   Irigaray: *Sexes*, p. 66. See also Whitford: *Irigaray*, pp. 145–6.
[64]   Luce Irigaray: *Speculum of the Other Woman*, trans. Gillian C. Gill (Ithaca, NY: Cornell University Press, 1974), p. 275.
[65]   See Luce Irigaray: *An Ethics of Sexual Difference*, trans. Carolyn Burke and Gillian C. Gill (London: The Athlone Press, 1984).

within which human beings appear as themselves at all. Thus she writes of the restoration of the intimacy of the mother–daughter relation, in which woman may be born into desire,[66] and of woman's recovery of the divine, through affirmation of her own mystical experiences.[67] These are linked in Irigaray's notion of the "sensible transcendental," not a deity in whose mind subjects are already formed, but a God who "comes into being through us,"[68] and thus who urges us into "a more perfect becoming."[69] This unauthorized version of the subject is Irigaray's attempt to articulate an other symbolic outside the masculine economy of signification. Abandoning the dialectic that seeks some higher reconciliation or overcoming, she affirms an unrepresentable identity for woman, the language of which is to be grounded outside authoritative grammar, since she is outside its subject in her multiplicity.

Running through these various signs of a disturbance within the language of subjects is the sense of an absence, the sense that what once was there in the subject is present no longer, that the subject has gone missing or that, in Butler's words, we keep losing track of the subject, and cannot seem to discipline ourselves to stay on it.[70] This sense is registered in the last dimension of postmodern troublings to be considered here, for in Derrida's notion of decentring is an explication of that event of western thinking which gives rise to our sense that some thing has disappeared. In common with many twentieth-century thinkers, Derrida understands this loss to be related to a number of significant turning points, as science moves on from Newtonian physics, as world politics moves on from Eurocentrism, as the visual arts move on from representation, as man moves on from self-confident Enlightenment humanism. These changes are all signs of a new thing happening, a decentring of the universe as we know it, such that the fixed points of reference no longer give us the assurance of things hoped for, and the foundations on which we have built a culture of understanding are shaken. His analysis of this event follows the lead of Nietzsche and of Heidegger, by suggesting that what has happened is the ending, the death, of a certain construal of the world in western thinking, called the metaphysics of presence. This way of thinking the world is assumed in our language, as we believe that in speaking we are presenting, making present, that of which we speak. Derrida calls this "logocentrism," and like the

---

[66]   Irigaray: *Ethics*, pp. 69, 150.
[67]   Irigaray: "La Mystérique," in *Speculum*, pp. 191–202.
[68]   Irigaray: *Ethics*, p. 129.
[69]   Irigaray: *Sexes*, pp. 68–9.
[70]   Judith Butler: *Bodies that Matter: On the Discursive Limits of "Sex"* (London: Routledge, 1993), p. ix.

referential theory of language noted by Baudrillard, it is the rule of a dying *episteme* to and within which human beings have become subject. Derrida claims that "The ethic of speech is the *delusion* of presence mastered,"[71] and herein lies his critique of the privilege of speaking over writing.

The language of subjects is thus at an awkward moment in its history. Still assumed within it is the notion that subjects speak language, that a subject first comes up with a thought and then puts this thought into expression verbally, so that the thought is present(ed) in the words, even as the subject precedes the words and the thought, being fully present to itself. Notions that I might express myself in language, or that I make myself manifest in what I speak or write, are signs of this assumption of a presenting subject. What Derrida investigates in his book, *Of Grammatology*, is the way in which, however this presence may assert itself into words, our language says so much more than we intend. Indeed, the subject of language is already deconstructing itself from within, for every assertion of some thing to be taken for granted or guaranteed as obvious, always already needs the speaking of it to make it so. The subject of language thus masks its own absence, its own not-being-fully-there, indeed its loss of itself, in everything that is said or written.[72] Furthermore, for Derrida, it is language which produces the subject as its necessary speaker, so that the subject is the effect of language. Language effectively speaks the subject, giving it an ephemeral and contingent place within its grammar as a "subject-position," and nothing more. The gendered subject is thus located within a system of signification, its gender no longer something which it "has" or which characterizes its otherwise independent existence, but its gender as that which is said about it, as a citation, as a given gender within the context of a chain of meanings. These givens, being citations, are citable in other ways, and it is towards the openness of future significations of the subject that Derrida's emphasis on *différance* is directed. For *différance* is "a non-origin that is originary,"[73] which allows us "to think a writing without presence, without absence, without history, without cause, without *archia*, without *telos*, a writing that absolutely upsets all dialectics, all theology, all teleology, all ontology."[74] Into this writing

[71]   Jacques Derrida: *Of Grammatology*, trans. Gayatri Chakravorty Spivak (Baltimore, MD: Johns Hopkins University Press, 1976), p. 139 (original emphasis).
[72]   Jacques Derrida: ". . . That Dangerous Supplement . . . ," in *Grammatology*, pp. 141–64.
[73]   Jacques Derrida: *Writing and Difference*, trans. Alan Bass (London: Routledge, 1995), p. 203.
[74]   Jacques Derrida: *Margins of Philosophy*, trans. Alan Bass (London: Harvester Wheatsheaf, 1982), p. 67.

comes a subject without being, without presence, a trace that displaces the binary oppositions of gender assumed in the language of subjects.

These postmodern exposures and disruptions of the language of subjects are signs of a change of the times of our thinking. Each of the dimensions explored here as simulations, parodies, unauthorized versions, and absences open ways of discussing the problematic assumptions of the subject within modernism, and of coming to speak otherwise. What links the subjects together in this chapter is the notion of assumption, by which it is suggested that the subject is the assumption of a place within language. That modern notions of the subject as one who is revealed in language are still persuasive has been the continuing hope of feminisms, whose argument for women to take their place as public representative human beings sustains their ethics of gender. Such a notion also finds warm commendation by Charles Taylor in his *The Ethics of Authenticity*. Having completed a major work tracing the sources of the self in the western tradition, he writes of an enduring "ideal of authenticity," which guides the self away from the traps of individualism and fragmentation, and out towards its fulfillment within the horizon of "a wider whole."[75] He describes authenticity as "an idea of freedom; it involves my finding the design of my life myself, against the demands of external conformity,"[76] and in this is the assumption of the subject as a uniquely creative being, an individual who "has an original way of being human" that "can only be made by articulating it afresh."[77] Yet this sinks into mere "self-determining freedom" without some "horizons of significance" which give greater meaning to the choices we make,[78] for without these, authenticity subverts its own end and becomes violent in the presence of differences. Thus Taylor encourages the "promotion of a politics of democratic empowerment" in which the subject of language may come into its own.[79]

That the postmodern speaks of the loss, the disappearance, the hiddenness of the subject who both occupies and vacates its place in language, articulates the problematic of a subject who is assumed to be there. Postmodern notions of the language in which subjects are placed may prove less tractable to a specific politics, as perhaps also to an ethics, for the subject only comes here to be represented as it escapes its own representation, to find

---

[75] Charles Taylor: *The Ethics of Authenticity* (Cambridge, MA: Harvard University Press, 1991), p. 91.
[76] Taylor: *Ethics*, pp. 67–8.
[77] Taylor: *Ethics*, p. 61.
[78] Taylor: *Ethics*, p. 68.
[79] Taylor: *Ethics*, p. 118.

its authentic self as it eludes the hold of this revealing. These thoughts can be articulated in "the epistemology of the closet" as they cannot be in the modern *episteme*.[80] Sedgwick's exploration of the places of closeting within modern culture offers an analysis of some of the ways in which the assumptions of this place in language become conceptually mired. From the late nineteenth century, Euro-American discourses have been caught up in an exercise of "world-mapping," by which human beings are assigned a place according to a profferred definition of male or female gender identity, and within which sexuality has come to occupy "a more and more distinctively privileged relation to our most prized constructs of individual identity, truth and knowledge."[81] In the context of these "institutionalized taxonomic discourses," the closet appears as a set of relations that defy definition, that refuse location, that forget to appear as they should. These "relations of the known and the unknown, the explicit and the inexplicit around homo/heterosexual definition" are the ones that Sedgwick finds "peculiarly revealing,"[82] for they speak by their silence, by their place "at a crucial node of social organization" from which they offer us no new information about the subject. Indeed, the relations of the closet both manifest and render intractable at once "the same yoking of contradictions [that] has presided over all the thought on the subject,"[83] which therefore offers no redemptive knowledge but only continued opacities.[84]

Like bodies that matter, so too the language of subjects takes a postmodern turn into a troubling of the presenting subject. Within modern thinking, the subject sought to be represented in and by language, and in this a revealing of the authentic person was to happen. For feminists, language was to facilitate this revelation of woman as herself, speaking and writing in her own words, and in this was a challenge to what is understood to be the false inclusivity of the subject of language. Appropriate ideals and goals could now be conceived in women's own ethical thinking. In the process of this rethinking, feminists have emphasized the emergence of subjects within networks of social relationships. This opens the way for a new thinking of democracy, as an arena of public discourse in which particular diverse subjects can come to speak with integrity, debate with one another, and come to decision regarding the conditions of their lives. The

[80]   Eve Kosofsky Sedgwick: *Epistemology of the Closet* (Berkeley: University of California Press, 1990).
[81]   Sedgwick: *Epistemology*, pp. 2–3.
[82]   Sedgwick: *Epistemology*, p. 3.
[83]   Sedgwick: *Epistemology*, p. 90.
[84]   Sedgwick: *Epistemology*, pp. 7–8.

6

The Power of Agency

As with the other themes of these last few chapters, so the power of agency too comes to be understood in particular ways within modern thinking, ways that have made a difference to our conception of what it is to act as women and as men, and like the other themes, it is turned around by much that appears within postmodern thinking. Since Hobbes spoke of man as a maker of change, running through modern accounts of agency has been a sense of the unique place of human power, poised between heaven and earth, combining the potential of material and spiritual, physical and mental, rational and emotional capacities in its living. Agency comes to be particularly significant and problematic here, because it is understood to be the crucible in which these capacities are mixed together, combined and interacting, for an outcome to be forged that makes a difference to the future. Agency thus becomes a fulcrum for change, by which something new is brought to be, and in its realization the fullest potential of humanity is being utilized. For this reason also, the power of agency has been of considerable importance in the politics and the ethics of modern humanism, which have sought to develop the optimal conditions for this fulfillment. Thus for Hobbes, "The end of knowledge is power . . . and the scope of all speculation is the performance of some action or thing to be done."[1] What kind of circumstances are required in our life together and what kind of deliberation must obtain in personal life for human action to be all that it is meant to be, has been the special provenance of political and of ethical thinking, bringing humanity into the fullness of its life. Theologically understood, it is in the realization of agency that human beings are to manifest their special potential as those made in the image of the divine,

[1]   Thomas Hobbes, *Concerning Body*, I: 1, 6, in *The English Works of Thomas Hobbes*, ed. W. Molesworth (London, 1839–45), vol. 1, p. 7.

and to complete that purpose for which their lives are intended, both to reveal and to cooperate in what God has begun and will draw to completion. So it is that agency bears some of the weight of Enlightenment interest in illuminating and promoting what is distinctively human as its *raison d'être*.

With feminist critiques, such notions of agency are shown to be divisive of women from men, with the resulting devaluation, or the constant misplacement, of the "activity" of women as its passive opposite. So is exposed the hypermasculinity of modernism. With postmodernity, the ironies of this agency are explored as we come to speak of the production of the one who acts, not as initiator and sustainer of action, but as mythical origin generated by a system. Here we come to consider the conditions under which agency appears as a necessary sign of the human, and becomes associated especially with power, with potential that is to be realized through action. As products rather than producers, as acted upon rather than acting, postmodern thinking turns us anew into our humanity and reengages the question of what it is to act. That we are now in a time of "speculation to the death" becomes the end of thinking of agency as power.[2] In this question is implicated what it is to be a subject, for postmodern thinking suggests that the power of agency is derived from a subjection, in which we collude for our empowerment and for the reception of techniques for the making of a self. In this question also is implicated what it is that matters with bodies, for in postmodernity disobedient and displaced bodies become the locus for a disruption of power and a reconceiving of agency. To think the ethics of gender within this antihumanism may open up another way into unresolved dilemmas and troubled debates.

Human Agency

Modern understandings of agency have been troubled by the dilemma of difference that is gender. Those who would emphasize the common ways in which women and men are capable of acting have inherited a dualism that locates woman with material, physical, and emotional capacities, and man with those that are spiritual, mental, and rational. To be offered this dual structure as the context for the exercise of uniquely human capacities already disempowers woman from their full realization, as it privileges the

---

[2] Jean Baudrillard, "Symbolic Exchange and Death," trans. Jacques Maurrain, in Mark Poster, ed.: *Selected Writings* (Cambridge: Polity Press, 1988). p. 124.

location of man. Is a woman to be a man in order to act?[3] On the other hand, those who would emphasize the distinctive ways in which women and men act, find it harder to speak of the power of agency we might hold in common. We become divided by being two different kinds of agents, each with a different way of going about the actions that belong to our natures, each with a sphere of influence in which those activities become effective and sensible. So it comes to be said that men understand by action something akin to having an impact, causing a change, bringing off a project, making things happen, such that action men become effective doers of deeds, driven by a passion for accomplishments, for achievements that become the measure of his worth. By contrast, it is said that women understand by action that patient work of nurturing what is already given, of caring for things that are received, of letting things happen, so that their doing is more like a preparing, a providing for, a bringing forth, a cooperation in, a willingness to help what is to develop come to its completion. In this is a difference of power, understood as men's power to be able to make change, and women's to be able to receive it. Whether this difference of agency is to be affirmed as complementary, whether it is understood to be reunited in some other medium, whether it is to be transcended altogether, is the dilemma that difference leaves in its wake.

Into this diremption of modernism come two recent thinkers, a philosopher and a theologian, for whom the power of agency signifies the distinctive work of human beings. They offer models of agency that might transcend the gender divide, providing a common ground on which women and men might be understood to act humanly, and within which the accompanying social separations might be resignified. For John Macmurray, the prospect of defining *The Self as Agent* was a way of addressing "the crisis of the personal" into which he understood modern thinking to have steered its course, and his effort to manoeuvre our thinking out again provides an affirmation of humanism that resonates with much in contemporary pragmatism and political philosophy.[4] For Sallie McFague, the return to organic models of agency provides a way of avoiding both the arrogantly destructive ascendancy of technology and its divisive gender implications, in a way that resonates with much in ecopolitics and green

---

[3] See, e.g., the stories of early Christian women whose lives transgressed the boundary between active and passive by "becoming male" in their spiritual discipleship, "sometimes even cross-dressing and 'passing' as men." Grace Jantzen: "She will be called Man," in *Power, Gender and Christian Mysticism* (Cambridge: Cambridge University Press, 1995), pp. 43–58.

[4] John Macmurray: *The Self as Agent* (London: Faber & Faber, 1969).

theology. For both of them, the problem of the broken middle provides the dramatic context into which their actors are set and toward the resolution of which their actions are to be directed.

John Macmurray's Gifford Lectures were presented as considerations of the form of the personal, at the heart of which he understood to be the notion of agency. Protesting both the personal and political impact of modern descriptions of the self as a private thinker, autonomous in reflection and judgment, accountable to self and to God alone, Macmurray offered a philosophical case for the primacy of action and therefore of persons acting together in harmonious relation. Modern thinking has been characterized by a fundamental egocentricity, which devalues our embodied lives in the world and our relations with other people, an insight that is to resonate with much of the feminist critique of the western man of reason. What is needed, he suggested, is that we begin our philosophical reflection with the premise, "I do," rather than "I think," for the former postulates the unity of personal existence around a relation, of self with world and of self with other selves, a relation mediated by the sense of touch rather than the sense of sight.[5] Touch is a primary feature of our experience, for it is what reveals to us both the world as a real physical environment, and other people, whose agency we experience in bodily encounters with them, and it is growth in this tactile awareness that forms the central thread of our human development.[6] Thus from the moment of our birth, we discover the resistance of the material world to our movements, and we encounter other people as resistance to our intentions to act, as our differing purposes become entangled with one another. These experiences bring with them a practical knowledge about what is effective, and so we learn the ways of negotiating our way through an environment constituted by complex webs of interactions. We are then on our way to becoming persons who act, selves as agents.

At the core of Macmurray's account of agency is his understanding of action and of what it is to act. Action has to do with efficacy in the world around us, so that to act is to undertake some causal operation on what is out there, and it is for making this difference that our intentions are formed and our passions mobilized. The power of agency is its effecting change. Action necessarily involves us with other actors, since the "possibility of action depends upon the Other being also agent,"[7] and so we learn what builds good relationships in which we each may flourish. It is

[5]   Macmurray: *Self*, p. 84.
[6]   Macmurray: *Self*, p. 107.
[7]   Macmurray: *Self*, p. 145.

for action too that our knowledge is developed, for we come to know things, not for purely theoretical reasons, but in order that our acts may more effectively engage with the common world, and that we may extend our vision to the cooperative building of a society, and ultimately a just and peaceful international order, in which a community of persons may live in harmony. Thus Macmurray can say that "all meaningful knowledge is in order to action, and all meaningful action is in order to friendship."[8] Agency here is described in a way that avoids a purely mechanistic account of behavior as response to stimuli, and an organicism in which activities are understood to unfold in a continuum out of the biological realm. This is the middle ground Macmurray seeks between the detachment of determined body from free mind on the one hand, and a notion of action as mere behavior, a function of the natural organic world realizing itself through human being. It is the form of the personal expressed in agency to occupy this precarious place, at the site of a distinctiveness within nature, yet requiring this world as the context for its most human living.

There are hints in his writing that Macmurray understood the form of the personal to be inclusive of women and men, and thus to be offering a way of describing agency in which both could find themselves. His work, however, is evidence of the problematic that affects these mediating positions, which seek to rise above the unresolved conflicts of a tradition to a higher place of understanding, for he reconfigures the self out of a framework of oppositions whose fundamental terms may need to be questioned. Thus one must ask why it is "resistance" to the world and to other persons which is encountered in touching, rather than yielding, or permeation, or coming toward, or receiving from, and how it is that the notion of resistance already brings the matter of bodies up against the doing of human actions, which must then exercise power over matter. And women must ask why it is that agency begins in relation to the external world and to others outside of ourselves, so that the conceiving and bearing of a child cannot be an agency, and thus once again this reproductive activity is relegated to a devalued organic realm as mere biological function.[9] May women only be agents provided they put away the things of the flesh? So, too, we must ask whether this conception of agency does not already configure the ethical as a technique, a utility, for the happy accomplishment of one's intentions, so that one's ethical concerns are to do with how to achieve what one chooses to do with minimal interference from and

[8] Macmurray: *Self*, p. 15.
[9] So he speaks of human life as begining in infancy, i.e., after birth. See John Macmurray: *Persons in Relation* (London: Faber & Faber, 1991), p. 47.

disturbance to others. And again women must ask why it is that a community of mutual affection is the necessary matrix for this agency to be
fulfilled, which once again is modelled on the family, but most especially
on the mother–child relationship in which one's first encounters with the
resistance of an Other take place.[10] Is this supportive environment of love
what women, at least symbolically, again are assigned to provide? This
question haunts the enthusiasm for an ethics of care which Macmurray's
thinking already anticipated. Does not thinking with gender require of us
a deeper questioning of the terms in which the human place is to be
established within our modern inheritance?

A concern for revaluation of the place of the human finds expression in
the more recent theological writings of Sallie McFague, whose *Models of
God* are offered as new constructions of action more fitting for "an ecological, nuclear age."[11] Hers is an ethical concern for the impact which our
ways of thinking have upon our ways of acting, for "naming" can be
healing and helpful, or it can, like much "anachronistic naming" in Christian
theology, be hurtful.[12] Seeking precisely to displace modern anthropocen-
trism in our thinking, which she takes to be *andro*centrism, and to reunite
the human with the natural realm, she argues for the use of organic models
to heal the divisions resulting in technological devastation of the planet,
abuse of natural resources for human projects, appropriation of energies
for warfare and death, and violation of earth as a mere passive thing to
be exploited by human agents. Man and his God need to be dethroned
as monarchs ruling over the world, whose reign is characterized by
an "assymetrical dualism" of the powerful above the powerless, a lack of
concern for whatever is "outside the human sphere," and distant domination from a place of splendid isolation.[13] Understanding God to be mon-
arch results in "the wrong kind of divine activity in relation to the world,"
for here, "God's action is on the world, not in it, and it is a kind of action
that inhibits human growth and responsibility."[14] For this human responsibility to emerge, a "decentering" must occur by which humanity becomes "decentered as the only subjects of the king and recentered as those

[10] See esp. chapter 4, "The Rhythm of Withdrawal and Return" in which this
critical mother–child relation is described. Macmurray: *Persons*, pp. 86–105.
[11] Sallie McFague: *Models of God: Theology for an Ecological, Nuclear Age* (Philadelphia,
PA: Fortress Press, 1987).
[12] McFague: *Models*, p. 3.
[13] McFague: *Models*, pp. 64–9.
[14] McFague: *Models*, p. 68.

whose warmth of intimate feeling will overcome the coolness of distant technical calculation. Such an overcoming requires both a strategy and an ideological construct in which to assess decisions and consequences, and it is to provide these that the theology of God's body is written. To act now means to place the right significance upon my actions, to set them in a regime in which their consequences will be assessed, and to discipline them by this right thinking. It is the body that is to perform this discipline, for this is an ethics of action which seeks to control mind by body, so that body may more purely and immediately express its will, its intentions to act, its passions for justice, peace, and care. Yet here is a strange contradiction, for this is an interpreted body that effaces its interpretative work as it proceeds. We are offered the semblance of a body, a body that is there only as we think it to be, a body that we are deliberately to put in place so that it may do its ethical work on the planet's behalf, while the rhetoric relies upon our assuming it to be real. And who am I, where am I, what am I, who makes this deliberation? I must be still a displaced intellect, capable of roaming the universe looking for ways of causing trouble, but choosing a way of looking at things, a theological construction, to whose rule I submit even as I know that it is only a set-up. So that for me to be "at home on the earth" becomes a deliberate simulation of nature, put on for a higher purpose, an enactment of an interpretation. Thus is the spirit of humanity to rise over the antithesis to its fulfilment that stands in its way, by means of a resignification, a reinterpretation in which all things are to be re-placed into the most inclusive context yet imaginable, even as Hegel, and later Nietzsche, had foretold. A higher overcoming is here.

Already we can detect the shift into a postmodern milieu that takes place between these two understandings of action. Macmurray's ontology of action assumes an immediacy of presence, such that to act is to make present the distinctively human way of being, within a world really there to offer resistance to human touch. His is a form of critical realism, which presumes that the real world is there at some point of resistance to our pressure, and that what works or doesn't work there can be learned from experience in the company of other agents. There is an apparent directness and simplicity in this pragmatism that expects its significance to be obvious and beyond dispute. That this understanding of external world and of the power of action within it still carries the division of gender into its rendering of human being, is the argument made here. Women and men cannot find a common understanding of action here for, like so many attempts at a middle way, this one too carries the privilege that is man's into its thinking. So the rift is reiterated. McFague's construction of action as a hermeneutics of nature is already the expression of what is most cultural in human being. Her approach subsumes what is taken to be real about the natural world into the interpretative work of providing a changed "sensibility,"[22] a new construal of our understanding,[23] and in this, a cultural change from what has signified masculine action to what has signified feminine action is to take place. There is to be in this a changeover of the power from man to woman, which whatever it is that is "nature" is used to justify. Yet is this feminization of culture the location of a healing? Since, according to McFague, it is through our models of nature that we come to know and to love it, this already mediated knowledge allows us to make of it what we will, and it is toward the proper form of willing that her writing is directed. A deliberation that wills its power into action is a feature of a postmodern anxiety that already knows the "real" is no longer there and thus that willing is all there is left to do. In this theology, this empowerment by hermeneutics, the power of agency all depends upon how you look at it.

Acting Human

It is a feature of much postmodern writing about action that it enacts the displacement of this modern emphasis on human distinctiveness from centre stage, in its consideration both of systems of power in which agency is generated, and of agency itself as the performance empowered within these schemes. Such an overturning we have already noted in relation to bodies, which come to matter not so much through a free detachable decision, nor through natural life manifesting its potential forms, as through the performing of bodies in signifying acts. In these acts, we do not always know what we do, for the significance of action escapes us, only to be read in a reflecting back upon what has been enacted. Yet there is an ethics of this mattering, which refuses a closing off, which lets itself be carried away into the future, and which gives itself up to its performance in one through whom meanings will come to matter. Similarly, we have noted an overturning in relation to subjects, whose struggle for the power to speak demands their representation in discursive acts, that mask that about them which cannot be spoken. The language of subjects exposes this will to be known in speaking as a privilege in which gender figures, and so we are turned into ones who have been written about, spoken into

---

[22] See Sallie McFague: *Super, Natural Christians: How We Should Love Nature* (London: SCM Press, 1997) in which this word is repeatedly used.
[23] McFague: *Super*, p. 175.

subjection. In this too there is an ethics of linguistic acts, which attends to the hidden, which listens into the silences carried in what is said, and which bears us into speaking as ones effaced and given up into words. So far these hints toward an ethics of gender are given in the postmodern turn.

In relation to agency too there is an overturning, and further hints toward an ethics. Postmodern thinking has partly been constituted as critical cultural theory, critical, that is, of theories of culture that have appeared within modern thinking, and within which our understanding of agency has been shaped. The influence of Hegel has been significant in modern interpretations of culture. He argued that human agency comes into its own as it overcomes our first nature, expressed in physical life, and develops into its second nature in our cultural life. In the expression of culture, the spirit of man is to overcome the givens of the natural world in a subduing of nature, as in his actions he seeks a realization of that higher transcendent Spirit, or *Geist*, that is to unfold in human history. Culture is thus understood to be the creation of the manmade history in which the ideal human vocation is achieved. The logic of oppositions which this account carries has been challenged by feminists who see that in it is a claim that women are to nature as men are to culture.[24] By suggesting that the engagement between man's needs and the material world result in the historical change called production, Marx intended to turn Hegel's understanding of action into a dialectical materialism. Here it is not the realization of transcendent world spirit that inspires action, but the materiality of physical life, with its requirements for food and shelter. These challenge the creativity of man to transform the material world through productive activities that meet natural human needs. Again, feminist writers engaging in critical cultural theory have wondered about the meaning of reproductive activity in this production line of history.[25] So too with Freud appears a theory of culture as the harnessing of an archaic energy lodged in the unconscious, which is forced out through disciplined actions into the

[24]   Sherry Ortner: "Is Female to Male as Nature is to Culture?," in M. Rosaldo and L. Lamphere, eds.: *Woman, Culture and Society* (Stanford, CA: Stanford University Press, 1974); see also Seyla Benhabib: "On Hegel, Women and Irony," in her *Situating the Self: Gender, Community and Postmodernism in Contemporary Ethics* (Cambridge: Polity Press, 1992) , pp. 242–59; and Luce Irigaray: "The Eternal Irony of the Community," in *Speculum of the Other Woman*, trans. Gillian C. Gill (Ithaca, NY: Cornell University Press, 1974), pp. 214–26.

[25]   See, e.g., Michèle Barrett: *Women's Oppression Today: Problems in Marxist Feminist Analysis* (London: Verso, 1986); and Sheila Rowbotham: *Women, Resistance and Revolution: A History of Women and Revolution in the Modern World* (New York: Vintage, 1974) and *Women's Consciousness, Man's World* (London: Penguin, 1973).

forms required by effective human interaction. By his time, the joy of reaching out into the heights of spirit found in Hegelian idealism has become the neurosis of an acting that is driven but never satisfied, and so bears its sorrow into all that it does. Yet again, an oppositional logic is found here in which man is made for cultural, and moral, achievements that woman fails to attain.

In these cultural theories of agency, the dualism of gender is inscribed, and so it is in cultural critique that dualism too may begin to come undone. Critical cultural theory takes place in this context. Again Baudrillard is important here, as one whose attention to the ironies of human self-understanding we have already explored in relation to the philosophy of language. His two essays, "Consumer Society" and "For a Critique of the Political Economy of the Sign," engage in an autopsy of the human figure that appears in theoretical and ethical analyses of economic systems. This figure, *homo economicus*, is the one whose productive actions were understood by Marx to bear humanity into the future of material fulfillment. Such a man Baudrillard understands to be nothing more than a figure in "the mythological sequence of a fable: a man, 'endowed' with needs which 'direct' him towards objects that 'give' him satisfaction."[26] It is this mythic presence, lying within explanations of economic behavior and within the ethics of action that becomes utilitarianism, which Baudrillard exposes by his critique. For, he claims, the *idée fixe* of humanism has been an assertion of the human vocation to be distinctive, "to distinguish themselves from animals as soon as they begin to *produce* their means of subsistence," as in Marx, or to posit a spiritual self realizing its potential in relation to some transcendent final reality.

Baudrillard comes to such thinking, not by taking a place above it all, but rather by turning into the phenomenon of contemporary life and considering what it is to be made human in the culture of advanced capitalism. What he finds there to be experienced is a drive to consumption, a frenetic activity, and the victory of technique over thinking. Consuming things becomes the requirement of a system dependent upon their making. This system is fueled by advertising which posits the desires or needs that it feeds upon, and which requires of us a choosing, a constant and demanding choosing, as a result of which new desires and new choices are produced. And choice, Baudrillard says, is a strange imperative.[27] Choosing in turn is

---

[26] "Consumer Society," trans. Jacques Maurrain, in Mark Poster, ed., *Selected Writings*, p. 35.
[27] Jean Baudrillard: "The Masses," trans. Marie Maclean, in Mark Poster, ed.: *Selected Writings*, p. 216.

associated with a busy-ness that cannot rest, with activities that set ever shorter-term goals to be met, so that the things to be done generate an energy for the mechanism that requires them. The purported utility of these individual and collective actions masks the utter purposelessness of the system itself for which there is no end. Here is the promise of infinity, of productivity without end, of propulsion of myself into an unlimited future which Baudrillard notes in so many of his essays, and there is no stopping it. In its functioning, technique has come to prevail over thinking. The concentration of thinking upon endless devising of strategies for the accomplishment of things, gives an illusion of control, which again masks the powerlessness and exhausts the energy of those made to function within its logic. So thinking becomes a "speculation to the death."[28]

What Baudrillard's critique suggests is that there is a production of the human being to be active in a certain kind of way, and that out of this production is generated the myth of a preexisting human being, whose supposedly free desires and choices, whose independent rational thinking toward purposive activity, and whose unpredictable inventiveness, make this system what it is. Thus he notes "the well-preserved mystique of satisfaction and individual choice . . . whereby a 'free' civilization reaches its pinnacle"[29] and for whom this individual "has become necessary and practically irreplaceable."[30] The exposure of the myth, the autopsy of what is already a corpse lying within the process, directs our attention to what lies beyond us, that is, to what it is that is realizing itself through our acting and our thinking. For Baudrillard is concerned that in our continual reference to a human power of decision-making, of choice, of action, we feed the system that produced us. Thus our very references to transcendence are a joke played by culture upon our consciousness, a joke that repeats itself in each attempt we make to be really free or to take an independent decision, and only in the ironic seeing of this can another beginning be made.

As in the economy of production, so too in the psychic life of the subject, the notion of controlling agency sustains an economy of desire within a sex-gender system. In the work of Lacan comes an analysis of the symbolic universe which reveals itself in the language we use. It is within this language and out of these words that notions of the self are con-structed, forming the context of human thinking in which agency and power come to be understood. For Lacan, the symbol system which speaks itself into our words is phallocentric, that is, all meaning rotates around the centre of the phallus, which in turn provides the source of all

---

[28] Baudrillard: "Symbolic," p. 124.
[29] Baudrillard: "Consumer," p. 39.
[30] Baudrillard: "Consumer," p. 52.

meanings within it. The route to human self-understanding, he suggests, is not to be found by means of an investigation into being itself, an ontology, but rather by means of asking "How is 'being' instituted and allocated through the signifying practices of the paternal economy?"[31] Lacan thus directs his attention away from the Freudian emphasis on instincts as real biological drives that shape the psychic life of individuals, and toward an emphasis on these drives as linguistic constructions that shape what we think of ourselves within a certain kind of symbolic order. Likewise, attention to this order turns us from a view of human beings as morally responsible for controlling (or not) their instinctual drives, and toward a view of human beings as those who are spoken into the world by the language of a symbolic universe. Through our speaking and thinking in the ways that we do, the law of this order makes itself manifest, and comes to be instantiated and asserted as the real.

For Lacan, the sex-gender system is implicit within this symbolic order, sustaining the emergence of individuals into gender difference, as either women or men, and locking them into a pattern of opposing sexualities, of desire for the opposite sex. What moves through this system is desire, prefigured in Spinoza's notion of *conatus* as that endeavour of all things to realize themselves in the fullness of their potential, and it is in the arrangements for the functioning of this desire that sexual difference appears. The narrative Lacan tells of personal psychic history suggests the stages of emergence of a gendered body, a body that materializes as Butler would say, through the shaping of desire, as the imaginary body of our precultured, pregendered phase is submitted to language and to the cultural law of the Father in which the phallus reigns. The actions that we do are not the result therefore of some essential femaleness or maleness that determines the how and explains the why of these acts. Rather our actions are projections of ourselves as centres of control, a necessary fiction that masks as it repeats the loss of, and impossibility of, return to an original imaginary body. In Lacan's appropriation of Lévi-Strauss, action takes the shape it does within an economy of separation enforced by the incest taboo and the laws of kinship, from which he concludes, "There is something originally, inaugurally, profoundly wounded in the human relation to the world. . . ."[32]

[31] Judith Butler: *Gender Trouble: Feminism and the Susversion of Identity* (London: Routledge, 1990), p. 43. See Jacques Lacan, "The Meaning of the Phallus," in Juliet Mitchell and Jacqueline Rose, eds.: *Feminine Sexuality: Jacques Lacan and the École Freudienne*, trans. Jacqueline Rose (London: Macmillan, 1983), pp. 83–5.

[32] Judith Butler: *Bodies That Matter: On the Discursive Limits of "Sex"* (London: Routledge, 1993), p. 72, citing Jacques Lacan: *The Seminar of Jacques Lacan, Book II, 1954–5* (New York: Norton, 1985), p. 167.

In Lacan's analysis of this law of the Father, men are constructed as those who *have* the phallus, who have symbolic and cultural power, while women are constructed to *be* the phallus, and thereby to represent that reality upon which man's identity depends. There is here a locking into a matrix of heterosexual desire, such that the identity of the one is fabricated out of the unfulfilled desire for the imaginary of the other. We both become then constituted as objects of exchange which never satisfy, in the economy of desire that our actions reiterate as our speech reenacts. The potential that is here for a woman's imaginary to be construed from outside the significance of the phallus is explored by both Julia Kristeva and Luce Irigaray, who seek to open up the possibility for speaking otherwise.[33] Here is envisioned an enactment of *jouissance*, the quality that Lacan assigned to woman's position outside the phallic signifier, as a power to disturb and disrupt, ultimately to transform the symbolic order by a new poetics of love. Whether this affirms woman's position as a constructed other to man, or overturns this location with a new signifying practice, is the continuing debate within this attempt to think what might be outside, or beyond, sexual difference. What the debate suggests for purposes of this chapter is that a symbolic order performs itself through our actions, and embodies itself in our gendered selves, so that our lives come to enact its law. Our actions are thus not a function of the gender we are, but rather we come to be the gender our actions perform.

The presentation of agency in modernity finds its centre in the individual, who has the potential for self-realization through what she or he does, and whose power to direct her or his own path to fulfillment is the energy that moves intentions to their effects in the world. In the narrative of the modern individual, the power of agency becomes grounded in the natural world to which the material body belongs, and is governed by judgments about what is good and true and beautiful which are the work of the rational mind. Such a narrative is given gendered meaning as the agency of women is more closely tied to the requirements of nature and that of men, more fully related to the possibility for objective and detached

---

[33] Julia Kristeva: *Desire in Language: A Semiotic Approach to Literature and Art*, ed. Leon Roudiez, trans. Thomas Gorz, Alice Jardine, and Leon S. Roudiez (Oxford: Blackwell, 1993); Luce Irigaray: *Speculum of the Other Woman*, trans. Gillian C. Gill (Ithaca, NY: Cornell University Press, 1974); Margaret Whitford: *Luce Irigaray: Philosophy in the Feminine* (London, Routledge, 1991); Michele Le Doeuff: *Hipparchia's Choice: An Essay Concerning Women, Philosophy, etc.*, trans. Trista Selous (Oxford: Blackwell, 1991); Michelle Boulous Walker: *Philosophy and the Maternal Body: Reading Silence* (London: Routledge, 1998).

reasoning. Both Macmurray and McFague, in different ways, seek a healing of this rift of gender that runs through modern accounts, and in both,
the requirement for a new interpretation of this individual basis for agency
becomes pressing. Such attempts, however, reveal their modern inheritance in the language of human fulfillment and in the imperative to recon-
struct our interpretations of things, in both of which the diremption
implicit in the power of agency still figures.

In attending to the phenomenon of acting human as a bearer of cultural
and psychic significance, we are drawn by critical theory to the universe of
meaning that becomes known and performed in our acting. The work of
linguistic analysis since the late nineteenth century has been important to
the development of these insights, serving as an investigation of the ways
in which meanings appear in language. In the mid-twentieth century, this
fruitful interaction was given added impetus with the work of Ludwig
Wittgenstein and J. L. Austin, whose understanding of the ways we do
things with words opened up a consideration of the performative force of
language. With Wittgenstein's suggestion that the meaning of words is their
use in social contexts, Austin explored the intertwining of individual intention and institutional setting that made for felicitous speech-acts, that is,
for the happy performing of language. It has been the innovative work of
Judith Butler to draw out the implications of this understanding of language
for that of gender. For, following Wittgenstein, the meaning of gender words
is their use in context, and following Austin, their use is a performance, a
citation, in which the user is made into a subject of the order of meaning
in which such words are normally used, as this order in turn speaks itself
through the one who performs. These are the kinds of insights which
allow Butler to suggest that gender itself is a performative effect, no longer
understood as the foundation upon which my identity is constructed, but
as a result, an outcome, a consequence of the performing of language.

Her critique of the notion of agency is itself the performance of an
overturning, in which she challenges the belief that there is a doer behind
or before the deed, by speaking another way of bodily acts. Speaking of
gender as an action, she writes:

> As in other ritual social dramas, the action of gender requires a performance
> that is *repeated*. This repetition is at once a reenactment and reexperiencing
> of a set of meanings already socially established; and it is the mundane and
> ritualized form of their legitimation. Although there are individual bodies
> that enact these significations by becoming stylized into gendered modes,
> this "action" is a public action . . . the performance is effected with the
> strategic aim of maintaining gender within its binary frame – an aim that

cannot be attributed to a subject, but, rather, must be understood to found and consolidate the subject.[34]

In this turning over of the power of agency to the social world, whose modes of meaning are performed and solidified in individual actions, Butler seeks to emphasize the performative nature of our acts, not as acts which express or reveal some prior subject identity, but as acts that effect this identity in what is performed. Thus, "gender reality is created through sustained social performances,"[35] and in this is a strange empowering. For here I am no longer an individual centre of power, in my willing to effect changes in the world or at least in my understanding of it, nor am I the recipient of a power produced from relationships that enable us together to find fulfillment of our true selves. Rather, for Butler, am I empowered only as I am also subjected, made a subject through whom that which exceeds my grasp comes to be performed and in whose actions are recited the meanings of a tradition. No change in the world is thought here.

Such new ways of speaking that appear with postmodernity are openings also for theological ethics. For the performative nature of religious language has been investigated for some time as a fruitful way of understanding how it is that faith is enacted in the believer's life.[36] One kind of question has been to consider in what ways a religious tradition lives through repeated recitations in worship, creedal affirmations and prayer, by which the believer comes to be instantiated as subject of its meanings. This proves a most fruitful avenue of exploration in postmodernity as we turn to consider the tradition, less as a container of dead statements, than as a living body of thinking in which the believer finds herself or himself coming to signify. Another kind of question has been to consider in what ways faith comes to materialize in acts of charity that repeat patterns of holiness to be found within a religious community. Here the community bears the symbolism of a tradition into its various members whose performance reenacts that charity and bears that holiness into the world. My being faithful is thus understood to be a performative effect, less an independent decision prior to my taking up a good way of behaving, than a continual disruption of fixed identity by that which exceeds my knowing. Here is the power of agency turned into a love that alone enacts my human being.

---

[34]   Butler: *Gender*, p. 140.
[35]   Butler: *Gender*, p. 141.
[36]   See, e.g., Donald D. Evans: *The Logic of Self-Involvement: A Philosophical Study of Everyday Language with Special Reference to the Christian Use of Language about God as Creator* (London: SCM Press, 1963).

7

Engendering Ethics

In the last three chapters, we have been exploring some of the areas that trouble contemporary thinking at the interface of modernity and postmodernity. In this time in which we live and think, there is a reflection upon what has come to be taken for granted in modernity, and there is a realization that thinking is moving on into what will come next. Our lives are caught up in the changes that reveal these reflective processes at work in our culture, so that attending to these by means of critical cultural theory has become important to awareness of ourselves and our society. In addition, such reflective work requires a return to some fundamental philosophical and theological matters, and inspires a renewal of our thinking within these disciplines in particular as they set about their work. For here are disciplines that are meant for the exercise and guidance of human thinking, and few opportunities could be as richly stimulating or as profoundly unnerving as this. The matter of bodies, the subject of language and the power of agency are all questions that appear at this juncture, and that have become points of exposure of modern thought in its strengths and in its weaknesses. In each of these areas, postmodern thinking speaks out of a diremption in modernity, a diremption which has been there and which surfaces now, and challenges are posed to us regarding how it is we will proceed from this point.

Thinking with gender takes place in the midst of these disturbances, for it opens to us a consideration of the ways in which our understandings of women and men have been shaped by the intellectual assumptions and ways of reasoning about bodies, subjects, and agency that are our modern inheritance, and that bear themselves into our thinking as it participates too in this tradition. To become aware of this is discomforting, as is all serious self-reflection, and it is utterly and deeply self-involving, as is all wonder about who we are. The fundamental questions that come up at this juncture are ones concerning matter, language, and power, and here the ways of modern ethical thinking too are disturbed. For the question of matter is a question about the foundation upon which modern ethics of gender has been established, a ground that was held to be securely grasped through the biological sciences, and that could provide the justification for an ethics that fulfilled its necessities, biology as destiny, as also for an ethics that opposed its beckonings in a disembodied reason. Both the affirmation of and the resistance to biological necessity are founded on this place which the question of matter exposes. In what way(s) do bodies matter? So we are drawn back to basics here.

The question of language is one that concerns the central place given in modern ethics to the speaker, the user of language, through whose formulations and expressions a self-revealing was to happen. A modern ethics of gender has become concerned with the extension of this right to speak, with the recognition of the speaker's identity and standpoint, with the legitimation of speakers' concerns, and with the sustaining of an order in which this speaking might be heard, acknowledged, and respected. Much that has appeared in feminist ethics has assumed this project as its reason for beginning, while much that threatens to undo it is the realization that this may not be a sustaining end in itself. The question of language exposes the subject who is the rationale for this ethics, and asks after its authority for a self-revelation. Who am I in speaking? In what ways it is language that speaks subjects brings us again to fundamental considerations for an ethics of gender. Lastly, the question of power puts us in mind of the modern project as an acting out of a separation, of man and nature and of man and God, a separation that comes to be thought in a particular way with the birth of modernity, and in which human agency comes to be conceived as the making of changes in the world. That gender ethics is written into this division of labor is the rationale for its seeking another interpretation that will ground agency in the many-faceted construction of relationships. The melancholy that haunts this project, however, speaks in postmodern thinking with a question about the power of interpretation to effect this change by a willed overcoming of separation. Is this not to perform the diremption it seeks to bridge? And is there a healing act here? To be turned into my humanity in another way is the unsettling of power that postmodernity brings.

All of these things suggest that an ethics of gender will need to address a complex tangle of issues, in which human self-understandings and the most searching intellectual endeavors are involved. To discern the shape for an ethics of gender that takes account of the questions arising at this juncture of thinking, is the overall purpose of this book. In this chapter, it will help us to progress by considering the work of three people whose thinking has been forged in just this place, who are sensitive to the challenges of postmodernity, and who bring the concerns of gender critique and reconstruction to a place of prominence in their thinking. From a philosopher, a practical theologian, and a moral theologian come three proposals for engendering ethics appropriate to this context, which it will be fruitful for us to investigate closely. Two questions may guide our reading of them. What is the problematic of gender that each undertakes to address? What is the nature of the deliberative practice of ethics that each commends? With a critical understanding of some of the ways in which these questions are being handled today, our thinking towards an ethics of gender may be guided forward.

A Universalism of Capabilities

In the work of the philosopher, Martha Nussbaum, is presented a theory of human nature and proposals for a way of human fulfillment that are to address some of the major difficulties prevalent in modern ethical thinking. Reading ancient philosophers with problems of modernity in mind brings her to some important insights, about human beings and about the ways they reason, insights which are to bear fruit in her formulation of a scheme of reasoning about pressing ethical questions that is practicable in the contemporary world. She is drawn to the possibility of providing a neo-Stoic framework within which universal ethical and legal discourse may be conducted, which is firmly rooted in the most inclusive and the most basic description of fundamental humanness. The beginning of this thinking is a conception of "human being and human flourishing," which she claims "is our best starting point for reflection."[1] Such a concept "asks us to focus on what is common to all, rather than on differences . . . and to see some capabilities and functions as more central, more at the core of human life, than others."[2] The elements of this humanness she has set out in a detailed list of capabilities, which she takes to be essential to our being human at all, and the fulfillment of which she takes to be the purpose of a properly constructed ethical scheme. She offers this rational humanism, as an appropriate ethical universalism for our time, in which diversities may be

---

[1]   Martha C. Nussbaum: "Human Capabilities, Female Human Beings," in Martha Nussbaum and Jonathan Glover, eds.: *Women, Culture and Development: A Study of Human Capabilities* (Oxford: Clarendon Press, 1995), p. 62.
[2]   Nussbaum: "Capabilities," p. 63.

recognized and respected, in which cooperation for human flourishing between many peoples might be sustained, and in which sound judgments in particular cases might be discussed and concluded. Her prolific writing and enthusiastic energy for this project well suit her interest in providing the necessary argumentation for "a global ethic and a fully international account of distributive justice."[3] Within this large vision, there is to be found some consideration of the problematic of gender, as there is clearly commended a method of ethical reasoning.

For Nussbaum, gender is a non-essential dimension of our humanness, being one of the forms into which human beings are molded by society, appearing therefore in many guises and being endlessly manipulable. The raw materials of our human capabilities are shaped by social expectations and roles into recognizable patterns of gender, a shaping that varies throughout the cultures of the world, but a process that all cultures have in common. The problematic of gender, as Nussbaum understands it, is twofold. First, differences in the regulation of gender may inhibit the development of an awareness of shared humanness. We may take our social codes of gender so seriously, or root them in cultural practices or religious beliefs so unassailable, that we fail to see the fact that we are the same kinds of being underneath all of this. Although gender formation is a molding of the surface, a shape into which the clay of body is pressed, although it is therefore superficial to our essential humanness, it nonetheless can prevent us from a true seeing of who we are, for it clouds our vision with its power over our behavior and thought. To think with gender is, in this case, potentially disruptive, for it requires of us a rising above social formations to touch this basic humanness. We may not share the same codes of behaviour or dress, but we can recognize women and men anywhere as having been subject to the same kind of formation as we have ourselves. And it is this recognition, the clear seeing that comes when we attend properly to our experience, that matters to Nussbaum. The temptation of gender is that we will lodge our entire understanding of a human being in gender's terms, while to think with gender in its proper place is to question our socialization with a notion of what is more fundamental.

Which bring us to the second problem of gender as raised by feminists, to which Nussbaum is sensitive. All attempts at a supposedly gender-neutral account of our basic humanness, it is claimed, are driven by the interests of men, which are then projected onto the ideal figure of man,

---

[3]   Martha Nussbaum: "Human Functioning and Social Justice: In Defense of Aristotelian Essentialism," *Political Theory* 20:2 (May 1992), p. 205.

exclusive of woman, that lies within such accounts. Citing Catherine MacKinnon, that "being a woman is not yet a way of being a human being,"[4] she recognizes the gendered character of definitions of the human species provided so far. Nussbaum however claims that this need not necessarily be so, and in her own description of fundamental humanness seeks to provide both the most inclusive possible account, and the one which is most powerful as "a tool for justice."[5] What she seeks in her description of human capabilities is a notion that will be "harder to withhold," that will exert a claim upon our decision-making in debates about who is to count as a human being. Thus, reason is a feminists' best friend, disciplining arguments according to the requirements of syllogistic reasoning,[6] and exposing exclusivist or discriminatory claims as both irrational and unjust. Here too, the problematic of gender is an exclusion that results from not thinking clearly, the remedy for which is to disarm patriarchal accounts and denials of the full humanity of women with a thinking that is guided by reason. It is important therefore to learn to speak this language of our essential humanness, for it will be these words used in argument that will show "the power of a universal conception of the human being in claims of justice for women."[7] All social practices, all economic differentials, all religious beliefs, all traditional patterns, all institutions in which gender is formed are to be brought before this court of reason, in which the commitment to human flourishing will be tested against a common standard.

Already the outlines of Nussbaum's understanding of the deliberative practice which is ethics are becoming clear. She writes in the tradition of liberal philosophy and politics, with a deep commitment to the autonomy of individual subjects in exercising their capacity to reason clearly, and with a concern for the potential anarchy of these independently formed decisions, without some proper, full, inclusive, and persuasive framework into which good judgments may be set and determined. We are thus to be free within reason. Nussbaum is cautious about postmodern fragmentations, which break up the framework of common humanness into endless small diversities that are incommensurable, for these threaten to obscure the fact

---

[4] Nussbaum: "Capabilities," both text and footnote, p. 96.

[5] Nussbaum: "Capabilities," p. 96.

[6] Most simply, such a syllogism would be: 1st premise: A human being is a creature with certain capabilities which exert a moral claim. 2nd premise: This creature beside you has these capabilities, which you know from experience. Conclusion: Therefore this creature is a human being and deserves to be respected as such.

[7] Nussbaum: "Capabilities," p. 98.

"that we do recognize others as human across many divisions of time and place," and that these recognitions are the basis for developing a fuller account of "those features that constitute a life as human wherever it is."[8] She is also highly critical of those anti-essentialist arguments of postmodernity that suspect all universalist ethics of destroying cultural differences and "the beauty of otherness."[9] Against these positions, Nussbaum sets out her "historically grounded empirical essentialism,"[10] which is "emphatically not metaphysical" in that "it does not claim to derive from any source external to the actual self-interpretations and self-evaluations of human beings in history," but which does aim "to be as universal as possible."[11] The deliberative practice of ethics is to bring us in touch with our human foundations, which lie in this mutual recognition and this broadly shared consensus, and on that basis, to encourage expression of the compassion and respect for human beings that are so necessary in the contemporary world.

There is a sense in which Nussbaum's ethics of gender may be understood as agreeing with the Nietzschean critique in which much postmodern thinking is born. With him, she recognizes "that the news of the death of God brings the threat of nihilism,"[12] since it renders a naive metaphysical realism, that attempts to establish a transcendent ground of value, no longer possible. For her however, this strengthens the case for ethical evaluation firmly rooted in human experience, and therefore for a realism that is not from above or from outside, but from within, from the wholly human. She mocks the shame that is felt by those who would consider this an unworthy basis for ethics, as indeed she is critical of the disruption of Christianity to "the emerging feminist consensus" in the humanism of the Hellenistic period.[13] For her approach to ethics rests upon the belief that human interpretations play a part in our understanding of reality, and thus upon the significance of the act of valuing itself. Nihilism is to be avoided by the appearance of a conception of our humanness which commands our assent, debated and examined reasonably in public, to which appeals can be made universally, which serves to discipline our acts of valuing should they attempt to stray outside its hold. Furthermore, and tellingly, she writes: "We do not grasp the significance of suffering or lack or

8   Nussbaum: "Aristotelian," p. 215.
9   Nussbaum: "Aristotelian," p. 204.
10   Nussbaum: "Aristotelian," p. 208.
11   Nussbaum: "Aristotelian," p. 215.
12   Nussbaum: "Aristotelian," p. 213.
13   Nussbaum: "Capabilities," p. 98, n. 86.

impediment unless and until we set it in the context of a view of what it is for a human being to flourish."[14] Thus is this conception of our fundamental humanness, this "view," to perform the work of a mediation, providing the medium in which our compassion and respect for one another is to be felt, mediating our actions and thoughts (rather unforgivingly it has to be said) before the court of justice, and finally, providing the bridge over "the gap between potential humanness and its full realization,"[15] which facilitates our acceptance of its moral claim upon us and holds nihilism at bay.

This suggests, however, that there is another sense in which Nussbaum misses altogether the self-referential character of Nietzsche's critique, which turns back to reflect upon what is happening in the act of valuing itself. It is in this further going within that Nietzsche understood our humanity to be held, and it was here that he heard its anguish. For in the demand for a valuing is both the will to power expressed and a further subjection enacted, over and over again, and in this understanding a deeper nihilism comes to dwell from which there is not an escape. Nussbaum offers one, by means of right knowledge, and in that offer is the will to power repeated and a subjection reinvoked. For hers is a higher view which allows us to speak of "the human body" as that in which we live, a body that comes to matter as a set of limits and of possibilities, which are the stuff of objective judgments upon them from this high place. Hers is an assertion of the speaking subject in whose words is to appear the image of the human before us, and in whose careful teaching we will learn to think rightly about who we are. Hers is a call for the power of the human to take its world into its own hands, to liberate itself through its own deliberate work on behalf of those values that all reasonable human beings agree upon. To ground our thinking in this truth is to rebuild the walls of the *polis*, wider and more flexible than before, but resistant nonetheless to the return of the unreflected upon whose brokenness it has been established.

Practice of Transformation

Another way of approach to an ethics of gender is one that considers the centrality of practice in the formation and transformation of human life. Here attention is given to the social relationships within which human beings are formed in gender, to become themselves the bearers of social

14   Nussbaum: "Aristotelian," p. 239.
15   Nussbaum: "Capabilities," p. 89.

values and norms. Like the previous approach, this one too understands gender to be a social construction, a complex pattern of behavior and of self-understanding within which human beings come to be recognized and accepted and effective in interpersonal relationships and social activities. Gender is understood to be ubiquitous, some formation of our lives as women and as men taking place everywhere, so that gender becomes one of the basic categories through which we come to know ourselves and to reflect upon who we are and what we do. On the whole, this approach is reluctant to turn to some notion of humanness that stands outside social practices, even one that strives to be as empty of specific details as does Nussbaum's framework of human capabilities. This reluctance is based upon the assumption that the social precedes the natural, that social practice forms what is believed to be human nature, and thus that all attempts to get behind or above practices to establish abstractly an essential concept of humanness to serve as a foundation for judgment fail. They can only repeat the particular located practices out of which they have arisen. What we must attend to therefore is these practices in themselves, to discover the techniques of their operation, and in exposing these manipulations, to find the ways of breaking open and of transforming practices.

This approach may be illustrated in the work of Elaine Graham, a pastoral theologian, whose interest is in demonstrating how such transformations might be conducted within the practices of Christian churches. Her work is set within the broad stream of liberation theologians, who have emphasized that theology is most fundamentally a reflective practice, that is, one that both reflects upon and itself determines practice. She too understands this method of thinking to be necessary for the time in which we live, "an age of uncertainty,"[16] and effective in shaping more just practices for the future. With the collapse of a broad vision to provide meaning in postmodernity, and with widespread suspicion of any new grand scheme as a reassertion of power, she turns to investigate human agency and practices. It is here that we may begin "to identify the possibilities of grounding Christian pastoral practice in alternative values than those derived from rational ethical discourse."[17] Her hope is that local church communities can become places in which such reflection is nurtured, and in which people can continually play a part in the shaping of its activities to reflect a commitment to openness and to dialogue. The church becomes then the model for transformations that are possible within all

[16] Elaine L. Graham: *Transforming Practice: Pastoral Theology in an Age of Uncertainty* (London: Mowbray, 1996).
[17] Graham: *Transforming*, p. 112.

social practices, so that to consider its own practices self-critically is the most important work of a pastoral theology whose care is for all people. Again, it will be helpful for us here to consider what Graham understands the problematic of gender to be, and what she outlines as the deliberative practice of ethics appropriate for postmodernity.

Sympathetic to much contemporary theory, Graham too writes of gender as "a fundamental form of social organization," which is "but one manifestation of human social relations."[18] She situates this understanding between views of gender, on the one hand, as "an ontological state" and, on the other, as "an intrinsic property of the individual." I take this to mean her expressed concern to occupy a place between determinism and voluntarism, that is, to argue that the categories by which we draw distinctions are not permanently fixed and ahistorical, nor are they merely chosen by some "disembodied pre-cultural pristine self." Rather, she writes, "the experience of living in any human society is one of being an active, creative agent, whilst simultaneously recognizing the constraints and sanctions . . . which proscribe a wider set of choices or lifestyles." It is this which makes the category of gender "self-reflexive," which Graham understands to mean, "allowing for human agency and critical scrutiny whilst not underestimating its power to determine our lives."[19] Thus the problematic of gender is in our thinking, in a failure to be reflexive, such that we slide into one of the extreme and mistaken positions, either ascribing gender some pre-social reality or seeking a non-gendered position from which to interpret it. This failure of careful thought results in an unwarranted "privilege" accorded to gender "as non-relational, acontextual and reified."[20] The injustices of gender, such as exclusion, devaluation, and subordination, are taken here to be the results of such mistakes in our thinking, in consequence of which our social practices cannot be all they are meant to be, in allowing human agency to flourish and to be continually renewed and transformed.

Graham thus calls for a critical phenomenology of *praxis*,[21] a technique of examining practices or regimes of gender, to uncover patterns of exclusion and of failed recognition within them, and then of considering alternatives which would keep open the boundaries for, and affirm the value of, each human agent. For this task, two of the insights of feminism are especially

[18] Elaine L. Graham: *Making the Difference: Gender, Personhood and Theology* (London: Mowbray, 1995), p. 217.
[19] Graham: *Making*, p. 218.
[20] Graham: *Making*, p. 221.
[21] Graham: *Transforming*, p. 140.

important. The feminist emphasis on situated knowledge maintains "the absence of transcendent truth-claims," such that "the purposeful practices of a community may be held to constitute epistemological and normative standards. . . ."[22] There is not an outside place from which to judge *praxis*. Within this awareness of the limits of our horizon, the second insight is significant, for with it we are directed to attend to the repressed 'Other' that is "created by the assertion of a unitary and dominant perspective," and that challenges univocal ethical authority.[23] Disclosure of the needs and experiences of women, for example, hitherto covered over, may open the way for a reordering of the norms and the values embodied in a given set of local practices. So it is that "gender challenges pastoral practice to refuse any system of sources or norms which lies in metaphysics or beyond human agency or mediation," and, in what amounts then to a reversal of the method of ethical deliberation commended by Nussbaum, "reliable and verifiable norms" are to be "established from within the reflexivity of *praxis* and community."[24] Graham claims: "The impasse of postmodernism is resolved not by turning away from its critique of metaphysics and dominant rationality, but by insisting that purposeful, coherent and binding values can be articulated from within the core of human activity and value-directed practice."[25] Thus the work of a theology of gender is to "address itself critically to the contribution of Christian practices, values and theological metaphors to the creation and maintenance of specific gender ideologies and relations."[26]

This concentration on the technique of deconstruction and reconstruction requires a vision within which it may be held and sustained. There are times when Graham writes of this as a vision of practice itself, such that our thinking is ever turning back to reflect upon the *praxis* out of which it has emerged. The cycle of practical reflection becomes in itself a demand, an internal necessity imposed by social life upon its members, so that "a vision of practice emerges which *insists upon* individual actions as both constructed by, and transcending, relations of power."[27] Here is a discipline for individuals, to remember where they belong and to attend to their origins, always returning their "transcending" to serve the needs of and effect changes to the practices that give them life. Because *praxis* is believed itself

---

[22]   Graham: *Transforming*, p. 156.
[23]   Graham: *Transforming*, p. 193.
[24]   Graham: *Transforming*, p. 141.
[25]   Graham: *Making*, p. 227.
[26]   Graham: *Making*, p. 231.
[27]   Graham: *Transforming*, p. 107 (my emphasis).

to "constitute epistemological and normative standards,"[28] and to generate "ethical and epistemological values,"[29] it is the task of interpretation, of theological wisdom and reading, to disclose these values so that a transformation of practice may be effected within this horizon. The transformation is a recovery and a naming of the ethical authority of the repressed, by which "distortions and universalized prescriptions" are revealed and fundamental values are reordered.[30] To continue in this line of thinking, however, requires of us to ask what kind of practice this practice itself is, as it enters into this logic of valuations in order to effect an empowerment. The central point of this thinking for a theological ethics is in the assertion that ". . . if practice actually *constitutes* human identity and meaning, then action is not the outworking of faith, but its prerequisite."[31] So whose action? Which faith?

That we are the ones who make the church "to proclaim and enact the Gospel in human society,"[32] is the conclusion of Graham's feminist critique of patriarchal practice, that seeks now to engage in a *praxis* with a difference. Such becomes an ethical definition of faith, which emphasizes human agency as socially formed at the centre of a mediation, from which the new is to be generated. We are to reveal, to enact, to name, "to ensure that the disclosive imperatives of transformatory practice determine the self-understanding of the community of faith, and not the other way around."[33] But is this not already "the other way around"? Is this not already the self-understanding of a community which has come "to regard all theological discourse as grounded in human agency,"[34] from which *praxis* one is able to quote with approval the quite astonishing claim of Peter Hodgson that "The presence of God may indeed be a function of our ability to speak meaningfully of God"?[35] In what is this faith? That we are the ones responsible for a revelation becomes "the imperative of hope,"[36] such that "[a] notion of transcendence is therefore generated through the immediacy and concretion of pastoral encounters and practices impelling human communities to transcend their own finitude and limitation."[37]

---

[28] Graham: *Transforming*, p. 156.
[29] Graham: *Transforming*, p. 161.
[30] Graham: *Transforming*, p. 193.
[31] Graham: *Transforming*, p. 205 (original emphasis).
[32] Graham: *Transforming*, p. 204.
[33] Graham: *Transforming*, p. 206.
[34] Graham: *Transforming*, p. 204.
[35] Graham: *Transforming*, p. 172. Quoted from Peter C. Hodgson: *Winds of the Spirit: A Constructive Christian Theology* (London: SCM Press, 1994), p. 65.
[36] Graham: *Transforming*, pp. 206, 210.
[37] Graham: *Transforming*, p. 209.

This generation of transcendence by our own *praxis* cannot, however, account for Graham's claim that the vision which maintains such disclosive practices is "grounded in a pre-commitment to a common humanity and the possibilities of ethical action,"[38] a commitment whose place is the unacknowledged point on which the whole project turns. So the problematic of gender brings a trembling humanity to the working-out of its own salvation in fear of a disempowering.

A Revaluing of Nature

Yet a third approach to an ethics of gender in which postmodern unsettlings of matter, of language, and of power are at work is that proffered by the moral theologian, Lisa Sowle Cahill. Understanding that sex and gender expose "the cracks in Christian morality's epistemological foundations,"[39] she seeks to reground an ethics of gender in a natural law theory, combining elements of Nussbaum's universal humanism with an emphasis on the historical practice of transformation. Her work is thus at what many feminists would deem to be the most difficult interface of gender thinking and the Christian tradition, living at the front line of what she has called a "head-on" collision between a discourse that has a reputation for the "rigidity and stringency" of its moral norms regarding sexual sin and its "proper hierarchy of gender" on the one hand, and "historicized or 'postmodern' interpretations of moral systems" on the other.[40] This opposition "between rationality and the authority of tradition"[41] appeared with the Enlightenment and has shaped moral reasoning through the modern period. Christian tradition has seemed to provide timeless foundations in scripture or the natural moral law, deemed to hold truth claims regarding sex and gender, whose authority was realized in the "deductive casuistry"[42] of moral reasoning. Modern moral philosophy, under the influence of Kant, has sought to ground moral reasoning in the autonomous structure of human rationality, and not in the order of things either scripturally or naturally known, and in this is the appearance of an anti-foundational epistemology. The purely formal nature of moral reasoning required here is taken to its logical conclusion in postmodernity, according to Cahill, for in its

[38] Graham: *Transforming*, p. 173.
[39] Lisa Sowle Cahill: *Sex, Gender and Christian Ethics* (Cambridge: Cambridge University Press, 1996), p. 14.
[40] Cahill, *Sex*, p. 1.
[41] Cahill: *Sex*, p. 40.
[42] Cahill: *Sex*, p. 12.

exposure of rationality itself as a totalizing consciousness, postmodern thinking presents us with an anti-rational and fragmented approach to moral
questions. Cahill's work is an attempt to demonstrate that natural law
theory is both a foundational and a rational approach to moral questions
that can heal the rift presented with modernity.

This resolution, for Cahill, depends upon the reappearance and revaluation of the body and of embodied experience, and it is thus in relation
to the real lived body that we are to think through the problematic of
gender. Since "an Aristotelian or a Thomistic approach to ethics depends
on some biological continuities,"[43] Cahill claims that the body "as such
and in its physiology, is relatively invariant over space and time," that
bodily experience is engaged and given form by cultural institutions, and
that "a critical and normative stance" toward the body is possible, without
succumbing either to modern abstractions of disembodied reason or to
postmodern deconstructions of the body altogether.[44] She assumes that
there is "cross-cultural differentiation of the human body into the male
and female sexes which cooperate for reproduction," but with sensitivity
to the feminist critique, disallows that this universal sexual dimorphism
should "provide the basic category for organizing human persons into
social relations, and especially not for establishing social hierarchies."[45]
Thus, while the "human body provides the specific nexus around which
social relations are built,"[46] and yields certain basic realities for our moral
attention, Cahill is clear that the "human moral project . . . is to work
upon, with, and out of, our innate bodily needs, capacities, and tendencies
(whatever and however we may discover those to be) in order to achieve
the virtuous and happy life for human persons."[47] So, she argues, gender is
a "moral project" that "entails the social humanization of biological tendencies, capacities, and differences, including the social ties that they, by
their very nature, are inclined to create," and in this, is an affirmation of
the body as "more opportunity than limit." For the sexual cooperation
necessitated by biological sex differences, and the social partnership spon-
sored by male and female parenthood, together provide the "ground and
content for the human virtues of love, commitment, respect, equality, and
the building of social unity toward the common good."[48] The norms of

[43] Cahill: *Sex*, p. 75.
[44] Cahill: *Sex*, pp. 79–80.
[45] Cahill: *Sex*, p. 82.
[46] Cahill: *Sex*, p. 76.
[47] Cahill: *Sex*, p. 77.
[48] Cahill: *Sex*, p. 89.

this moral project of gender are to be guided by discernment and realization of these human values.

The deliberative practice required for this project is to be found within a framework of Aristotelian–Thomist natural law, providing the "reliable and effective" source of intercultural critique and of motivation for social change[49] necessary for the work of revaluation. In natural law theory, she explains that "the concept 'nature' is a means to establish moral goods or ends on the basis of human experience itself," the notion of law is "to give goods a morally compelling character by presenting them to choice as a 'law,' " and the natural law itself "as derivative from the divine reason or the 'eternal law' " is a way "to set human goods and morality with the larger scheme of divine providence."[50] Such an understanding emphasizes the inductive method for arriving at moral principles from ordinary human experience, which are legitimated through the continued exercise of discerning what is actually good for human flourishing, and which are understood to be an expression of the God-given "inclination of every creature to the proper ends and actions intended for it by God."[51] Accordingly Cahill seeks to demonstrate that "the realization of the *equality of the sexes, male and female*" is the condition for human flourishing as sexually embodied beings, and that "*reproduction, pleasure*, and *intimacy*" are the further values, which "the institutions gender, marriage, and family should *ethically and normatively* be responsive to and should enhance. . . ."[52] This reasonable critique of human practices helps to provide "the directions in which sexual value and happiness generally lie," and so too "a better *apologia* for a humane and Christian approach to sex and gender."[53] Such a method is flexible to accommodate cultural diversity and historical change, realistic in expectation and commitment, revisable through conversations about common experiences, and oriented toward the fulfillment of the good for which life is created by God.

For Cahill, the moral project of gender becomes a way of restoring a "theological notion of reason,"[54] in which authority and rationality are both to be respected and fulfilled in a discipline of transformation. For this

---

[49]   Cahill: *Sex*, p. 45.
[50]   Cahill: *Sex*, p. 46.
[51]   Cahill: *Sex*, p. 47.
[52]   Cahill: *Sex*, p. 110 (original emphasis).
[53]   Cahill: *Sex*, p. 117.
[54]   Cahill: *Sex*, p. 69, quoting from Jack A. Bonsor: "History, Dogma, and Nature: Further Reflections on Postmodernism and Theology," *Theological Studies* 55 (1994), p. 311.

project, "we will have to rediscover or reinvent a reasonable account of knowledge and truth, and of the 'universals' in human experience," such that reason may replace the exercise of sheer power in public affairs.[55] This rediscovery/reinvention involves attention both to "sex and gender as representing human realities," and to the discernment of underlying values by which these may become "informed by . . . Christian materials,"[56] – herein the content of the project, and it involves a continuous process of "refinement, expansion, and replacement of values"[57] in a spirit of collaboration with others, by which the various institutionalizations of natural sexual differentiation can be assessed – herein its methodology. The pattern of such moral reasoning as a Christian practice of faith is, for Cahill, well exemplified throughout the scriptural and later traditions, and is at the heart of discipleship.

> Christian discipleship transforms the human realities of sex and gender by respecting both their embodied and social aspects, and their interpersonal and intentional dimensions. Christian sex and gender ethics, as a transformative ethics of discipleship, builds on but reforms human cultural practices so that they better represent the Christian values of incarnation, community, solidarity, fidelity, compassion, and hope that moral and social change are possible.[58]

In this ethics of gender, a faithfulness to the authoritative presence of God's will for humanity set within human nature, and a willingness to work with the possibilities of its reasonable reinterpretations, are combined.

The revision of natural law ethics, of which Cahill's is one example, has become important in the continuing dialogue of moral theology with contemporary philosophy, and for this reason lives at a number of the awkward junctures exemplified in debates about sex and gender. The recovery of a tradition in order to address these concerns is ever a troublesome project, bearing questions about what it is to be faithful in a tradition, and of what it is to risk an interpreting. One would not be surprised to find these troubles also manifesting themselves here, leading us to a closer consideration Cahill's revisionary efforts. The question of faithfulness appears in her use of the concept of nature. Cahill suggests that an understanding of nature is something that emerges when people come together to consider their common experiences, and thus that it is not so

[55] Cahill, *Sex*, p. 69.
[56] Cahill, *Sex*, pp. 108–9.
[57] Cahill: *Sex*, p. 109.
[58] Cahill: *Sex*, p. 257.

much a statement about "the 'natural order' of things,"[59] as it is an inductive generalization we can come to recognize that we share. At the same time, she speaks of this nature as a kind of biological continuum which underlies all things, so that our attending to it, even with suspicion, is a way of being faithful to the Aristotelian–Thomist tradition. Is this so, however? This pragmatic epistemology begs the question which was surely essential to this tradition, namely that concerning the nature of nature, by which we ask whether nature is to be as a temporary hyperreality conjured up in discourse to serve as a ground and a context for human decisions, whether nature is to be as "a means to establish" anything at all. This question requires of us a further self-reflection upon what it is that we call "the natural," and upon the way in which it comes to stand for the very emptiness of meaning it so badly seeks to fill. The nihilism of postmodernity, which already knows that the foundations are not real, speaks itself into this projection of the natural, which thereby reveals the speaker rather than the spoken about, and in that sense is not what was happening in Aristotle or Thomas. One must ask in what way this is faithful to the question of truth within this tradition.

This question comes to rest too on the matter of bodies, and particularly in the reliance upon the body to provide the "anchor" for discussions "about human needs, goods, and the ways of life that best fulfill them."[60] One senses here the law of the body emerging to hold us in place. Cahill is clear in her rejection of "physicalism,"[61] and yet speaks of "the most basic and widespread forms of our materiality" as the existence of a matter we share with others.[62] The heuristic fiction which is required here disarmingly acknowledges its interpretative origins by bracketing "the body" so that we know it to be really unreal,[63] and then by placing the reader before the alternative of directionless drifting. To cling to what we know to be reifications, that nevertheless serve us in providing stability and order to our moral thinking, is to act out a morality we do not believe; it is thus a bad faith, in which our acting, our pretense, protects us from the very involvement of self that is required of a faithfulness. To what are we then

---

[59]   Cahill: *Sex*, p. 72.

[60]   Cahill: *Sex*, p. 13.

[61]   Cahill: *Sex*, p. 73.

[62]   Cahill: *Sex*, p. 76. It is for this reason, among others, that I find Cahill's to be a form of naturalistic feminism. See Susan Frank Parsons: *Feminism and Christian Ethics* (Cambridge: Cambridge University Press, 1996), pp. 141–3.

[63]   Cahill: *Sex*, p. 76. There is a curious use of brackets around words in this section. Why?

being called by the thinking of body into which Cahill directs us? There is here a combination of both the abstractions of modernity, by which we arrive at general claims regarding, for example, what is "innate," what is "continuous," or what is "differentiated," – for how else could we come to say these things in this way without modernity's reason? – and the deconstructions of postmodernity which ask the reader to collude in the pretense with a knowing wink. Thus her calling in the law of "a reliable and lasting sense" to cut short Butler's self-reflective questions about the materiality of bodies[64] is not so much the protection against the troubles of postmodernity Cahill intends, as an expression of them. Is our obedience to the necessary anchorage of bodies that comes to appear as law a way of faithfulness to truth as it appears in this tradition?

The trouble with truth of course is that in our time, postmodernity reads itself into all of our interpretative acts, demanding of us a revaluing by which truth is to be secured by will, and placing us before a choice – either this or chaos. So we have been carefully taught to accept that all searching for truth is really a self-seeking of power, which we too must engage in if we are to be empowered as human selves and not be swept out in the tides of history. Already this necessity speaks into the place of a loss of authority, and thus, into the emptiness brought by the death of God, it ventures with the seemingly more modest proposal of an authority taken up by humanity, the authority of a valuing, which requires only to be able to set its particular concerns into some larger scheme. The necessity for the repeated affirmation of values, and for their refinement and revaluing in further affirmations, is the postmodern appearance that qualifies and disturbs Cahill's task of interpretation. To interpret here means to value, to recover what it is that was valued by people in the past, to recollect the values that have been consistent through the Christian tradition, to reassess these values in light of our present human situation, and to reaffirm the values by which living today is to be ordered, and all of this I can enter into without myself being called into question. For it seems that I am not at stake here in this moral project which is gender, but only the values by which I am to be represented are in question, so that in this is not a self-involving interpreting which belongs in the act of faith, but an exercise at one remove from myself, an argument about how I am to appear, in which I can remain as one untouched. So this interpretation never comes to the question of who I am in the interpretative act and thus never really comes to the matter of the inclination of my soul to the presencing of God.

[64] Cahill: *Sex*, p. 87.

These three proposals for an ethics of gender are shaped in the context of the juncture of modernity and postmodernity, and share in a common concern to protect and enhance human being in a time of unsettling and uncertainty. With the first proposal, is a way of coming to know what are the capabilities essential to our humanity, and of using these to guide decision-making in the affairs of personal and social life. The problematic of gender is rendered here as a wrong thinking, which intrudes non-essential characteristics into our self-understanding, and which can be corrected through the deliberative practice of reasonable judgments, that aim to restore the horizon of a universality. This noble effort of reason offers to us the prospect of being able to present ourselves in full human dignity and to work together for human flourishing in the details of our lives. With the second, is a way of acting to make of the future something different out of the problems of the past. The problematic of gender is here the practice of an exclusion which enacts a subordination and a devaluing, and it is to be transformed by the deliberative practice of a reconstitution of its meaning and value in new patterns of communal activity. In this is a generation of values, upheld by a vision of liberating the repressed, and offering a way for the making and remaking of the human within a horizon of possible expectations. With the third, is a way of revaluing a traditional framework of moral reasoning, in which the concept of what is natural can be shown to be adaptable to contemporary needs and compelling for the purposes of human fulfillment. The problematic of gender here is an inflexible and overextended institutionalization of the differences that appear with the body, to be revalued by a deliberative practice of ordering our social structures by those values that can be recognized to be universally human. The moral project of gender thus contributes to an overall humanization of society, itself transformed by Christian values that present the possibilities for change. Considering these proposals for engendering ethics takes us further into the question of our humanity and into the thinking of the ethical that informs our time.

8

Conceiving of Difference

The proposals for an ethics of gender we have briefly considered suggest various ways in which we can be responsive to the times and to the search for the good human life within these times. All three proposals are shaped by the turn into postmodernity which we are living through, and thus appear no longer entirely within forms of modern ethical discourse. These three proposals reveal a commitment to an equality of women and men which is taken to be essential to our humanity, so that this truth becomes the guide for ethical thinking with gender. Always the guiding matter is before these proposals – in what way can this truth come to be realized and practiced in our daily lives and relationships? Commitment to this truth is a way of expressing what are the most treasured insights that appear with modern thought at the time of the Enlightenment, and in that sense, these proposals continue the modern agenda of affirming the value of the human and the equality of all those understood to be human. Each has also been critical of modern developments in ethics, especially as these have resulted in the problematics of gender which characterize our thinking today. The irrational use of gender as a discriminatory category that denies our fundamental common humanity, the malformation of social groups and institutions in which the equal dignity of woman and man cannot be practiced, the troubled understanding of nature and of what is natural which has been used to repeat the hierarchy of gender that devalues women in relation to men – all of these patterns of thinking with gender have been challenged by ethical discourse throughout modernity, and are indications of the running rift of gender that comes to be so problematic to us today.

Postmodern thinking, then, already disturbs these proposals, so that they each manifest a disquiet with modern ethics – with its clinging to irrational partisan loyalties, with its inconsistency in the application of its principles, with its failure to historicize nature – and so each speaks already with the voice of the critique of modernity that appears today. While there is a holding to the truth of equality voiced in a particular way with the Enlightenment, there is also a recognition that this project was not fully carried out, and furthermore, that today its realization is threatened in all sorts of ways by the troublings of postmodernity. The awkwardness which is revealed in each of the proposals is that described by Foucault in his essay on enlightenment. We are living with a paradoxical situation, in which "the relations between the growth of capabilities and the growth of autonomy are not as simple as the eighteenth century may have believed." While its great promise "lay in the simultaneous and proportional growth of individuals with respect to one another," our situation today presents us with the question: "How can the growth of capabilities be disconnected from the intensification of power relations?"[1] Each of these ethical schemes is troubled by the prospect of the loss of hope for equality, and so each is driven to find a way through to its assertion, to provide the necessary ground and horizon for an ethical humanism. So they are characterized by a protectiveness of the truths about our humanity that cannot be denied, by an impatience with the abandonment of even small expectations of social change, by a disquiet with the continuous unravelling of the foundations that ought really to stop somewhere, and thus they too speak with a voice that assumes and intensifies a power. Yet the paradox of which Foucault wrote, that the acquisition of capabilities may no longer be compatible with the struggle for freedom, is the troubling question that weaves its anxious way through these proposals.

The ethics of gender that has emerged with modern humanism remains therefore in many ways tied to Enlightenment ideals, and to the method of critical thinking which accompanies these. Taken for granted is the notion that the human person is the unit of freedom, exercised in her use of reason and her involvements in relationships, which is to be the measure of good. Modern ethics of gender is founded upon this freedom to deliberate concerning the things she should do to sustain herself in reason and in relationships, and for this she needs to develop principles to follow and some conception of the end which is to be attained by means of them. She can then make her way as a centre of freedom into the confused and violent world of human affairs, and can exercise the critique of all that does not yield to reason and that hinders the full partnership of equals. These become the interests within the various forms of feminist critique,

[1]　Michel Foucault: "What is Enlightenment," trans. Catherine Porter, in Paul Rabinow, ed.: *The Foucault Reader* (Harmondsworth: Penguin, 1987), pp. 47–8.

which are carrying out this project into each sphere of life. Within these interests are to be found a revaluation of the material world, an assertion of the subject, and an assumption of power, in each of which the birth of modern humanism is repeatedly performed. Thinking with gender becomes then a critique of the body with its determinations of reason and relation- ships, a critique of language that does not engage the authentic subject who speaks, and a critique of agency for its failed inclusivity. How it is that women and men might meet as centers of freedom, acknowledging the revalued matter, the asserted subject, and the assumed power of each one is the vision that guides modern ethics of gender.

What comes to be possible in postmodernity is both that this critique turns against itself, and we have explored some of the ways in which this has happened, but also that there begin to be heard new ways of saying what it is to be human. The critical thinking that calls for a revaluation of matter turns back to ask, after all, what it is that appears to be the matter, and thus to consider anew the notions of materiality with which modern thinking is encumbered. With this, comes the possibility to think in what way gendered bodies come to matter. So the critique of hindrances to the assertion of subjects turns back to ask how it is that certain knowledge of my self comes to be the expression of me, and thus to think anew the epistemology of the subject in which modernity is embedded. With this comes the possibility of hearing the language of gender in an other way. So, too, the critique of exclusive limitations of power turns back into the modern assumption of what it is powerful to be, and thus questions the agency that comes to power in this time. With this comes the possibility for thinking with gender as the performance of the modern subject, and thus for thinking anew in what way it is human to act. With these next three chapters, we turn into some of these new ways of thinking, to listen to what is being said specifically within gender theory, and to move through some of the openings presented there for a renewed theological ethics that may be sensitive to the gender critique. Some tremors have already begun to be felt through our thinking – from the matter of bodies to bodies that matter, from the subject of language to language of subjects, and from the power of agency to performances of power. Attending to these closely, we may find the openings necessary for discerning what may be the way of the human today, and in what may be the way of human knowing of God, in whom our beginning and ending in good is to lie.

Three areas in particular will be of interest here to take our enquiry further into the fundamental ways of ethics. In this chapter, we will consider the way in which sexual difference is thought to be that original form of our humanity that brings us to our being as woman or as man, and that seeks to realize itself in our bodies and in our embodied relations with others. Might we conceive of an indifference, in which there is a turning from the repetition of a binary regime, into a holding open of the future for our becoming in faith, so that the opening of an other way in which we may be faithed into God becomes the question with which the ethics of gender has to do? In the next chapter, we will examine ways that the subject has come to be informed by the discourse concerning persons, human and divine, and how it is that a revelation of the subject within has come to concern the human being of modernity. Might there be in this a form of subjection from which speaking no longer sets free, but which awaits a being-spoken, a call, into which I may come to live, and in this might not the ethics of gender be turned into a hearing of the vocation of the human? Finally, we will consider the way of thinking in which gender comes to be as an assignment to represent the human in modernity, binding us together in a common humanness in which is held my particular place. Would there be an other way to think the form of the human, as that which I come to be in asking that God comes to be in the place of my life, and thus that only in love am I turned into who it is that I am to be, so that the ethics of gender is entirely emptied out into this tenderest meeting of the soul with God? It may be that in these ways, of faith and of hope and of love, another kind of theological ethics begins to be heard through the troubled thinking with gender of our time.

Presentations of Difference

One of the interesting, and often amusing, discussions of the ethics of gender in recent years has centered on the commonality of the themes of sexual desire and of sexual difference, as these have appeared in the writings of John Paul II and of Luce Irigaray.[2] To find that papal commendations for the recovery of bodied love between woman and man in the maintaining of their complementary differences, should resonate with the outrageously playful and suggestive writings of one of the leading theorists of feminism, is cause for comment and for closer investigation. Between the two of them,

---

[2]   See the several pieces on this topic by Tina Beattie, most recently "Carnal Love and Spiritual Imagination: Can Luce Irigaray and John Paul II Come Together?," in Jon Davies and Gerard Loughlin, eds.: *Sex These Days: Essays on Theology, Sexuality and Society* (Sheffield: Sheffield Academic Press, 1997), pp. 160–83. See also Fergus Kerr, OP: "Discipleship of Equals or Nuptial Mystery?," *New Blackfriars* 75:884 (July–August 1994), pp. 347–8; and the chapter on Irigaray in his *Immortal Longings: Versions of Transcending Humanity* (London: SPCK, 1997).

they present a case for the enhancement of sexual difference in which our true humanity may come to be manifest. For both, there is a concern that sexual love present itself into human relationships, so that there may be a new joyfulness in sexual pleasure that is generative, self-giving, and procreative, as is divine love, for it is in this coming together of woman and man in the authentic difference of true loving that the communal nature of human persons is realized. For both, the problematic of gender is the failure of difference to come to be known, and thus ensues the impoverishment of only one being present. Herein lies the solitude that prevents our living out the fullness of human being, our being able to give of ourselves one to another, and our transcending of human love into the divine in which all love is gathered up. For both, then, the deliberative practice of ethics is to seek the return to an original community of two, woman and man, that lies as a founding moment of our humanity, and then to restore the presence of difference between us in which may be found true sexual giving and receiving.

In 1997, some of the writings of John Paul II on love were gathered together in one volume, entitled *The Theology of the Body: Human Love in the Divine Plan*.[3] The title suggests the importance of the matter of bodies which, as we have seen, has become central to one kind of recovery of a natural law tradition of ethical thinking. Of interest for us here is the Pope's reflection on the original unity of man and woman, contained in the first short book of this volume, and by giving attention to the major points in his exposition, we can come to see a way of presenting the difference of gender which is to find its place and its significance in the celebration of the body. The particular moral question that inspires this reflection is that of the indissolubility of marriage, as it seeks to deepen our understanding of Jesus's saying that "the two shall become one flesh" in marriage with reference to what has been "from the beginning."[4] It is this "from the beginning" that brings John Paul II into an extended catechesis on the two accounts of the creation of man and woman in the Book of Genesis, in which lies the theology of the origins of our being human. While the newer account of Genesis 1 "conceals within itself a powerful metaphysical content,"[5] by which man is defined and valued, in the older

---

[3] John Paul II: *The Theology of the Body: Human Love in the Divine Plan* (Boston: Pauline Books and Media, 1997). This volume contains the material originally published in four separate books: *Original Unity of Man and Woman, Blessed are the Pure of Heart, The Theology of Marriage and Celibacy,* and *Reflections on Humanae Vitae.*

[4] Matthew 19:4.

[5] JPII: *Original*, p. 29. See Genesis 1:27: "God created man in his own image; in the image of god he created him; male and female he created them."

account of Genesis 2, there is a more subjective, even psychological character to the self-knowledge recorded.[6] These metaphysical and subjective
dimensions are both important in the teaching here.

What the Pope takes to lie within both accounts is "a condition,"
which he describes as "man's original solitude," meaning here man as
Adam, as human. The creation of Adam is into a solitude, not a condition
of "man the male, caused by the lack of woman," but a solitude "derived
from man's very nature, that is, from his humanity." In this solitude,
original man becomes self-aware and conscious of the human body, as he
discovers in the visible world that "he is a body among bodies,"[7] and as he
"acquires a personal consciousness in the process of distinction from all
living beings (animalia),"[8] especially known through his naming of them.
So also in this solitude, man is to find the very definition of human in
which his identity appears, for here is the "ontological structure" of being
made in the image of God, in which is to be found "the meaning of his
own corporality."[9] Thus the "somatic homogeneity," by which man alone
knows himself to be distinctive within creation, and in which is the
identity of human nature as *imago dei*, defines the condition of the human
in its original conception, a creature placed between heaven and earth,
bearing alone the sign of the Creator in his body and knowing his unlikeness
to all the others. The human body thus comes to bear the significance of
God's sovereign rule over all things, as alone the Creator, and it comes to
hold for human consciousness a continually presenting awareness of
human distinctiveness. In terms both of his self-consciousness within the
natural world, and of his being as defined and given significance by God,
both subjectively and objectively, original man is conceived in solitude.

In the Pope's reflection, this original solitude prevents, in the sense of
"goes before," the appearance of the original unity of man and woman,
which comes with the creation of woman, and thus solitude goes before
the appearance of man specifically as male human being. Both the meaning and the substance of original solitude are prior to and become part of
what is meant in the original unity of man and woman. This solitude is
carried through into unity, as an underlying, a beginning substance, which
is taken up into the relation of man and woman that is to come, and
which remains as a weighty origin within this relation. So appears "from
the beginning," the significance of this original unity of man and woman
"as an overcoming of the frontier of solitude" through masculinity and

[6] JPII: *Original*, p. 30.
[7] JPII: *Original*, p. 38.
[8] JPII: *Original*, p. 45.
[9] JPII: *Original*, p. 39.

femininity,[10] such that man "is not only an image in which the solitude of
a person who rules the world is reflected, but also, and essentially, an
image of an inscrutable divine communion of persons."[11] The creation of
difference in unity becomes the passing over of a frontier and the sign of
a further unfolding of the divine being as communion. This "communio
personarum"[12] is then the significance of the unity of man and woman, in
which the difference of gender is presented.

The ethics of this gender is found in the self-giving of one to other,
without shame and without constraint, a purity of communication between
two which is mediated by the body. In their original unity, man and
woman "were both naked and were not ashamed,"[13] a text which is taken
to express not the lack of some feeling or self-awareness, but rather "to
indicate a particular fullness of consciousness and experience" which is
given with "the happy discovery of one's own humanity with the help of
the other human being."[14] In their self-giving, man and woman are "both
to reach and to express a reality that is peculiar and pertinent only to the
sphere of person-subjects,"[15] so that nakedness "signifies all the simplicity
and fullness of the vision through which the 'pure' value of humanity as
male and female, the 'pure' value of the body and of sex, is manifested."[16]
What lies at the root of every experience of self-giving of man and woman
is the fundamental and radical gift of God, who calls all things into existence from nothingness, and who creates Adam as the one capable of
receiving the world as a gift to him and of becoming himself a gift to the
world.[17] This relation of mutual gift is available for Adam to know in the
fulfillment of his original solitude as original unity of man and woman. So
it comes to be that "masculinity and femininity – namely, sex – is the
original sign of a creative donation and an awareness on the part of man,
male–female, of a gift lived in an original way."[18] The theological significance of the body then, is the "deep connection between the mystery
of creation, as a gift springing from love, and that beatifying 'beginning' of
the existence of man as male and female. . . ."[19] This nuptial meaning of
the body as masculine and feminine is already "conditioned 'ethically'," so

---

[10] JPII: *Original*, p. 45.
[11] JPII: *Original*, p. 46.
[12] JPII: *Original*, p. 56.
[13] JPII: *Original*, p. 55.
[14] JPII: *Original*, p. 55.
[15] JPII: *Original*, p. 56.
[16] JPII: *Original*, p. 57.
[17] JPII: *Original*, p. 59.
[18] JPII: *Original*, p. 62.
[19] JPII: *Original*, p. 61.

that "it constitutes the future of the human ethos", as *communio personarum*, as the meeting and giving themselves to each other in the fullness of their subjectivity,[20] as "the disinterested mutual gift."[21]

What sustains this ethics of gender is knowledge, the self-understanding of man and of woman, in their difference one from another. Woman is to know herself as one who is originally given by God to man, so that in each giving of herself, "the woman 'rediscovers herself' at the same time."[22] Woman's self-understanding is formed "through the offer of what she is in the whole truth of her humanity and in the whole reality of her body and sex, of her femininity," and in this, "she reaches the inner depth of her person and full possession of herself." She is to know herself to be as a gift, as one given, and is to reenact this origin in her own self-giving. This is the meaning which is carried in her sex, in her body, which gender makes known. The mystery of this giving which is woman is "revealed in motherhood," which otherwise would remain "hid" within her body, and in which she becomes "the subject of the new human life that is conceived and develops in her."[23] To know her body to become "the place of the conception of the new man" is not "a passive acceptance of one's own determination by the body and by sex, precisely because it is a question of knowledge."[24] Here is not a "naturalistic" mentality, argues the Pope, but a responsibility to know oneself in a particular way, of interpretating oneself, in which gender comes to signify an original giving. Man is to know himself as the one to whom "the woman is entrusted to his eyes, to his consciousness, to his sensitivity, to his heart," and in this, is a responsibility for receiving, for accepting, the gift. His self-understanding is of his responsibility to "ensure the same process of the exchange of the gift, the mutual interpenetration of giving and receiving as a gift," since it is through this reciprocity that the "real communion of persons" is created.[25] In this "ensuring" of the economy of love lies something of man's difference, for "the acceptance of the woman by the man and the very way of accepting her, become, as it were, a first donation."[26] Otherwise he too is to give of himself in response to woman, and in that gift, is to manifest "the specific essence of his masculinity, which through the reality of his body and of

[20] JPII: *Original*, pp. 73–4.
[21] JPII: *Original*, p. 84.
[22] JPII: *Original*, p. 71.
[23] JPII: *Original*, p. 81.
[24] JPII: *Original*, p. 80.
[25] JPII: *Original*, p. 71.
[26] JPII: *Original*, p. 71.

sex, reaches the deep recesses of the 'possession of self'."[27] He is to know that his "masculinity conceals within it the meaning of fatherhood," by which he is to be dispossessed of self alone. So it is that in difference is the fullness of the original unity which sustains both "the generative and the nuptial meaning of the body."[28]

In this presentation of difference, there are three interwoven strands – substance, matter, and knowledge. The substance of our human being as distinctive person–subject and as *imago dei* begins in solitude, and the trace of this original is still to be found within sexual difference. The meaning of this substance is to be carried to completion in the communion of persons that crosses its frontier into difference, and it remains there as an underlying reality of one flesh, in which origin is reconceived difference again and again. On this basis, the Pope argues that the coming to matter of man and woman as different sexed bodies, is both what makes available this substantial origin to us as the founding meaning of our created lives, and what necessitates a return to the one flesh in which is to be found the redemption of the body. For in the mutual giving between man and woman is the coming to matter of one flesh, in which "a primordial sacrament is constituted," a sign "that transmits effectively in the visible world the invisible mystery hidden in God," a visible sign in the body, in "visible masculinity and femininity" of the invisible "economy of truth and love, which has its source in God himself. . . ."[29] As the matter of bodies allows us to participate in the mystery of the divine life, so it necessitates a saving return. For "the path of the redemption of the body, must consist in regaining this dignity . . ." in which "there is simultaneously accomplished the real meaning of the human body, its personal meaning and its meaning of communion."[30] For bodies to matter in this way, knowledge of truth is required. Regaining the body's dignity is facilitated by what is given, by what is there for us to know: "Sex decides not only the somatic individuality of man, but defines at the same time his personal identity and concreteness."[31] It also requires of us a certain knowledge, which "inscribes a living and real content." For "the biological determination of man, by his body and sex, stops being something passive. It reaches the specific level and content of self-conscious and self-determinate persons."[32]

[27] JPII: *Original*, p. 72.
[28] JPII: *Original*, p. 85.
[29] JPII: *Original*, p. 76.
[30] JPII: *Original*, p. 89.
[31] JPII: *Original*, p. 79.
[32] JPII: *Original*, pp. 81–2.

Thus is our responsibility for this knowledge, for a decision in the light of truth, to come to the matter of our bodies in which lies the full integrity of the human subject.

The ethics of sexual difference presented in Irigaray's writings bears some striking resemblances to much that is said here, at the same time as it plays on the substance, the matter, and the knowledge given in the Pope's catechesis. We have already discussed Irigaray's challenges to the subject of language, a subject which is presumed to originate in and be assigned to a prelinguistic necessity that continues to regulate the presentation of this subject in its speaking. Such would be the assumption of a founding moment of the human person-subject in original solitude, a moment that continues to undergird the presenting subject in everyday life. For Irigaray to question whether this original is not already a male projection of his own existential subjectivity into the first position, assured by an horizon of divine giving, is to unsettle the normative meaning it carries into sexual difference for women. So, also, she asks whether the bodies that matter in difference are not constructed from man's self-understanding. The pattern of woman as the one given and man as the one receiving is the first completed donation that is to come to matter repeatedly in the difference between them, and in this, woman's giving of herself depends upon her first being as one who is given in an economy of love that is to be ensured by man. In this is not a difference, but a one constructing its other as complement to itself. Lastly, knowledge as obedience to the truth of this version of the sexed body is, for Irigaray, entirely a deprivation of woman, for she is absent both from the difference that her body might make to this text, and from the very possibility of knowing otherwise in which genuine difference might make its appearance. The truth regime that excludes woman's knowledge thus cannot come to sexual difference at all.

Irigaray's unauthorized version of texts teases out the traces of man in the presentation of difference, to open up a way for women to come to the matter of their own difference, in an identity that is unrepresentable in terms of one and its other, which is the typical language of sexual differ-ence conceived by man. What is necessary for the presenting of difference with a real difference are three tasks for women: – to touch the essence of her own deepest awareness of being as woman, to discover the feminine in the matter of women's sexed bodies, and to articulate a feminine symbolic in which a different knowledge of the divine may come into being with women. For the first task, Irigaray offers critical readings of the western philosophical tradition in its rendering of sexual difference. Phallocentric culture has so deeply buried the feminine in its texts that women have become adjusted to their absence, and have therefore lost touch with themselves. One of the ways for modern thinking to assert the presence of woman has been to claim equality with the man who is present, to insist upon the equal value of woman and man, but this Irigaray believes is a form of destruction of woman as herself. For equality masks heteronomy, the law of the other, in which woman can either choose to be a man or to be man's complement – it makes no difference. Irigaray writes with the dilemma of these alternatives in mind, and so her own presentation of difference is both a disruption of existing gender categories and a securing of "a place for the feminine within sexual difference."[33] She therefore is prepared to take "the risk of essentialism"[34] in urging that women construct and deconstruct their own identities, their essences, and with this pragmatic strategy, to open a way for women to refigure the difference that they are, to present their difference, into culture.

Irigaray's emphasis on a feminine morphology suggests that it is the lived body of woman which is to bring her difference to matter, and in this is a second step in her ethics of gender. Irigaray understands by body, not merely anatomy or physical flesh, but the coming together of given matter and transcendent spirit, the place of a becoming spiritual and cor-poreal which are inseparable, for which the embodied figure of Christ is significant. For Irigaray understands every moment of his life to be "an event of the body,"[35] an incarnation, which means not only that embodi-ment must be central to theological ethics generally, but also that women may find something of the meaning of a feminine morphology in his being incarnate. A renewed appreciation of the symbolic body may allow woman to affirm what is important in the feminine body, especially its innerness and its self-intimacy,[36] in which her sexed difference comes to matter. The recovery of innerness is to reverse the Genesis account of her "being born from man's envelope, with God as midwife," for in this "the feminine has no conception."[37] So in the Christian tradition "Woman,

---

[33] Luce Irigaray: *This Sex which is not One*, trans. C. Porter with C. Burke (Ithaca, NY: Cornell University Press, 1985), p. 159.

[34] Diana Fuss: *Essentially Speaking: Feminism, Nature and Difference* (London: Routledge, 1989), p. 70. See also Elizabeth Grosz: *Sexual Subversions: Three French Feminists* (Syd-ney: Allen & Unwin, 1989), p. 113.

[35] Luce Irigaray: "Equal to Whom?," *differences: A Journal of Feminist Cultural Studies*, 1:2, p. 65.

[36] Luce Irigaray: *An Ethics of Sexual Difference*, trans. C. Burke and G. C. Gill (Lon-don: The Athlone Press, 1993), p. 68.

[37] Irigaray: *Ethics*, p. 93.

who enveloped man before birth, until he could live ourside her, finds herself encircled by a language,"[38] such that "conception is the privilege of the masculine"[39] in which her body does not matter. The enveloping which women know in innerness is that "between mother and daughter, daughter and mother, among women," an enveloping that "must not become closure," but which becomes "a love of the same, within the same . . . a form of innerness that can open to the other without loss of self or of the other in the bottomlessness of an abyss."[40] In this is to be found a real life-giving on her part, which means that her body is not simply to be as given to man. So too self-intimacy, of which Irigaray writes in "When Our Lips Speak Together," becomes a return to woman's sexed body, to her own sexual pleasure, which "cannot be projected, or mastered," and which is exiled within the distinctions and oppositions of man's sex.[41] To come back from this displacement is to affirm a woman's love of self and of other women, in which being longed for as a daughter allows her to be born anew into feminine desire. In this she can make her appearance as different.

The third task is for an other speaking of God as women come to know the divine. Man's God has been a projection from his own lived sexed body, and in man's religion, woman is made to occupy a redemptive role "through suffering and chastity."[42] It is after she has been fitted up in man's symbolic order and conceived in terms of that "Old Dream of Symmetry,"[43] that the sacramental value of her relationship with man in nuptial love is realized as one flesh. In this, is a fundamental sameness reasserted, in which women are alienated from themselves, as they are "deprived of God" and "forced to comply with models that do not match them."[44] So genuine difference is impossible, until women fully come into being with reference to their own God, in whom is their gender reflected back to them, and within whose horizon becomes possible the full realization of their being as woman. This recovery of the transcendent for women emphasizes especially the importance for Irigaray of women becoming

---

[38]   Irigaray: *Ethics*, p. 94.

[39]   Irigaray: *Ethics*, p. 92.

[40]   Irigaray: *Ethics*, p. 69.

[41]   Irigaray: "When Our Lips Speak Together," trans. C. Burke, in *Sex*, p. 212.

[42]   Luce Irigaray: *Sexes and Genealogies*, trans. Gillian C. Gill (New York: Columbia University Press, 1987), p. 66. Cf. Margaret Whitford: *Luce Irigaray: Philosophy in the Feminine* (London: Routledge, 1991), pp. 145–6.

[43]   Luce Irigaray: *Speculum of the Other Woman*, trans. Gillian C. Gill (Ithaca, NY: Cornell University Press), Part I.

[44]   Irigaray: *Sexes*, p. 64.

divine, of their conceiving of God in the matter of their own bodies in which their sanctification is to happen. Here too, innerness and self-intimacy are significant as ways of knowing the presence of God, "More intimate than the 'soul' even," in whose reciprocal sharing "she loses all sense of corporeal boundary" and "is transformed into Him in her love."[45] This is the coming of the transcendent in woman, in which she is present as *imago dei*, that prevents, that goes before, her coming together with man in genuine difference, for "It takes two to love."[46]

In the presentation of sexual difference that Irigaray offers are also the strands of substance, matter, and knowledge. What founds and underlies the existence of a woman is an essential feminine, conceived not as solitude, but as the most intimate union of women with God and with one another. This is her being in the image of God in which she knows herself to be primordially enfolded by divine love, and from which she is torn by the erection of man's oppositional schema. The essence of her difference then remains veiled to her and obscured to human relationships. In the love in which she is conceived and born of woman, and in the morphology of her own sexed body, does the matter of her difference come to be, and in this she too finds a way back to the divine origin. So Irigaray reads the Pope's understanding of the sacrament of the body with a difference, a difference to which women must return before the union of two can happen. She must come to matter again through the encrustations of phallocentric culture before the genuine engagement of two in the creative union of love can begin to be known. Irigaray speaks of this knowledge as a woman's coming to know the truth of herself, and in that sense there is realization of what lies in her embodied sex. What prevents this from being a rigid essentialism, is her recognition that this knowing of herself is to be an ongoing project for woman, in which is not a new ontology, but a thinking and speaking that resists definition or prediction. Both in her disruptive influence in existing systems of knowledge and in the potential multiplicity of her voices, woman disobediently breaks open and destabilizes any fixed binary distinctions. What she knows is thus uncontainable in a single original word of truth.

Indifference

One of the questions around which contemporary gender theory has been focussed is that of sexual difference. Initially this was a question concerning

---

[45] Irigaray: *Speculum*, p. 201.
[46] Irigaray: *Ethics*, p. 71.

the potential for a biological determination of gender role and value on the basis of the sexed body. The separation of gender from sex thus became a critical stance that shaped early explorations of gendered behaviour and thought, and a commitment to the transformation of the relative positions of women and men. Gender came to stand for the historical and socially changeable features of being woman and being man, and thus required continuous revaluing and replacing within present situations. As gender theory develops, there is a closer investigation of the implications of this separation, both as it carries within it a more general critique of the divisions that appear with modern humanism, and as it brings more sharply into focus the matter of what it is to be, as woman or as man, as human. The presentation of difference, and the return of the body to gender, is one expression of this wider dissatisfaction with modern ways of thinking. Both John Paul II and Irigaray are critical of the language of mere equality in which comparison difference cannot come to be known, for the abstract measures of its implementation do not touch the heart of the relation of woman and man, that is more than their status alone can say. To return to the body is to find the way of a redeeming relationship, in which love between two may both affirm the difference that each one is and simultaneously manifest the divine in their midst. Difference is more than itself for, as it comes to matter between man and woman, so also does God. An ethics of gender difference stays close to this epiphany, for in it lies the origin of our humanity in which we are founded and set upon our human way in the world. The presentation of difference is thus a re-presentation of this original form, veiled by patriarchy or fallen into objectifications, but nonetheless the true, the essential, that which subsists to be known and of which my life is to be a further embodiment.

To bring into focus the question of what it is to be, has been the remarkable work of Judith Butler, whose elusive and allusive ponderings of gender and sex suggest that the return of the different body may not hold the redeeming being that it promises for us. The difference rooted in origins, which seeks to realize itself into the existing of particular bodies, is a way of saying something about our beginning to be human, that somehow always remains as a bar to our actually beginning to exist. The founding image it shows and the order that it brings to bear in the body prevent the very coming to birth of the human which they intend, and thus can only be the cause of a redeeming that happens elsewhere, but not in me. The paradox, the impasse, of this way of thinking it has been Butler's task to articulate, and in so doing, to touch on a number of fundamental philosophical questions that come to matter in a theological ethics. As is often the case with people who speak and write in a new way,

Butler's style of expression has been criticized as inscrutable and muddled, and many a first reader may be put off by the difficulties.[47] So, too, the turns and twists of her thinking that she invites her readers to follow are deemed by some not to be worth the trouble. However, it is because what she has to say is not something to be recognized, but to come to be known for the first time, and because she is so constantly self-reflective, that her words are performative, doing what they say, and calling us too into the performance of our lives.

We have considered already, briefly, two of the themes that appear in Butler's work, in her speaking of bodies that matter and in her critique of the identity that becomes gender. Along with other thinkers of postmodernity, Butler has asked what it means that we understand matter to be the preexisting stuff of which the world is constituted. Suggesting that this is a matter of signification is a challenge to the "empiricist foundationalism" that undergirds the presentation of difference in much thinking with gender. The notion of bodies that matter is a way of saying that the body is as performance, as the material presentation of that which comes to signify in the living of my life, as the physical form in which my care is revealed. With this is a dislodging of the body from a certain kind of metaphysics in which philosophy has been interested. Again, Butler's critique of the subject reveals her disquiet with the stable identity that is supposed to materialize with being woman or man. Her "losing track of the subject" as she tries to think about the boundaries of the gendered body, is the awareness of a discipline, of a constraint, that keeps trying to hold her in place, and that subjects her to its regulation even as it promises her liberation.[48] Here it will be useful for us to develop these ideas more fully, to demonstrate how a disturbance of gender difference brings us before our humanity in another way, and leaves us with a question of how we are to be, in which the question of the way of a redeeming is opened anew to reflection. Specifically, we can see how Butler investigates the desire that underpins the matrix of heterosexual relations, how she understands the formation of bodies within the regime of difference, and how it is that in the knowing of this, the future is at risk.

The context for Butler's consideration of gender is partly made up of the narrative of desire that weaves its way through modern humanism, and that Butler holds in question in the way that Foucault and Nietzsche had

[47] See Martha C. Nussbaum: "The Professor of Parody: The Hip Defeatism of Judith Butler," *The New Republic*, February 22, 1999, pp. 37–45.
[48] Butler: *Bodies that Matter: On the Discursive Limits of "Sex"* (London: Routledge, 1993), p. ix.

done. Nietzsche's attention to will to power as it appears in the modern upsurgence of the human subject into nature and into politics, and Foucault's analysis of the assumption of a life-force that sustains the human when man is invented to be an object of study, both of these suggest for Butler that there is also desire in this modern humanism. With Nietzsche, this desire appears to hold something of self-promotion in it, and with Foucault, this desire seems to be the positing of a natural power that underpins our existence so that we can come to be at all. Thus desire is already in modernity something of a projection, a project of the human to come to exist in this way, and a projection from the human of that which is most needed to sustain this existence. Butler holds this desire in question insofar as it is also that which underlies the modern account of sex as the difference of two, and insofar as continued appeal is made to it as the logic, the word, of our origin. The negotiation of sexual difference that has featured in modern humanism requires this foundation in desire, from Spinoza's presentation of *conatus* as that endeavour of all things living to realize themselves in the fullness of their potential, to be what they are, through to Lacan's analysis of the symbolic law of this desire that forms individuals as gendered. It is this desire out of which the requirement for heterosexual relationships is produced, and which forms individuals into the power of this order of life. Butler is aware that critical thinking with gender already has made the separation of gender from sex as formed of desire; what she moves on to consider is the nature of the sex from which gender has distinguished itself, and so to ask what it is to be as one formed of desire.

This question moves through her thinking about bodies that matter, and her suggestion that it is through the significance bodies are given for the expression of this desire that bodies come to matter as differently sexed, as male and female bodies, constructed in difference for the further manifestation of the desire out of which they have been formed. Bodies come to matter as male or female in their being rendered meaningful, and in this process is the formation of an order in which some bodies materialize and some do not, some can be conceived and others cannot be conceived, some can be loved and others cannot be loved. So to be as embodied is an assignment; it is to be as the saying of something which the body materializes in its fleshliness, a something which the body does not itself wholly contain but which it manifests in the ways of its coming to matter. The particular schema of desire that happens to have formed during modernity has been a heterosexual matrix, in which space is provided for the bodies that can continue to reproduce its underlying drive, the man's body and the woman's body which are meant for each other, and outside of which is the pile of rejected bodies that are refused materialization in the order of difference. This other place, this outside, this place of the "cannot be," is the place of abjection under this symbolic law, and for this reason, as Lacan has noted, "there is something originally, inaugurally, profoundly wounded in the human relation to the world."[49] For Butler, thinking that bodies come to matter is a way of thinking anew about what it is that is called "real," or "natural," and her thinking that these are conceptions which are constructed to form the foundations of sexual difference, and that therefore they follow from rather than precede this difference, is her way of suggesting that what we deem to be prior prevents, in the sense of "hinders," what is to be revealed in actual bodies. So for us to be as embodied is to bear the signs of a prior signification in which and for which we are made to come to be.

To think this way is to open ourselves to the future. Again, modern humanism has emphasized the future as the place for a realization of potential, for the expression of the power and value that already belongs with the human, unfolding as what is natural for the human to be, and valued as that in which the human being is to appear fully. The future becomes then the happening of the past. Butler is critical of this kind of thinking within naturalistic feminist ethics, which seeks to centre a feminist praxis on the irreducible materiality of woman's body, that is now to be revalued apart from its place of degradation in phallocentric thinking. To revalue woman is to lay hold of the power to originate the discourse of woman and then to seek a realization of this different original as each woman comes to identify with it. To be identified, to be known as woman in this difference, is to get real, and with this kind of essentialism, there is "an attempt to preclude the possibility of a future for the signifier."[50] In this metaphysics of difference is woman still seeking her equal status with man since, for all her criticisms of equality, this is also what Irigaray's ethics of sexual difference comes to in the end.[51] Butler precisely sees that in this revaluation is a continued subjection to the law from which it seeks to escape by establishing a separate, distinct, and really different foundation. For the law of difference, which has presumed to enjoy "a separate ontology prior and autonomous to its assumption is contravened by the notion that the citation of the law is the very mechanism of its production

[49]   Butler: *Bodies*, p. 72.
[50]   Butler: *Bodies*, p. 219.
[51]   See, e.g., Luce Irigaray: *je, tu, nous: Toward a Culture of Difference*, trans. Alison Martin (London: Routledge, 1993); *Thinking the Difference: For a Peaceful Revolution*, trans. Karin Montin (London: The Athlone Press, 1994).

and articulation."[52] For us to conceive of difference is to recite its law into significance for us, thereby binding us to its requirement as the primal source of value, and to resite its living expression into the matter of our bodies. Butler asks whether there is an other way to think the future that does not come to be as the repetition of the past. Her hopefulness is in the continuous rearticulations, recitations, that now characterize what it is to be in postmodernity, in which the possibility of thinking the body anew, not as a thing of the past, but as a coming to matter towards the future, appears. Thus, unlike "the necessary and founding violence of any truth regime," here "The task is to refigure this necesssary 'outside' as a future horizon, one in which the violence of exclusion is perpetually in the process of being overcome."[53] In this, one takes an ethical risk of being open for the future.

That this threatens the very possibility of the formulation of an ethics at all is the anxiety that finds expression in Nussbaum's review of Butler's work. Nussbaum's defense of an Aristotelian essentialism, with which we are "able to form a conception of the good and to engage in a critical reflection about the planning of one's own life,"[54] is simultaneously an attack on the "anti-essentialist conversations" she hears from "hip, defeatist" postmodern thinkers.[55] Her ethical humanism, and that with which Cahill also seeks to revise the authorized version of papal teaching regarding sexual difference, are both attempts to resignify the body into a more flexible and situationally sensitive citational chain, but nonetheless ones which necessitate the realization of what is already a founding moment, and which, in the drive to be as inclusive as possible, will "domesticate all signs of difference,"[56] taming all disagreements into versions of itself. The metaphysics of morals that underpins this humanism reveals a concern to secure the future so that one may know when one has been good, and will recognize the product of ethical thinking and practice when it appears. Butler's thinking has heard the Nietzschean announcement of the nihilism that lurks in this metaphysics, as it projects the anxious subject of modern humanism into the horizon of its own potential, so that for her to notice this same emptiness also in the metaphysics of gender also takes the risk of being destructive, of seeming to leave one open to the sheer chaos of endless

---

[52]   Butler: *Bodies*, p. 15.
[53]   Butler: *Bodies*, p. 53.
[54]   Martha C. Nussbaum: *Sex and Social Justice* (Oxford: Oxford University Press, 1999), p. 41.
[55]   Nussbaum: "Aristotelian;" see especially pp. 202–5.
[56]   Butler: *Bodies*, p. 53.

valuings, or of leaving everything alone since a better vision would repeat the problem.

Butler's work is thus situated at a critical point in philosophical and theological thinking, a point at which gender appears bearing its concerns for matter, for substance, and for knowledge into the problematic of contemporary ethics. There is little doubt, I think, that, while she rarely cites him, Butler is reading carefully Heidegger's critique of ontology, and of a theology which finds itself within these parameters, and thus also of an ethics whose work it becomes to match the existence of beings to the essence of Being. The difference between these is what the bridge of gender is constructed to bear, and across it, the presentations of sexual difference appear to carry us over. In the papal writing, there is the sincerest concern that we be held in faith by a teaching that God comes to be known in the bodied encounter of woman and man, which becomes then more than itself as, through this giving and receiving, we participate in the giving of God to us, now present in our midst. Our faith is to be in the knowing of this truth; faith comes to life in truth's light, and in this is a redeeming. One hardly knows how to take Irigaray's presentation of difference, and indeed this might exactly be her point, since it is undertaken with entire self-awareness that this is set up for women for the purpose of their becoming divine alongside men. Faith here becomes a willed imitation of truth, and in so far as it pretends to know what it is committed to, it effaces itself with irony even as it calls forth our trust in its alluring words. This is already a postmodern posture of faith in which the light of truth gives its own game away. Butler's indifference to these alternatives brings me to the question of faith by another way.

For she suggests that "the symbolic law in Lacan can be subject to the same kind of critique that Nietzsche formulated of the notion of God: the power attributed to this prior and ideal power is derived and deflected from the attribution itself."[57] The presentation of difference according to gender complementarity is a law of nature and nature's god that both expresses the impoverishment of the human state in which it is conceived, and simultaneously reinstates this condition by requiring our failure to live up to its ideals. Each time we speak into this difference, we own our distance from it, so that even in the call from feminisms that we revalue difference, overcoming the hierarchy of value that has dominated women's lives and presenting a different kind of god for whom these higher values matter more, even in this, is a repetition of the law of ontological difference into which gender is constructed. Here, as Nietzsche understood in his analysis

[57] Butler: *Bodies*, p. 14.

of sin, is the place in which "the cry for redemption" is heard, and in which a theological ethics struggles for the breath with which to come to faith.[58] So Butler asks, ". . . to what extent does this conception of the law produce the very failure that it seeks to order, and maintain an ontological distance between the laws and its failed approximations such that the deviant approximations have no power to alter the workings of the law itself?"[59] Neither the escalation of value into which feminisms have been driven, nor the search for valued gender identities established within a different law, can escape the inflationary spiral of this economy that reinforces the laws that bind us, and thus cannot bring us into a redeeming.

Is there here a place for a theological ethics to speak anew what it is that marks the turn from a life according to the flesh into a life according to the spirit, by means of which St. Paul sought to interpret the change of life in which a redeeming comes to be possible? For if a Christian ethics of gender is to say something here, it must be about the coming to possibility of faith, in which one agenda is laid down, no longer holding sway, and another is assumed in response to a call, a call into a becoming in the indifferent form of Christ, in whom is neither male nor female, which it is the work of faith to take up. In this taking up, in this coming to assume the form of the human in Christ, is the shedding of the garments in which we have been working out our salvation, a saving by gender or a saving by sex, and a letting oneself be drawn into the life of one who was not ideal, but in whose human form I am freed most entirely to come to be as myself in God. The strange crossings-over of human and divine which enflesh this possibility for me, I hear as a word that truths for me, that comes to matter as true in me, and that therefore calls me not to copy a previous model, but to be formed as one who faiths into a future. In this is to be my becoming as divine, as one in whom God comes to be lived. The call of this faith is thus to be as something which is spoken with a life, in a performing, in a living from the future, and thus in enactments by which the desperate process of commodifications without end that materializes in our culture is broken, and the requirement of perfect representations of an identity is left behind. In these acts, in these speakings, the horizon of the future is held open by faith in the indifferent coming of God to be known amongst us.

---

[58] Friedrich Nietzsche: *The Genealogy of Morals*, trans. Francis Golffing (Garden City, NY: Doubleday Anchor, 1956), p. 278.
[59] Butler: *Bodies*, footnote 13[sic], p. 247.

9

Subjected in Hope

Conceiving of difference brings us into the problematic that manifests itself in thinking with gender today. In the previous chapter, we began to discern the ontological question that troubles ethics as it seeks a sure foundation for its praxis. One rendering of this ontology, this logic of being, is that which presents a dual-nature anthropology, man and woman in their being different understood as a gift to each other of love, a love that exceeds the bounds of their relation in making present the love of God. The mystery of this being together in love is that of sacramental presence, in which the source of being comes to be known in the things that are, as they in turn reveal this coming and this ultimate belonging with God. A different logic of being is presented in the ontology that is not one, that intends to disturb the categories of being as it urges women to be present with a difference that is multiple. Here is a deliberation toward the provision of a foundation for an ethics of sexual difference, in which woman and man do not so much return to an original form of being, as they imaginatively project the vision into which the full expression of their gendered being can come to be expressed. Both of these presentations are thrown into question by the reading of ontology in our time as the attempt to fill up the empty place of God. Modern thought bears its history unavoidably into our present ways of thinking and speaking, and there is no place hidden from its impact. With that body of thought come the declarations of independence from the divine in which the modern subject makes its appearance, so that to reclaim the ground and recover the lost property of this division is to try to effect a redeeming through the very thinking in which the problem came to be manifest. A thinking with gender which speaks without ontology, without the logic of being, but within the existential matter of what it is to be, may be a thinking in which a redeeming can come to be performed in faith.

We are brought then to the question of who is concerned with this thinking, with this faith that lives into the open future of God's coming. Who am I, who is the one that matters, if not one made to be as woman or as man from the beginning, and if not one who can make it all up for myself in the effort of the imaginary? If the ontological grounding for an ethics of gender were understood to be removed, if it were known already to have disappeared in the age of the modern so that its recovery is no longer possible, what then about myself, and the subject that I am to be? The question of the subject is newly brought into consideration with postmodernity, and as we have already discussed, the assumption of its priority is undermined. That it may not precede its own speaking but rather be the one who is spoken, finding itself speaking without prior authorization, as Butler says,[1] that it may not initiate its own action but rather be the product of a being acted upon, these thoughts trouble the subject today. In their thinking, we come closer to an awareness of the uncertainty with which the modern subject has been born, and of the structures with which it has attempted to frame a secure existence for itself. Feminist and gender theories have been exposing this subject at its work and now find themselves caught up in the implications of its demise. For the hope with which theories initially sought reconciliation with one's authentic identity, or revaluing for a truer becoming myself, or reconstruction for a more humane enculturation, this hope has been itself thrown into question. Thus with the subject is the matter of hope, of the assurance in which it is to be held, and so we consider in this chapter how it is with this subject in its hoping, and how it is with the hope in which the human being today may rise up into its calling.

Hopeful Subjects

In his book, *Sources of the Self*, Charles Taylor traces the development and analyzes the major dimensions of what he calls "modern identity."[2] Clustered together in this word, "identity," are notions "of what it is to be a human agent, a person, or a self," notions which he seeks to demonstrate are "inextricably intertwined" with those of "the good" or of morality. Moral sentiments and reactions are affirmations of some understanding of

[1] Judith Butler: *Excitable Speech: A Politics of the Performative* (London: Routledge, 1997), p. 163.

[2] Charles Taylor: *Sources of the Self: The Making of the Modern Identity* (Cambridge, MA: Harvard University Press, 1989), p. 3.

what it is to be a person, so they assent to "a given ontology of the human."[3] This "background picture" forms "the only adequate basis for our moral responses, whether we recognize this or not."[4] Part of his concern in this book is to investigate the shape of this moral ontology in modern thinking, and so he attends to the particular appearance in modern western thinking of the notion of rights, of "subjective rights", with which "the place of the subject" begins to be articulated, and in which modern concerns about autonomy, suffering, and living well are to be expressed. It is within these modern ideas of the self that the meaning of human life is sought in our time, as it is also here that contemporary "disenchantment" with the notion that there is a meaningful order is experienced.[5] Recognizing that today there is widespread suspicion of ontology, we both feel the threat of a loss of meaning and find ourselves on a "quest" for making sense of human life, and it is to this problematic that he seeks to offer "a believable framework."[6] A framework provides both the horizon at the furthest reach of our thinking, toward which moral action is to be directed, and the overall context in the midst of which we find our positions and carry out the business of our daily lives. A framework allows us to take a stand as a human being, and thus to identify who we are in relation to a particular standpoint. No one, Taylor argues, can live as a human being without some overall framework of meaning, and thus human identity is bound up with having an orientation, with being able to take up a place in relation to issues of importance.

Thinking with gender about this presentation of the modern subject brings to light the question of its being as a single self-centred one, or its being-as-related-with-others. Generally, the feminist critique of western thought in this respect has been that its assertions of the self-centred being of the subject have justified a politics in which individual freedom is believed to be unbound, have expressed the man's quest for independence from all things earthly, natural and womanly, and have left women behind as morally immature and religiously inadequate subjects. Modern politics has emphasized the right of the individual to make decisions on the basis of rational principles, and has thus been constructed around the belief in a core centre of freedom in which this independence of mind and choice is held and protected within each one of us. In this emphasis, many feminists have detected a desire not to be tied down by relationships which would hold

3   Taylor, *Sources*, p. 5.
4   Taylor, *Sources*, p. 10.
5   Taylor, *Sources*, p. 17, quoting Weber.
6   Taylor, *Sources*, p. 18.

the mind back from its free explorations and exploitations of the universe. Because women's lives are bound up with those elements from which men seek to escape, there is a sense in which those dimensions of life associated with women accordingly are devalued. Feminist writers in recent decades have been seeking to set out an alternative self-understanding which begins with the assumption of being-in-relation, and which attends to the networks of relationship in the context of which meaningful personal life is to be found.[7] To understand myself to be constituted by relationships is to realize the sociality of my being, formed in the midst of people living and speaking together in a culture, and thus shaped in my identity by all that weaves its way into my life. In this view, there is to be less concern for the demarcations between one ego and another, more respect for the nurturing of good relationships in which persons may flourish, and a desire for just attention to the different voices in which women speak their moral concerns and insights.

This relational understanding of the self has been developed by a number of feminist thinkers, who have found in it a challenge not only to the assumptions of modern ethics, but further, to the support given these assumptions by Christian theological claims about the divine being. In a work such as Daphne Hampson's *After Christianity*, the individual subject, sustained from the heavens by a God who "is self-sufficient, alone, not in any way constrained, and not needing to take into account what is other than 'himself'," is exposed as an idol, a projected model of a male being complete in himself. For Hampson, transcendent monotheism is "instrumental in consolidating a gendered conception of reality,"[8] which, even in its trinitarian formulations of relations between the divine persons, expresses man's anxiety about mutuality and presence of one to another.[9] Within such a framework, women are constructed into the position of "other," and the rich spiritual understanding of interconnectedness that women treasure becomes merely "a mirror which allows man to find his own reality."[10] Women today are coming "to see themselves and to be accepted as subjects in their own right,"[11] within a lifestyle, a value system, and a way of conceiving the self that feminist ethics provides.[12] Here is "a

---

[7]   See esp. Carol Gilligan: *In a Different Voice: Psychological Theory and Women's Development* (Cambridge, MA: Harvard University Press, 1982).
[8]   Daphne Hampson: *After Christianity* (London: SCM Press, 1996), p. 125.
[9]   Hampson: *After*, p. 157.
[10]   Hampson: *After*, p. 169.
[11]   Hampson: *After*, p. 208.
[12]   Hampson: *After*, p. 85.

different conceptual space from which one can see"[13] the ways in which centredness of self is formed, not having "rigid ego boundaries," but having a certain integrity and agency" that "finds itself through deep connections with others."[14] Only with a renewed ethics and spirituality in which connectedness and relationality provide the framework for understanding the self can women and men place human beings "at the centre of their world,"[15] and come to their full humanity as simply "people – people set in the midst of the glory and the wonder of our world."[16] Hampson's hope is for setting aside the history of harm done to women's self-understanding within Christian culture, by means of a new conceptualization of God as "a dimension of the totality that is,"[17] the totality within which the mutual interrelatedness of God, ourselves and the world becomes both conceivable and healing.

Hampson's acceptance of the Enlightenment "turn towards the subject," in which "[H]uman subjectivity acquires foundational status" as the basis for our knowledge of God, is explicitly challenged in Kevin Vanhoozer's description of "Human being: individual and social," in which he sets out an anthropology derived from theology. Vanhoozer understands the authorized version of the subject that appears with modern thinking always to be in danger of losing its hold on human uniqueness, even as it establishes the conditions for its own autonomy, and so he recommends a return to "the meaning of the human story . . . as it is lived out before, with and by God."[18] To secure the subject is a framework of theological affirmations regarding the origin and the end of human life that establishes the indicative and imperative dimensions of our being human, for "what we should do follows from the kind of creatures we are."[19] We are those creatures who are called to be "echoes of God's evocative creative, reconciling and redeeming action,"[20] enacted whenever we go out of ourselves in communicative action for the sake of entering into a dialogical relation with another.[21] There is a twofold movement

---

[13]   Hampson: *After*, p. 87.
[14]   Hampson: *After*, p. 106.
[15]   Hampson: *After*, p. 284.
[16]   Hampson: *After*, p. 285.
[17]   Hampson: *After*, p. 231.
[18]   Kevin Vanhoozer: "Human Being: Individual and Social,"in Colin E. Gunton, ed.: *The Cambridge Companion to Christian Doctrine* (Cambridge: Cambridge University Press, 1997), p. 159.
[19]   Vanhoozer, "Human," p. 183.
[20]   Vanhoozer: "Human," p. 183.
[21]   Vanhoozer: "Human," pp. 176–7.

here. In our origin, "[I]t is the individual in his spiritual interiority that corresponds to the one God in his divine sovereignty,"[22] so that there appears the "irreducible ontological reality" of persons "that cannot be defined in terms of something else."[23] In our end, we are to relate as persons, as "agents able to initiate and respond to communication,"[24] and in this, relationships are established between us that witness to "the image of God as relatedness,"[25] by whose self-communicative activity we are first formed and for whose glory we are meant to live. Our vocation is thus to engage in "faithful speech," defined as "the religious relation to one's own words," such that "Christian existence is a matter of the relation a speaker bears to his own words."[26] By this, Vanhoozer seems to be suggesting that we are to mean what we say, and in that authenticity, the truth of our personhood is manifested as it points beyond itself to its transcendent foundation in the life of God.

To set such an account alongside Hampson's brings out the distinction between the subjects, as ones who go out of themselves to relate with others, or as ones whose relation with others constitutes the centre in which they find themselves. There are also common elements here that characterize moral ontologies of the subject emerging in modern thinking. There is a tension in both of these descriptions of the subject, between the independent centred-self and the self-in-relation, a pull in one direction or the other which reveals, not so much their opposition, as their interdependence. Vanhoozer's sovereign spirit held within its own interiority comes to be known by going out of itself in an act of self-communication that enters into personal relations,[27] while Hampson affirms for the relational self a "differently nuanced" concept of autonomy, perhaps as "inter-dependent autonomy,"[28] in which it still makes sense to speak of "coming into one's own." There is a different pattern of movement in each, but between the same two poles in which their difference is held. For each account, this description of the subject becomes the basis for the imperative of truth, so

---

[22]   Vanhoozer: "Human," p. 164. Note the parallels here with the exegesis of John Paul II, with the distinction that Vanhoozer understands Adam, not as generic man, but as a male whose "loneliness in the absence of a female partner indicates the social, not merely sexual, character of the difference between male and female," p. 165.

[23]   Vanhoozer: "Human," p. 175.

[24]   Vanhoozer: "Human," p. 175.

[25]   Vanhoozer: "Human," p. 177.

[26]   Vanhoozer: "Human," p. 182.

[27]   Vanhoozer: "Human," p. 177.

[28]   Hampson: *After*, p. 104.

that some form of faithfulness to the origin and destiny we are given is essential to being human. Being authentic to oneself is thus a sign of that which transcends one's particular life and circumstances, for it testifies to the truth in which it is held, as that truth in turn comes to dwell in oneself, a mutual confirmation which it is the covenant relation for Vanhoozer, and the matrix of being for Hampson, to sustain. The same logic of decision seems to be involved in these presentations. Finally in both accounts, there is a sense of the subject as the one in whom a redeeming possibility is made known, which it becomes the task of a religious ethics to lay hold upon for the sake of the world. Human beings are given to be a certain way in order that there may be a creative healing, a reconciliation between persons, the world and God, in which the hope of redemption is expressed. To engage in this healing in faithfulness to truth is the work of hopeful subjects.

Thinking with gender through such accounts brings us before the question of equality and the matter of difference, for these modern ethical concerns have provided the means and the language for our critical reflection upon ontologies of the subject. They present us again with the dilemma of a one-nature or a two-nature theological anthropology. Is there one common concept of the human in which the different subjects of man and woman are grounded and in which the meaning of their individual lives is to be conceptualized? Are there two accounts to be given of the human, clearly gendered anthropologies conceived and affirmed by women and men separately and thus belonging to each separately to live and to think within? With these questions, a further set comes to our attention. If the former shared framework is sought, who is the subject who will adjudicate the question of equality, ensuring a just apportionment of elements, of goods, of values between all who come to be fairly represented there? If the latter separate accounts are given, who is the subject who is able to read them both, and in that reading, to conceive and to value the matter of difference as it appears between them? The pattern that emerges in these self-reflections draws us to an awareness of the ways in which our conceptions of the subject are meant to provide the grounding, the under-pinning, upon which a hope can be formulated, an assurance that the things which are to come between us will be good and healing, honest and real, and a certainty that an ethics of the gendered subject will keep us on the right track of salvation.

These points may be demonstrated in an analysis of one theological attempt to speak of the subject-in-relation in a way that may be less gender-specific, and to retain the connection with traditional Christian theological proclamations. In Alistair McFadyen's *The Call to Personhood*, is an interpretation of individuality created in God's image, which seeks "the most adequate way of doing justice to the reality of personhood."[29] Two features of this account are interesting for our discussion here. The first is McFadyen's argument that a person is not constituted of a substantial core at the centre of the self, but rather is centred through "dialogue and dialectical interaction" with others.[30] There is an intrinsic relationality to personhood that "makes it impossible to think of us as having a clearly defined 'centre' or 'foundation,'"[31] and thus that speaks about the processes of relationship into and out of which persons are formed. An understanding of the social formation of persons leads us to find the individual at "a distinct spatio-temporal location in both the physical and social worlds,"[32] from which position an individual's identity, viewpoint, and experiences become centered through self-understanding. Thus McFadyen argues, "there is no substantial personal core, but . . . personal centring is enabled by holding a belief or a theory about oneself, without which personal life in the network of responsibilities which constitute a morally structured world would be impossible."[33] The achievement of this centering is the project of communication to effect, and in it is to be revealed the divine community of Persons in whose relational image lie our human origins. Woven together here are three elements: – a "natural state" of being "in need of community with another," a "structural openness" in which is "a social refraction of the openness to God" built into our human being,[34] and a moral demand to participate in relationships, in a dialectic of mutual understanding in which we are informed and transformed by the image of God. This image stands beyond us, not as a static ideal nor as an internal attribute which we might "have," but as a quality of relationship into which our relations with others are to be guided.[35]

To interpret our personal lives into this matrix hinges in a critical way upon the difference gender makes to relationships, for McFadyen proposes that "male–female relatedness is a structural paradigm of human life in the image" of God.[36] This relationship becomes a medium of signification between the divine and the human, in which we are able to read and understand both the ideal image of God and the particular circumstances

[29] Alistair I. McFadyen: *The Call to Personhood: A Christian Theory of the Individual in Social Relationships* (Cambridge: Cambridge University Press, 1990), p. 17.
[30] McFadyen: *Call*, p. 10.
[31] McFadyen: *Call*, pp. 9–10.
[32] McFadyen: *Call*, p. 77.
[33] McFadyen: *Call*, p. 93.
[34] McFadyen: *Call*, p. 33.
[35] McFadyen: *Call* , p. 31.
[36] McFadyen: *Call*, p. 36.

of our lives. On the one hand, "[T]he divine image represents an ideal codification of relations, which, as ideal, is universal and socially abstract," and on the other, it is through this image that God communicates to us in concrete situations the form our specific relationships are to embody. This paradigm is thus the form of personal relatedness into which the socially relative content of our particular locations is to be understood. So the difference of gender is more than "physical sexuality," "specific sexual organs," or "forms of bodily sexual union," all of which have to do with a "specific medium or content;" instead it signifies a "dialogical pattern of mutual whole-person orientation."[37] While the image of God is not to be equated with human existence as male and female, as the means of our understanding what this image entails, male–female relatedness is important for "the structure of distinction and relation in dialogical encounter which it contains."[38] Through this heterosexual matrix we are to learn what it is to be a centered self with an identity-in-difference, and what it is to communicate from one to an other in openness and honesty. Therefore, the importance of this paradigm is not in its gender or sex definitions, for these, McFadyen says, it cannot produce, but in its suggestion of "the orientation of the different upon one another,"[39] to be manifest in genuine truthful communication and in "an appropriate mutuality of understanding."[40] So it is that the formation of persons as centred relational beings requires a faithful interpretation of one's self through the medium of male–female relatedness, and in this is the ground of hope for redemptive relationships.

The investigation through this section reveals the strain of thinking that comes upon hopeful subjects within the constraints of the logic of being as it emerges in modernity. For the question running through these accounts is whether the sense of emptiness which the subject seems to bear can be filled by saying otherwise, by the positing of a fullness out of which the subject is to understand itself to be born. If only I could believe that to be true. The work of this subject is to interpret itself to be as an image, as one who is to become the full person whose image, or whose ideal, as Hampson might prefer to say, lies in its beginning. These three accounts describe that beginning as in some way relational, so that the ontological foundation of human life and the horizon of meaning given for its completion are there to be taken up, to be appropriated by particular persons in their different locations as they come to understand themselves aright. Each

---

[37]   McFadyen: *Call*, pp. 36–7.
[38]   McFadyen: *Call*, p. 38.
[39]   McFadyen: *Call*, p. 39.
[40]   McFadyen: *Call*, p. 162.

account suggests that this beginning is a divine communication which speaks itself into the founding of the human, so that we come to be as its word, and whether that word comes from on high, from a wholly other one whose self-emptying this creation exemplifies, or whether that word comes from the spirit of relationality whose presence already infuses all that is, makes no difference to the subject. This is the division which gender has come to signify in theology and in ethics, pointing beyond itself to the source of its meaning, so that as women and as men we are to repeat what it says in our lives, truthful to the end. Is there hope in this? Is this still the bearing of the hollowed-out self of modernity, hoping that its effort to replace a lost horizon will cause it so to be, and that its faithfulness to the relational form, for the sake of the form, will effect good relations between us? Thinking with gender brings us to these problematic questions of who I am to be, and in what way is the future.

Revealings of Children of God

In offering answers to the question of who I am, the approaches considered here seek to describe the nature of the person I am, and in that description to find the underlying truth of being which founds and sustains my existence in particular. Within this ontology is a framework of meaning to be discerned, to which my life is to adhere for its authenticity, and which promises to me a fulfillment of self in relationships, to myself, to others and to God. Characteristic of these accounts is the importance of inter-pretation, of right understanding by which I come to know myself as a subject whose existence is sustained in this matrix, and in remaining true to this vocation, the person I am is revealed. Already we have examined some of the ways in which this reading of the presenting subject is dis-turbed in postmodernity, challenged by an antihumanism that unsettles the language of subjects to its roots. Sedgwick's investigation of the epistemo-logy of the closet suggests that a "yoking of contradictions has presided over all the thought on the subject" in modernity, defining what it is the form of the personal to be and at once hiding away whatever does not fit and proves intractable to the description. Her claim that the "impasse of gender definition" exists also within this "field" opens a way for us to ask whether there is anything further to be said about the gendered subject, and thus to consider another way of hope.[41]

---

[41] Eve Kosofsky Sedgwick: *Epistemology of the Closet* (Berkeley: University of Cali-fornia Press, 1990), p. 90.

Certainly this impasse is felt to be running through the theological anthropologies considered above. For the realization that inclusive descriptions of the subject create exclusions, and that the voices of the excluded require that their own descriptions of the subject be understood to be the truly inclusive, enters a cycle of representations and counterrepresentations that cannot be resolved into the happy commonality from which each believes it began. The burden of this reconciliation either falls to women, who are deemed to understand this message of relationality and whose lives will bear the burden of relationships for others, or it rests upon each of us taking up some increasingly abstract notion of humanity, emptied of content, so that the form of relatedness alone may carry us forward. What Sedgwick calls a "minoritizing taxonomy" operates here in our attempts to represent our personhood to ourselves,[42] so that the history of anthropologies bears its politics into our ways of thinking what it is human to be. Each effort to be the most inclusive possible description of the human meets the challenge from the minority whose lives it neither explains nor values, and the stakes are then raised. Thus it is that a culture becomes absorbed in "the volatile, fractured, dangerous relations of visibility and articulation," which Sedgwick investigates in relation to the possibility of homosexuality, and the "panic" of which threatens exposure of the whole modern enterprise of representing the human. The politics is here revealed as a controlling endeavour, to be the ones who know what God knows, and who are able to say that and demonstrate what that is like, and in this rendering visible and in this saying, a violence has come to live even in our most noble efforts. Whoever would seek to climb above the fray for a higher viewpoint is encumbered by the untidy bits that keep falling out of the bag, and has to discipline these with a moralizing look that says it all.

Sedgwick therefore undertakes a reading of those "unarticulated assumptions" that are so obvious we don't say them aloud,[43] as a way of turning to the phenomenon of human experience. What is self-evident to each of us is the complexity of differences between people, and the facility we have for knowing this about one another and about ourselves. The highly nuanced tapestry of an individual life is not only continuously escaping the attempts to classify its various dimensions according to some scheme or other, but contributes, in spite of our efforts to think otherwise, to that richly diverse "human social landscape" with its "possibilities, dangers, and stimulations."[44] Her question is then "how certain categorizations work,

---

[42] Sedgwick: *Epistemology*, p. 20.
[43] Sedgwick: *Epistemology*, p. 22.
[44] Sedgwick: *Epistemology*, p. 23.

what enactments they are performing and what relations they are creating, rather than what they essentially *mean*,"[45] and in this is an opening up for persons to come to be as themselves. The question becomes then what kind of enactments are performed in our culture and what relations are created between us by gender, which has become

> ... the far more elaborated, more fully and rigidly dichotomized social production and reproduction of male and female identities and behaviors — of male and female *persons* — in a cultural system for which "male/female" functions as a primary and perhaps model binarism affecting the structure and meaning of many, many other binarisms whose apparent connection to chromosomal sex will often be exiguous or nonexistent.[46]

Attending critically to the significance gender has come to have as a marker in personal and cultural life, and to the explanatory power it is given in reading our history and our texts, can again allow us to state the obvious. For Sedgwick suggests that an unavoidable and "damaging bias toward heterosexual or heterosexist assumptions" in gender analysis[47] may inhibit our notice of the incongruous operations, different structures, and complex intersections of human embodiments one with another, which bring "different axes of oppression" that cannot be ranked, or understood *a priori*,[48] or indeed eradicated by thinking these are "only" cultural.[49] Attending to gendered subjects may not therefore free us from the particular oppressions that its schema brings to our attention, but reconsign us to its framework of understanding.

Already we have noted the critique that Butler makes of gender categories, which posit as an original identity what is the effect of cultural assignments. Her genealogical critique is a refusal "to search for the origins of gender, the inner truth of female desire, a genuine or authentic sexual identity that repression has kept from view,"[50] not simply to destabilize these categories, although that certainly happens, but, in the end, to get to the subject. For underneath these formulations of what is woman and what is man is a supposedly original subject, and Butler is interested in disclosing the production of the subject as an effect of power, and in analyzing the

---

[45]   Sedgwick: *Epistemology*, p. 27.
[46]   Sedgwick: *Epistemology*, pp. 27–8.
[47]   Sedgwick: *Epistemology*, p. 31.
[48]   Sedgwick: *Epistemology*, p. 33.
[49]   Sedgwick: *Epistemology*, p. 41.
[50]   Judith Butler: *Gender Trouble: Feminism and the Subversion of Identity* (London: Routledge, 1990), p. x.

reproduction of the subject in the form of subjection. "In effect," she argues, "the law produces and then conceals the notion of 'a subject before the law' in order to invoke that discursive formation as a naturalized foundational premise that subsequently legitimates that law's own regulatory hegemony."[51] Her challenge is not only to forms of naturalism which posit some essence that all women or all men represent, but also to the notion of "a pregendered 'person' [who] transcends the specific paraphernalia of its gender."[52] Both of these are operations of "juridical power" which "inevitably 'produces' what it claims merely to represent,"[53] and in exposing this operation, Butler realizes that an ethics of gender is also undermined. Insofar as this ethics is a politics which seeks fair and equal representation of the subject, and the empowerment of the subjugated, then the power of this law in its production and regulation of subjects is not broken, but repeated as subjection. If the subject is not the independently formed foundation and rationale for the changes to be performed in ethical action, so that it can be realized in its authentic being through this ethics, then what hope is there?

The answer to this question is not to look for a pristine, precultural location for the subject, for Butler understands this to extend the regime of law and the boundary of the polis into our metaphysical speculation. In saying this, her thinking is a challenge to the task of theological anthropology which resites the modern human subject into a transcendent kingdom of being in which it may safely dwell. Butler takes these questions quite deeply into her study of *The Psychic Life of Power*, in which she examines the phenomenon of subjection, that paradoxical human condition in which "[t]o desire the conditions of one's own subordination is . . . required to persist as oneself."[54] This paradox she describes as the empowering of the subject by the very conditions of its subjugation is a way also of questioning the requirement in ethics that, to operate at all as a moral subject, presupposes and repeats one's subjection to its conditions of possibility. In ethics, therefore, is no lofty expression of human freedom and dignity, but a pathos of repeated guilt in which subjects reinstate themselves into the conditions of their subjugation. In this critique is a reading of Nietzsche, and post-Nietzschean questions which she asks. How is a resistance to be formulated? In what gaps in the iterative cycle might a break appear?[55]

---

[51]   Butler: *Gender*, p. 2.

[52]   Butler: *Gender*, p. 3.

[53]   Butler: *Gender*, p. 2.

[54]   Judith Butler: *The Psychic Life of Power: Theories in Subjection* (Stanford, CA: Stanford University Press, 1997), p. 9.

[55]   Butler: *Psychic*, p. 12.

And in her questions can be heard also Nietzsche's understanding that this is the place where the cry for redemption is sounded.[56] For exposing the foundational myths of modernity, and of modern theology, is not, for her, attempting to overthrow one kingdom for the sake of another. It is rather to find a way of articulating the place of the birth of hope, and thus the place in which such hope may be sustained in a living beyond our status as subjects, and in this, Butler too is looking for a language of a redeeming hope.

This investigation resonates with a most difficult debate within Christian ethics about the place of law in the life of faith. For Butler's questions resonate with those of many in the Christian tradition who have wrestled with the paradox of St. Paul, namely that the law, which sustains one's own self-understanding and moral action, so exercises its dominion that it cannot bring life.[57] Being found in Christ opens up the subject to live in grace, to be revealed as the glory of one made to be godly in an utter generosity of Spirit, that puts away the old ways of thinking and brings in the new. The possibility for grace, and thus the place in which hope for a turn from the old to the new, from death to life can be spoken, is what Christian ethics in every age must find a way of saying. Today that demand comes from within gender theory, as it uncovers the ways in which we are subjected and looks for the saying in which that condition is turned into hope.

One suggestion for this articulation comes from the Greek Orthodox theologian, John Zizioulas, whose discussion of a different ontology of the personal may open up further consideration of this subject.[58] Zizioulas recognizes that "a true ontology of personhood" is problematic "unless certain drastic revisions of philosophical thinking are introduced."[59] Two would be outstanding among these requirements. In the first revision would be a refusal of ontology as a static level of being, somehow fixed and not subject to changes of time, on the stage of which my particular person comes to be acted out. Much that has been spoken about gender identity and representation continues to be subject to this assertion of what is permanent, of what is the truth that ultimately transcends our fleeting

---

[56]   Friedrich Nietzsche: *The Genealogy of Morals*, trans. Francis Golffing (New York: Doubleday Anchor, 1956), p. 278.

[57]   See esp. Romans 5–8.

[58]   John D. Zizioulas: "On Being a Person. Towards an Ontology of Personhood," in Christoph Schwöbel & Colin E. Gunton, eds.: *Persons, Divine and Human* (Edinburgh: T. & T. Clark, 1991).

[59]   Zizioulas: "On Being," p. 34.

and particular grasp upon it. Such thinking will ever lock the individual into becoming a representative of the essence which it is true to be, or will subject us to some abstracted form of the personal or the relational by which our obedience to this truth can be enacted. This kind of thinking "makes a personal ontology impossible,"[60] an "inability" which Zizioulas finds throughout the history of philosophy, and which brings him to consider the interface of the philosophical tradition and Christian theological claims upon and within that tradition.

For the second revision requires us to speak of the horizons opened up by faith, that take us to the matter of our beginning and our end in the Person of God. Here what Zizioulas emphasizes is twofold. There is the claim that our beginning is not in a universal substance that underlies or precedes the existence of individual subjects, but in a particular Person, whose self-revealing is "a reality of communion" in which relationship "constitutes an indispensable ontological ingredient."[61] Thus for us to be at all, for us to appear as persons, is for us to participate in this communion upon which all being ultimately depends, and to which faith witnesses. This beginning in a Person calls me to be personal, and that means to find my beginning not in some definition of "what" I already am, whatever authority that might claim over me, but rather in a call, a vocation, to be "who" I am to be, and in this does my "absolute uniqueness" become the future horizon into which I am to grow.[62] Further, Zizioulas speaks of a requirement of "the category of *ethical apophatism*," which means that "we cannot give a *positive qualitative content* to a hypostasis or person, for this would result in the loss of his absolute uniqueness and turn a person into a classifiable entity."[63] Suggesting that the personal always escapes or transcends any qualitative *kataphasis* is to remind us that what constitutes our being personal is our relating, not as ethical actions of forming relationships, but our relating as being formed in and by that which exceeds us, a relating that faith takes on and hope sustains. In faith, I am born into that mystery of the personal who is Christ, and in hope I live from beyond myself in an "expectation of the transformation of the world."[64] Therefore this living as personal is an always living from above, from an excess to myself in which my being as subject no longer is determinative. In this Zizioulas finds that "relating is not consequent upon being but is being

[60]   Zizioulas: "On Being," p. 36.
[61]   Zizioulas: "On Being," p. 41.
[62]   Zizioulas: "On Being," p. 45.
[63]   Zizioulas: "On Being," p. 46.
[64]   Zizioulas: "On Being," p. 44.

itself. The *hypo-static* and the *ek-static* have to coincide,"[65] and in this are the revealings of children of God.

Here too, as with faith, the ethics of gender comes to the birthplace of a theological virtue, with a question about my being in God's future. Zizioulas offers here a fruitful description of this timely living. He suggests that the *hypo-static*, that is, that which lies at the bottom, or which sediments underneath in my being subject, comes alive as personal in its living from beyond itself, from the *ek-static*, and this means from allowing itself to be put out of its place as ground and to be taken up in a future that is yet to be. There is something in the ethics of relationality, as described by both Hampson and McFayden, which suggests a concern to discover and to articulate this movement of the subject from the relational web in which it sediments as a particular person, out into the forming of relations with others. The question Zizioulas encourages me to ask of this approach is whether it does not fall rather too heavily on the *hypo-static* to bear out into the world the relationships it knows in its beginning, and thus to seek to cause these to be formed elsewhere, and thus to communicate what it knows to be true in its foundation as the ground of its hope for a future that is relational as the past has been. In taking up the *ek-static*, which is also in my being formed as personal, is an acknowledgment that that which exceeds me is already borne out in all that I am, and that my attending to it is not so that I can find a place at the beginning in which to locate my original being as self-in-relation, but so that I can become now a place in which that which underlies me and that which displaces me come together, in other words, so that I may begin to be, here.

Such an approach places less emphasis on the importance of self-disclosure, as some kind of revelation of the person I am, in which I present, or make present to others in a communication something about my identity, as it has been forged within and by a network of definitive relationships. Rather it turns my attention to the ways in which the performing of my self *is* a relating, and thus is a locus for the coming together of what I am given to be and what I am yet to be, and thus asks of me that I think what I am doing here. The virtue of hope is in part a holding open of the future *in* what I am doing, by a confident refusal of any closures that attempt to end my life before it has begun, and that knows, in this performance, the keeping open of the future for any ones whose path crosses mine, with whom is also this fragile and precious possibility of finding themselves awaiting a beginning. The virtue of hope is also that assurance with which I may abandon myself to the grace of this coming future, in which the

---

[65]   Zizioulas: "On Being," p. 46.

breaking open of the psychic life of power begins in my taking hold of a future possibility for life given from ahead of me in God, and the ending of the law of subjection happens as I think that I am one whose requirement to persist as myself, *kata sarka* as Paul expressed it, matters less in me than the person I am to become in God. These are elements in the revealing of hope, in the living of life *kata pneuma*, which a Christian ethics of gender may perform.

10

For Love of God

In her conclusion to the chapter on the epistemology of the closet, Sedgwick writes of "the impasse of gender definition" in which an understanding of what gender is has become mired. Such difficulties we have been investigating throughout this study, since an attempt to formulate an ethics of gender has also become entangled in these disputed identities, these erectings and crossings and transgressions of boundaries, these disclosures and concealments, these ontological foundations and relational matrices, these philosophical conundrums, into which the discourse of gender plunges us, somewhat unprepared and always vulnerable. In the end, for Sedgwick, this comes to an incoherence, "a highly structured discursive incoherence," at what she calls a "crucial node of social organization" carried into our lives as women and as men.[1]

A point of incoherence may be a place in which we abandon hope, for all efforts to find a way out of the morass seem closed to us, each way so highly defended or so morally exacting that we lose hold of the question in the following of it. So we give up the struggle to begin, to come to ourselves in the horizon of the future, and scurry around to make the best of a bad situation. It occurs to me that such is the thinking, at times, that upholds the move into pragmatism, by which the gender critique seeks simply to hold in check the worst impulses to unkindness, and in balance the interest in fulfillment which each one person brings to bear in a discussion. Have we come all this way for that? So too, a point of incoherence is a place in which faith may be most unacceptable, seeming to be only the nostalgia for a once-coherent world, or the busy production of a present reality that might look the same as our imagined one. Such is the

---

[1] Eve Kosofsky Sedgwick: *Epistemology of the Closet* (Berkeley: University of California Press, 1990), p. 90.

thinking that tries by reinterpretation to re-create what has gone, or to reclaim the world by the power of our saying it is so, and in these works, the postmodern performs itself against our will, its nihilism undoing our best efforts to be faithful.

Yet such incoherence of gender is the place in which we find ourselves, a place, Sedgwick says, that bears "all of its violent and pregnant modern history" into our thinking and speaking. The violence, we know, for it lives in exclusions and prejudices, in emotional torment and struggles to speak, in silent suffering and righteous anger, in dashed hopes for revealing and faith enfeebled by power. Thinking with gender brings us to an extraordinarily violent place, which is where we are now, and which will be manifest in one way or another in all that we do. Few will need to be convinced that this is a violent place. Indeed, the intention of our study here has been to raise sensitivity to and develop understanding of the modes of operation of this violent enactment as it comes among us, and seeps into our thinking about what it is to be human. But pregnant? Why is this a pregnant history – and with what? That there might be a birth in this violence is a stunning thought, and Sedgwick uses words here of the "generative," or the "unfolded," which is what history does as it moves from one thing to the next, giving birth to new generations. What has come, or is coming, to be born today? Yet her study seems to suggest, not that the birth, but that the conception with which pregnancy occurs is what matters here, and thereby it turns our attention to the conceiving in the present, and to the ways in which a conceiving might be happening among us.

Sedgwick raises these points in the context of a discussion of epistemology, and along with many critics of modern ways of knowing deemed to be masculine, she too is doubtful of the view from above, the God's-eye view that takes in the whole at once, deciding where and upon whom to alight. The conceiving which is to come here will not be by an intrusion from outside, for she claims to have "no optimism at all about the availability of a standpoint of thought" from which we might intelligibly, never mind efficaciously, adjudicate the matters of this incoherence of gender.[2] So there is no outside source here, and arguments over whether it is to be your source or mine that is life-giving are entirely beside the point. The point of this incoherence is that it is the only place in which to think, and the things that have come to matter here, and the forms of subjection which are experienced here, and the power that is operative in our contested discourses – these are the things that are found in our

[2]   Sedgwick: *Epistemology*, p. 90.

thinking. Our calling as philosophers is to say in what way truth is to be conceived here, and our calling as theologians is to bear its cry for redemption into the coming of God. The place of our most difficult work as philosophers, turning into our time to think truth as ones who are entirely formed in its midst, is also the place of our most urgent work as theologians, in faith – letting God come to matter here, and in hope – standing at the threshold of glory.

These difficult callings bring us to the question of love. For love is at stake in this violent and pregnant history, that carves so deeply into the body of gender theory the marks of all that stands between us, and that ever divides as it seeks to hold together. This history becomes the text of our lives, the signs of its ruptures found too in our flesh and the tangled web of its citations holding our thinking in thrall. The anguish of these oppressions wherein we are mapped onto the geography of the social world, and the cautious politics with which we maneuver the tangled complexities of discourse, have together formed the broad stream on which the ethics of gender appears in our time. This ethics comes forward to perform the mediations that will let us reveal ourselves, that will heal the scars left by our violent schemes, that will bring us to one another in care for our giving and receiving. It is here that the necessity for love begins to be articulated, in our reaching out for transformation of the past into a better future, in our realization that without the presence of new life this one remains subject only to death, in our search for the bridge that will cross our divisions. How attentive must be our listening to hear the tonalities of these articulations, and how exacting must be our thinking so that the conditions for the possibility of love may be opened out and sustained. This too is the work of philosophy, in its best efforts at human self-understanding, and this too is the work of theology, in its proclaiming the coming of love. For speaking of love is asking after the way in which a tenderness and a generosity might come to be formed among us, and it is transcending into the coming of love so that its gentleness may find a place to live here, and it is knowing a joy for love of God as we ourselves are turned into ones who love. In its attention to the reason for my existence, and in its call to know the place I am given to be, the title of this chapter brings me before the possibility of love, and asks that faith and hope find their greatness there.

These themes find some resonance in the work of feminist philosophers of religion, who explore the conditions of human understanding within which our transcendence into the divine may be enacted. Grace Jantzen's investigation of the way of becoming divine is one such work, in which the feminist critique of reason and of reasonable misunderstandings of religion is developed further into the formation of a feminist religious language.[3] Jantzen is concerned, like Sedgwick, to understand a violent and pregnant history, as this is manifested in accounts of religious experience and belief. Here at the meeting place of the divine and the human, at the point of a transcending in which faith and hope and love come to be born in the human soul, is a most fragile moment, and thus it is here Jantzen finds the possibilities for the destruction or for the birth of the soul into God so starkly exposed. It is our ways of thinking about the human subject that require critical investigation at this point, for Jantzen understands that "the task of becoming divine, of realizing divinity in our individual and collective lives, is obviously a task which cannot escape problematization of our selfhood and its dimensions."[4] It is, after all, in me that God comes to be born, and what kind of a place is prepared for God there is crucial, and what kind of bearing I, in particular, may have toward the possibility of this birth, or this death, is the story of the past that brings me towards a place of meeting.

To examine this preparation for faith is the task of philosophers of religion, and Jantzen approaches this work with a clearly stated conviction that gender figures in this work. We cannot proceed into a true under-standing of the human encounter with the divine unless and until the gendered subject is taken into account. For gender comes between us, both because it prevents our understanding and thus our appreciation of the forms of religious experience and expressions of religious belief that come differently to women and to men, and because its presence as a category of our thinking about who we are as human beings stands in the way of our approaching the divine. Jantzen is persuaded that the difference of gender matters here, and specifically that women's experience and belief cannot be authentically known within the framework of philosophical accounts that ignore this difference. A feminist philosophy of religion thus seeks "to develop ways of 'thinking differently,'"[5] and in this work, to set humanity before the starkest choice, between a way of life or a way of death, upon which ways of understanding, our becoming divine depends.

For Jantzen, the violence in the history of the philosophy of religion is the combined impact of its having been written from man's experience and self-understanding, thus bearing man's body and language and categories into the account, and of its projecting the existence of a deity fashioned in

[3]   Grace M. Jantzen: *Becoming Divine: Towards a Feminist Philosophy of Religion* (Manchester: Manchester University Press, 1998).
[4]   Jantzen: *Becoming*, p. 27.
[5]   Jantzen: *Becoming*, p. 26, quoting Foucault.

man's image, whose otherness from the world, whose very transcendence, above all things, both reveals man's awe of power and at the same time allows him privileged access to it. Her task is to demonstrate "the bias and sterility of masculinist (supposedly neutral) pursuits of the discipline,"[6] in which women either do not recognize the subject who figures in the account, as in much British analytic philosophy of religion, or find themselves to be deliberately excluded, as in the Freudian heritage of Lacan's "there can be no women subjects."[7] Revealing this violence within a discipline is sustained by Jantzen's interpretation of the male imaginary as trapped within its own oppositional binary constructions, and as driven by a will to power so that his place in the scheme of things may be secured. In this context, women are present, or indeed absent, as those subjects who think differently, and who therefore need "to explore other conceptions of the divine," since this is "not the only concept of God available."[8] Here the concern for the pregnant history appears, for Jantzen needs to explain "from where shall such conceptions be derived, and why would they be persuasive?"[9] With these questions, she seeks to locate the beginning of a different philosophy of religion.

What inspires Jantzen's approach is the possibility of a feminine imaginary, as this finds expression in Irigaray's unauthorized versions of the subject, and as Jantzen herself has examined in those women of the Christian tradition who write of their spiritual lives.[10] These past and present writings reveal the potential for "the achievement of women's subjectivity,"[11] through speaking from a world-affirming "imaginary of natality" that "recognizes our rootedness in the physical and material,"[12] and from "a symbolic of flourishing" that belongs at the heart of our understanding of salvation.[13] It is this "emergence of women into speech" that can change "the symbolic

---

[6]   Jantzen: *Becoming*, p. 17. In this sense her work here continues that of her earlier book on mysticism, in which she exposes the pretense of philosophical neutrality, arguing that "the various social constructions of mysticism have been bound up with issues of power and gender," a fact that goes "largely unrecognised" within philosophy of religion. See Grace M. Jantzen: *Power, Gender and Christian Mysticism* (Cambridge: Cambridge University Press, 1995), p. 342.

[7]   Jantzen: *Becoming*, p. 43.

[8]   Jantzen: *Becoming*, pp. 75–6.

[9]   Jantzen: *Becoming*, p. 76.

[10]   See esp. Grace M. Jantzen: *Julian of Norwich: Mystic and Theologian* (London: SPCK, 1987).

[11]   Jantzen: *Becoming*, p. 171.

[12]   Jantzen: *Becoming*, p. 145.

[13]   Jantzen: *Becoming*, p. 171, quoting Irigaray.

of western culture,"[14] which has become trapped in the vicious cycle of a necrophiliac imaginary, its preoccupation with death and its valorization of infinity wreaking havoc and visiting injustice upon the world and its peoples. Through the potential of their imagining, their thinking, a "new religious symbolic focused on natality and flourishing rather than on death, a symbolic which will lovingly enable natals, women and men, to become subjects, and the earth on which we live to bloom,"[15] will become incarnated and salvation made available. With this turn to earth as divine embodiment, in a form of pantheism, Jantzen concludes with Irigaray that "there is strategic value in rethinking religion rather than in acquiescing in an already masculinized secularism, not 'awaiting the god passively, but bringing the god to life through us' – through us and between us, embodied, transcendent, the projection and reclamation of ultimate value, the enablement of subject-positions as women, natals becoming divine."[16] Thus will the earth save itself through the perfection of the female divine, accepted and welcomed by women, for "It is within the world, not in some realm beyond it . . . that the horizon of our becoming must occur."[17]

It is important to give considered attention to this kind of account, for it touches our questions here regarding the possibility of love at a place of special significance within feminist discourses, and in a time of profound experience of the problematization of the Christian theological tradition. Here are the intersecting trajectories of the postmodern critique of the western *episteme* within which theology has come to be formed, the feminist assertion and revaluation of the difference gender makes within this culture, and a theological apologetic that unsettles the language of its time by speaking differently within it. Jantzen takes hold of the opportunity that is here to give expression to an ethics of gender that is to be known in "solidarity and compassionate action for love of the world,"[18] wherein is the end of faith. Her affirmation of the place of woman, embedded and embodied wholly in the world, and her confidence that the setting free of the power of the feminine imaginary will redeem this world, loving it back to itself and restoring its best life-enhancing possibilities for human fulfillment, are the logical conclusion of the ideology into which feminism is solidifying. In its vision, women are offered to the world, as models for a relational way of living and exemplars of an ethic of care, an

14 Jantzen: *Becoming*, p. 171.
15 Jantzen: *Becoming*, p. 254.
16 Jantzen: *Becoming*, p. 275.
17 Jantzen: *Becoming*, p. 274.
18 Jantzen: *Becoming*, p. 263.

offering in which there is an integrity of spirit that ennobles those who seek to take it up for the good of all.

Many women have been willing to establish their ordained ministry within the Church in the place of this conception of God, presenting themselves to be its servants with their lives, body and soul, and offering the spirit of their gentle and healing touch to renew what appears to be its failing life for the sake of the world. It is here that there has been the making of their bodies into a living sacrifice.[19] Women have received this vocation to a discipleship of service deeply into their hearts and have heard also, and themselves have suffered, the cry of despair of an anguished world so badly in want of love. The difference of gender comes here to signify the possibility for a redeeming, the offering of the different gifts and perspective of women to be the medium through which the world may be taken over from death into life. Thus, it is no surprise that women are unhappy with the boundaries around institutional church, or even around Christian tradition, that would confine the possibility for a redeeming to its territory, and that there is a reaching out in collaboration with women of other faith, and with women of post-Christian and post-traditional theologies, who understand this want and believe in this healing. So too it is an occasion for joy that women come forward to offer their love – the energy of their passion for life and the exercise of their intellect for the struggle to think and to say in what this life may be truly known. There are precious gifts here.

Yet the very seriousness of the matter of redemption and of the coming to birth of love, and the very urgency with which the world awaits the conceiving of God into its life, lead us to pursue the problematic voice that speaks in this offering, and to ask of it the questions that trouble the soul in its readiness for faith. What appeared in Ruether's question so many years ago, "Can a male saviour save women?" – a question that women initially articulated on their own behalf –,[20] has been turned around by much that is feminist theology, so that it becomes an assumption of redeeming work by women themselves for others' sake, indeed for the sake of men.[21] In this voice, there seems to be too ready a deflection from

---

[19] Romans 12:1.

[20] Rosemary Radford Ruether: *Sexism and God-Talk: Towards a Feminist Theology* (London: SCM Press, 1983), chapter 5.

[21] See esp. Angela West: *Deadly Innocence: Feminism and the Mythology of Sin* (London: Mowbray, 1995); Laurence Paul Hemming: "The Nature of Nature: Is Sexual Difference Really Necessary?," in Susan Frank Parsons, ed.: *Challenging Women's Orthodoxies in the Context of Faith* (Aldershot: Ashgate Press, 2000), pp. 155–74.

the speaker herself, and thus from her own need and condition, such that she becomes wholly invested in the message, in what is to be communicated to others that she has come to know by wiser means, and must summon up the intention and the feelings for others by which this restoration of our humanity and re-creation of the world is to be accomplished. Hers must be a voice of power and conviction, of commitment and strength of will, that knows what it has to say, and in that very necessity, that "must be so," lurks its pain. For therein comes a nihilism also to be spoken in this voice and performed in its ministrations, and therein, in the very condition of this necessity, is the place that cries out for redeeming. This kind of feminist theology, by turning our attention to women as redeemers by their words and by their actions, leaves women themselves before the question of the possibility for redemption, and that is to be before the question of Christ.[22]

What feminist theology is so reluctantly coming upon, and what Jantzen's book is itself an effort to mollify, is that nihilism in which is also our violent and pregnant modern history, and out of which gender has emerged as the accountable representation of our humanity. In his tracing of "the strange twists and turns of human thinking that led to nihilism," Michael Gillespie tells a story that may assist our understanding of "the character of modernity," and open a way for the intensification of our questions regarding a redeeming love.[23] Describing modernity "as the realm of human self-assertion," Gillespie looks to its origins in the notion of absolute will. Initially he claims, this finds its place in Ockham's idea of an omnipotent deity: "To say that God is all-powerful is to say that he can do everything that is possible and this includes everything that is not contradictory. Omnipotence also means that everything is or occurs only as the result of God's disposing will and that there is no reason for creation except his will."[24] With this assertion of God's power as a transcendent deity, it becomes possible to characterize the human being also as will, as one by whose will this deity is conceived subjectively, for thereby the human subject finds "a secure basis" and constructs "a bastion against the transrational God of will."[25] Thus what is claimed to be the character of the objectively distinct being of God is, at the same time, an assertion of the subject of human being.

---

[22] See Susan F. Parsons: "Accounting for Hope: Feminist Theology as Fundamental Theology," in Parsons, ed., *Challenging*, pp. 1–20.

[23] Michael Allen Gillespie: *Nihilism Before Nietzsche* (Chicago: University of Chicago Press, 1995), pp. xiii, xxiv.

[24] Gillespie: *Nihilism*, p. 16.

[25] Gillespie: *Nihilism*, p. 41.

Like many who interpret modern thought, Gillespie also ascribes special significance to Descartes, in whose notion of self-consciousness is not a victory of reason, *contra* numerous feminist readings of his work, but a precedence of will over reason, such that all thinking becomes "a formative willing of the world."[26] In Descartes is an understanding of the world as "reconstructed by the will," and thus of the world as representation for which there is no "real" with which it can be compared: "The will thus takes possession of the world on the most fundamental level by recreating it so that it is always in its very being *mine*. The self in this sense is not just another object but the essential ground for the whole representational re-creation of the world."[27] With this way of thinking begins a nihilism which says of the world that ultimately it is nothing, "devoid of form and purpose,"[28] and which realizes that, in the end, "it makes no difference whether there is an omnipotent God" since "Man is able to reform the world by virtue of his will."[29] Not in the freedom of reason, therefore, but in the unlimited power of will is the nihilism of modernity conceived, and the separation of God and humanity wrought into a metaphysics of absolute difference.

It is this nihilism of which Nietzsche writes, and the continuing controversy around his speaking of it appears also in Gillespie's work.[30] Nevertheless, what comes to light by his notice of the death of God is that the "history of modern thought has thus been the ever more explicit revelation of the hidden foundation of modern reason in will,"[31] and further that the God to whom omnipotence was first attributed has come to live in the human subject. The necessity which conditions the postmodern, therefore, is that of having to think within the terms of this disclosure, in which is the Enlightenment darkened, the discipline of the subject of ethics mocked, and the human being as framed by gender deconstructed. This is the condition that shapes the ethics of gender, its moods variously shifting from stoic resignation to what is good for us, to heroic fervour for deliverance to a better state, to brave resolve that this is to be understood as God's world after all. The perplexing of philosophy and the exhausting of theology that come to be experienced in this time are thus also determinants

---

[26]   Gillespie: *Nihilism*, p. 51.
[27]   Gillespie: *Nihilism*, p. 51.
[28]   Gillespie: *Nihilism*, p. 53.
[29]   Gillespie: *Nihilism*, p. 54. Cf. p. 255.
[30]   Gillespie's central thesis is "that Nietzsche was mistaken about the origins of nihilism and . . . equally mistaken about its solution . . . ," *Nihilism*, p. 254.
[31]   Gillespie: *Nihilism*, p. 256.

of this ethics, whose best efforts are rendered possible and barren in the same breath. In this appears the necessity for redemption. In this comes the foolishness of faith to dwell, precisely in the places of our greatest discomfort and impotence, as it takes hold of the coming to matter of God in Christ, and as it speaks anew of that on which it stumbles in its very longing for truth. In this is the certainty of hope founded in all that escapes its grasp and yet is most intimately present, that compels the sight of an empty tomb to become the knowledge of life in God, and that leaves us ever walking along the edges of its disclosure in our midst. Thinking with gender brings us before the question of the redeeming of Christ in an unavoidable clarity, and asks theology to say what it means here.

It will be clear from what has been said so far that I am less sanguine about the possiblity of a feminine imaginary which takes up the baton of this modern project, and seeks so fervently to prepare a kinder, gentler version of its terrible regime of will than Jantzen or Irigaray seem to be. While there is the most sincere effort in this to prepare the place for a conception of God in the human soul, and to turn us from a violent past into the dawning of a new day, such must be sustained by precisely the act of will of a subject, which begins in the Cartesian project of self-securing, and which ends in the simulacrum of postmodernity. By concentrating on the epistemological dimension of modernity as if it had only to do with reason, with the exercise of thinking as a detachment of mind and with the content of what is thought as objective truths, Jantzen, along with so many feminists, misses the dimension of will, and thus the will for a voice, for a privilege, continues to speak in her critique.

The trouble to which Butler attends in the modern understanding of gender lies in the very subjection of this subject, who must re-present itself in the world as an identity, sustained by a will and rationalized as the consequence of its own free choice, and who is therein made, produced, to be one who repeats this history of self-assertion. The appeal of feminism to locate the will of this power in the natural world, rather than beyond it, does not thereby escape its clutches, as though a different willed version of transcendence could save us, for in this is no difference, but a repetition of the same problematic of which the modern has been constituted. Butler is not a popular figure amongst naturalistic feminists, precisely for the reason that she calls the bluff on this game, refusing its consolations, parodying its pretentions to be real, and remaining firmly at the points of difficulty in our thinking. Thus she allows a way for us to attend to the question of transcendence and of love, as this appears in gender theory.

After Nietzsche's proclamation, and in a time of such challenging re-thinking of the tradition that has come to live with us, the way for an

ethics to be formulated also becomes problematic. We have seen much of
the difficulty already, in the disturbances rendered by postmodernity to the
ideas of freedom, of the subject, and of agency, and we have explored
some of the schemes, sensitive to these changes, which are offered as a
way through the complexities of this discursive incoherence. Through
these last chapters, we have been exploring the boundary of philosophy
and theology, which is where ethics lives, to find there that thinking with
gender has become the focal point of some of the most difficult questions
within these disciplines, questions concerning the matter of origins, the
nature of subjects and the life of the soul. In our ways of thinking through
these questions, gender has been unavoidably present, requiring us also
then to consider the ethics of our thinking. For we can be dismissive,
hostile, welcoming, or generous to the problems brought to our attention.
This author has at least sought to be welcoming, finding in these problems,
new opportunities for the articulation of those theological virtues of faith
and hope and love in which the soul is born into the freedom of the
future. These new ways of speaking are a happy consequence of careful
listening to what it is that the critical theory of gender presents. It may also
be that there is generosity, for in this does love come to be conceived, and
so our attention may now turn for the conclusion of this chapter, and of
this study, to its ways of becoming in us.

One way of thinking toward the origin of love is found in the dense
and suggestive writing of Emmanuel Levinas, whose essay on exteriority in
particular can offer some help in considering our questions.[32] His approach
to an understanding of human existence, and to the significance of ethics
within it, begins with his critique of the ontology that has developed in
western philosophical thinking. Ontology, which is the study of being, has
been dominated by "the concept of totality," that is, by the notion of
being as that which is encompassable, as that totality within which particular beings appear, and thus as that realm from which the meaning of
individual beings is derived.[33] The prevalence of this concept in our thinking has resulted in two preoccupations of modernity, namely a concern for
the representation of the self as visible within the domain of the total, and
a concentration on politics as the adjudication of the space allotted to each.
Levinas understands this situation to require a reduction, a flattening of
human being, such that the possibility for its exteriority is lost to the
surface of an image, and further to require the production of war as the

---

[32]   Emmanuel Levinas: *Totality and Infinity: An Essay on Exteriority*, trans. Alphonso
Lingis (Pittsburgh, PA: Duquesne University Press, 1969).
[33]   Levinas: *Totality*, pp. 21–2.

"test of the real." He claims that, "The visage of being that shows itself in war is fixed in the concept of totality," for it is in this violence that the order of being is re-produced absolutely as that "from which there is no escape."[34] The inheritance of ontology, insofar as totality has come to predominate, is the violent destruction of the rich otherness to being, which we ignore, therefore, at our peril.

For what lies beyond totality is infinity, that which is *"a surplus always exterior to the totality,"* and thus that which must break in upon us by revelation of itself as "a primordial and original relation with being."[35] This in-breaking is announced through an eschatology, here an eschatology of peace, that "institutes a relation with being *beyond the totality* or beyond history,"[36] and it is this relation with infinity which it is the role of ethics to sustain. For ethics is the vision in which this breach, this rupture, is held, and thus in the thinking which is ethics, the precedence of metaphysics over ontology is enacted.[37] It is the significance of ethics to live in this borderland, in which what is natural is interrupted by what is revealed, and thus to "see" the situation of the infinite "where totality breaks up, a situation that conditions the totality itself."[38] The mode of this relation is determined by the presence of infinity in the strangeness of the Other, for in the face of the Other "is the gleam of exteriority or of transcendence."[39] The infinite, in which is our ultimate belonging, and that which finally conditions the reality of any totality by which we seek to define the nature of being, leaves its trace in the presence of an Other to me, so that it is by coming upon and by welcoming and by giving to the Other, that the true exteriority of my being is returned to me. The in-breaking upon the totality, by which "the same" is called into question, is brought about by the Other, whose face unsettles my spontaneity, who sees my world from another center, and who reminds me of the origin of my existence in that which surpasses my self. It is ethics that accomplishes this calling into question, by admitting the strangeness of the other, and thus it is ethics that concretely produces "the critical essence of knowledge"[40] as a return, "a tracing back to what precedes freedom," which is what it is to philosophize.[41]

[34]   Levinas: *Totality*, p. 21.
[35]   Levinas: *Totality*, p. 22.
[36]   Levinas: *Totality*, p. 22.
[37]   Levinas: *Totality*, p. 42.
[38]   Levinas: *Totality*, p. 24.
[39]   Levinas: *Totality*, p. 24.
[40]   Levinas: *Totality*, p. 43.
[41]   Levinas: *Totality*, pp. 84–5.

For Levinas, the possibility of love is "through the idea of the Infinite,"[42] by which the self-centred being of the ego, the will by which it invests in its own "inter*estedness*," and the desires in which its presence is constituted, are transcended, affected by the Infinite, passed over by that which is near, but different, separated from me, holy.[43] The face of the Other is the trace of the transcendent, and thus between me and the one who meets me, "[A] difference gapes open" that cannot be restored to a unity by thinking of some biological bond, a "brotherhood – conceived with the sober coldness of Cain" in which legal contractual arrangements are established between us. Levinas is clear that "[R]esponsibility for the neighbor is precisely what goes beyond the legal and obliges beyond contracts; it comes to me from what is prior to my freedom, from a non-present, an immemorial."[44] Thus the concept of my own ego is "extracted" from me, and I am assigned a responsibility in which is "a new identity," my obedience to the Other constituting an "augmentation of holiness" by which I grow towards the Infinite in an exhausting of myself.[45] The pure possibility of love is en-countered in "the non-desirable proximity of others" by which we are reoriented to our neighbours,[46] and in this turning appears generosity, as we bestow "the possession of a world . . . as a gift on the Other."[47]

Ethics is here not in consequence of the natural, and is not the deter-mination of law within the realm of Totality, but rather is in consequence of the revelation of Infinity, and thus the good which it seeks is known as "a deficit, waste, and foolishness in a being." For "to be good is excellence and elevation beyond being. Ethics is not a moment of being; it is other-wise and better than being, the very possibility of the beyond."[48] The Good, and the goodness of the Good, calls me from beyond my subjectiv-ity into the transcendence which is ethics, separating me from myself by the intrusion of the holy, so that I become a new subject only as a subjection to my neighbour, by whose strangeness I am compelled to goodness.[49] In this formulation of ethics as an adherence to the in-breaking

[42] Emmanuel Levinas: "God and Philosophy," trans. Richard A. Cohen and Alphonso Lingis, in Grahan Ward, ed.: *The Postmodern God: A Theological Reader* (Oxford: Blackwell, 1997), p. 62.
[43] Levinas, "God," p. 63.
[44] Levinas, "God," p. 65.
[45] Levinas, "God," p. 67.
[46] Levinas, "God," p. 63.
[47] Levinas: *Totality*, p. 50.
[48] Levinas: "God," p. 64.
[49] Levinas: "God," pp. 63–4.

of transcendence, Levinas is suggesting the way by which the will to power of my self may be disrupted in the face of the Other, confronted by that which exceeds it, and thus re-turned to itself via a transcendence in which its own power is now to be subjected. The violent barrenness of will to power is opened up to its true origin in the Infinite, an origin which is "inconceivable in a totality,"[50] but which encounter, engagement, and conversation with the Other now renders possible.

Such thinking offers a return to a kind of Platonism, in which the transcendence that is the Good is reaffirmed as that Otherwise-than-Being in which is the world's true beginning and end.[51] The presence of that which exceeds, of that from beyond, is experienced in human being as a summons, a challenge, to give over all that has mattered to me, to the Other in whom I see the look of Infinity, and is experienced as a responsibility to look after the Other whose interests, in justice, are higher than my own. In this respect for the exteriority of the metaphysical is a subduing of the impulse to control, to possess, and a subordination of life within the totality of things to a "freedom from the arbitrary," to which it is the essence of knowing to lead us.[52] Such thinking is a rich resource for the ethics of sexual difference. The imagery of Levinas draws upon a distinction between interiority and exteriority in the subjective life, a distinction that favours exteriority as that in which our liberation is constituted, as that presence of Other which outbursts interiority, and a distinction which comes to correlate with the feminine and the masculine. The place of the feminine is the dwelling, the home, the being-at-home, the interior, in which possessiveness and desire are normal, as that with which one lives. The presence of the Other is from outside, and comes to me as one who is to be welcomed in, who is not desired yet who is to receive all that I have, and to whom my home is to be opened, as the opening up of a soul to a strange coming.[53] Thinking with gender requires us to wonder whether this return to the binary symbolic is the only way for a conception of love to be affirmed in our time, and whether, in taking it on as our way of conceiving, we have not thereby given over our thinking once again to the determinations of a physical, a spatial imagery that divides what is here from what is there along gendered lines.

---

[50]   Levinas: *Totality*, p. 119.
[51]   Emmanuel Levinas: *Otherwise than Being: or Beyond Essence*, trans. Alphonso. Lingis (Dordrecht: Martinus Nijhoff, 1981).
[52]   Levinas: *Totality*, p. 85.
[53]   Levinas: *Totality*, pp. 170–1.

It is not clear to me that there can be satisfactory resolutions of these questions of gender within the terms Levinas sets. Indeed, it is interesting that such a re-ethicization of the world has been taken up so favourably, albeit with a difference, by feminists. The reclaiming of the space of interiority, and of the physicality of the elemental, is a project Irigaray undertakes for women, as she seeks to turn the location of the feminine in Levinas's imagery to the advantage of women, in their own coming to love and to value the transcendence which is the mother. In her poeticizing of the elements, the interior that has been assigned to women becomes what is willed by women, by an act of interpretative reimagining, so that by the choosing of a feminine imaginary of transcendence, women are to be brought to the truth of themselves with a difference.[54] The overturning of Platonic space is what Jantzen undertakes, as she rejects the notion of the transcendent as that which is above or beyond the physical, the Infinity in which the male god dwells untouched, in favour of the transcendent which is here among us, in the world itself, and thus which is finally physical. Here women can find a home within the present for their relational concerns, which resonate so favourably with those of Levinas, for the here and now contains possibilities for good enough forms of transcendence to keep us busy with loving our neighbours and doing the work of justice for the whole of our lives.[55] However, the question that appears in these attempts to turn Levinas to feminist purpose, is whether the reclaiming of territory or the overturning of space are a transcending, or are a re-sitation of the self as subject into the terms of its confinement.

For the situation of the subject is the problem in this spatialization of ethics, requiring me to think of my self as a centre, from out of which I go to meet the world, to believe my self to be that interior space in which are the desires that drive my possessiveness and the will that strives for power over the outside, and to be taken from the confinement of my self by means of an Other, who breaks through the boundaries that mark the limits of the claims I have staked out, with a voice from elsewhere. So it comes to be that the ethics required for this subject is the positing of a

---

[54] Luce Irigaray: *Elemental Passions*, trans. Joanne Collie and Judith Still (London: The Athlone Press, 1992). See also Luce Irigaray: *An Ethics of Sexual Difference*, trans. Carolyn Burke and Gillian C. Gill (London: The Athlone Press, 1984). See also Michelle Boulous Walker: *Philosophy and the Maternal Body: Reading Silence* (London: Routledge, 1998).

[55] Having refused Levinas's preoccupation with death in an earlier section, Jantzen then writes quite favourably of his ethics of relationship in the context of natality. See Jantzen: *Becoming*, pp. 133–6, 232–45.

higher judgment upon it, a judgment that comes through the presence of the Other, and that speaks with the authority of the Infinite in its final hold upon me. Is this not however the voice of the subject itself that speaks here? For this judgment is precisely what makes and keeps me subject, and is thus that which I have to say in order to remain knowable as subject within this metaphysics. This judgment re-places me into the situation of my subjectivity, so that my subjection to its higher claim upon my life, is, and can only be, a repetition of that in which my subjection has already been formed. We are now bound together, the Other and I, not so much for love of God, as for the certain knowledge of ourselves to be the subjects of it. And for woman, there is a double movement re-quired — first to will herself to be subject in the same way that men are, so that she assumes also the will to power, and then to submit herself to the rule in which this status can be maintained, formulated as pantheism in deference to her purportedly feminine sensitivities.

Still we are pondering in what way this history which is thought as violent may also be thought as pregnant, and now, with this examination of Levinas, this becomes a question about the way of our thinking ethic-ally. For Levinas, this thinking is the allowing from beyond, from the Infinite, to break in, and thus to open out a further horizon within which to think and to act. This horizon is present to me in my encounter with others, appearing at the moment of a realization that I am judged and held accountable by that which I may never grasp, but which holds me subject to it for the saving of my life, and the life of the world, from endless killing. A higher truth than violence comes upon us. Such an understand-ing of ethics offers a framework within which an ethics of gender may be enacted — as awe and respect before the Other, as humility in letting myself be judged by the Other, generosity in a willingness to give away all that I have for the need of the Other, as a sense of mutual responsibility that between us is the world upheld by the Infinite, and thus redeemed. In this is a conception of love.

The assumptions which have been at work in our study here, however, suggest another way in which we might begin in a conception of love. Throughout this study, I have been trying to think with the questions of Martin Heidegger, in an effort to open up the ethics of gender in a new way, and most especially in an effort to come upon the place at which a theological ethics might begin. What comes to light in his analysis of the history of philosophy, which is the history of our thinking of being,[56] is

---

[56] See esp. Martin Heidegger: *An Introduction to Metaphysics*, trans. Ralph Manheim (Garden City, NY: Doubleday, 1961).

that the emergence of gender as representation of human being, willed and constructed, has both been part of a much wider philosophical interest in the distinctive appearing of the human and, in our time, has come to be the locus of the most poignant cries for redemption which a theological word might enflesh.[57] Its violent and pregnant history is disclosed in this way as a relation with being, and its presenting as a coagulation of many diversely disputed strands, its discursive incoherence, comes to light in this context. This is the place in which the vocation of theology to discern the human situation in all of its poignant promise, and to become itself the thinking that will turn this into God, is to be realized. This is where it matters. If nothing else comes from the thinking with gender which is undertaken here, at least it may bring us to the point of a beginning, where the theologian picks up the threads of this genealogy and allows its troubles to live with her, and lets herself be led in a reflecting upon what has happened here so that it may come to know love.

The story of gender that presents us to the world has swept in on a tide of modern humanism, at the centre of which was to be the self-directed human being sustained from the heavens by the omnipotent authoritative deity, and ordered in his living by an ethics of human fulfilment. That this account has always carried a sorrowing hollowness has been the discourse of feminism to bring to light, its impulses directed towards a critique, but also towards a nourishment, a filling up of this place with meaning. Feminisms have been exercises in the conceiving of love, clearing away the space for a beginning, and treasuring the point at which new life might be conceived within this history. As the discourse of gender unfolds into the postmodern, the distinctions around which gender has been woven are both intensified and confounded. For the (re)production of the human as a centre of will has become the necessary myth that sustains the culture of late capitalism, an intensification of what has been thought most patriarchal about our humanity and masculinist in our ethics. With this intensity, thinking with gender now is shown to be an exercise of will, of the assumption of power by the subject, so that it may speak and act within its bodied life, and accordingly, a gendered ethics is shown to be the means for the accomplishment of this work. This unveiling of this intensity which is happening in our humanity is the consequence of the awesome truth that Nietzsche spoke, of human being as will to power and of the death of the god once thought to be its origin and limit. Humanist and

---

[57]   See esp. Martin Heidegger: "Letter on 'Humanism'," trans. Frank A. Capuzzi, in *Pathmarks*, ed. William McNeill (Cambridge: Cambridge University Press, 1998).

feminist ethics alike are implicated in the necessity for valuation which this brings.[58]

At the same time, there is a confounding of gender within the simulacra, which has virtually become our reality, and within which our hold on the true and the real slips from us in the very thinking of them. We are fascinated by the sheer multiplicity of representations and of embodiments that materialize before us, and are intrigued by what it then means to be a physical being. We are unsure of who anyone is, man and woman wise, and are no longer entirely clear why this identification should matter to us. This is the place of postmodern confusion, for which Plato's metaphor of the cave seems so entirely appropriate, explaining our situation to us, and directing us to think towards that other, that reality which lies elsewhere, some "where" that is definitive, by which this one is to be encompassed and valued. To gain access to that world in which truth and goodness and beauty are to be found, becomes the compelling desire for redeeming which so drives an ethics of gender in our time. The search for the original in which we can be known to have begun in our humanity, the grounding in nature which may constitute the real for us again if only we think it so, the matrix of relationality into which our lives are thought to be woven – in all of these an ethics of gender seeks the means to bring us to that essence of humanity, in which lies what is true and good and beautiful for human beings, and to place that humanity in the care and the love of God.

So, Heidegger writes, "[T]he desire for an ethics presses ever more ardently for fulfillment as the obvious no less than the hidden perplexity of human beings soars to immeasurable heights."[59] Thus the question appears and troubles us through an analysis of these alternatives, namely whether these do not still speak with the voice of the nihilism in which they are born, so that they manifest themselves as alternative accounts of truth that appeal to a freely deciding human subject, who is then replaced into the centre, re-formed as a subject of will, even as this will is effaced by its subjection to a higher truth. And in this, will not the same problematics of gender in which modernism has been mired come to be repeated? So that whether this is to be a man's or a woman's version of Platonism becomes the crucial question that has to be answered before access to its truth is

---

[58] See esp. Martin Heidegger: "Nihilism," vol. IV of *Nietzsche*, trans. Frank A. Capuzzi (San Francisco: HarperCollins, 1991). Cf. Heidegger: "Being and the Ought," in *Introduction*, pp. 164–7.

[59] Heidegger: "Letter," p. 268.

gained, and woman is once again made to find her discomforting place within the thinking enacted as will to power. Gender will come again between us in these ethics, to stand in the way of our knowing one another in love, to make us think of ourselves as "persons of gender," and to serve as a test for love of God.

My reading of Heidegger suggests that the exposure of nihilism allows a destruction to be present, a destruction in which a way of thinking can be seen to have come to its end, and I am the one who experiences the impact of this failure, in myself, in the place where I am. In reflecting upon this failure, in letting the overturnings of postmodernity unsettle the positions and resolutions of modernity, in allowing the contradictions and the concealments of this humanism to be thought, I may come to myself anew.

> Who can disregard our predicament? Should we not safeguard and secure the existing bonds even if they hold human beings together ever so tenuously and merely for the present? Certainly. But does this need ever release thought from the task of thinking what still remains principally to be thought and, as being, prior to all beings, is their guarantor and their truth? Even further, can thinking refuse to think being after the latter has lain hidden so long in oblivion but at the same time has made itself known in the present moment of world history by the uprooting of all beings?[60]

Yet Heidegger's approach does not turn me towards a metaphysics, as in Levinas, for "[M]etaphysics closes itself to the simple essential fact that the human being essentially occurs in his essence only where he is claimed by being."[61] For I am the one whose thinking is a performance of a relation with being, and thus one in whom that which has not been said in the conceptions of being that form our common history, may yet come to be disclosed as truth, in the place where I am. I am to be one who awaits this truth. This waiting upon truth is the beginning of a conceiving of love, for it is a place in which tenderness and generosity are born, and so in this, awaiting disclosure in the place where I am, do I come to be human and to think of my beginning and my end for love of God.

Such allowance then brings me to wonder about the place of ethics in the conceiving of love, and there to find a question – Is ethics in love's way? To pose this question of an ethics of gender is to consider what it is that our thinking with gender performs, and that means to wonder what is

---

[60]   Heidegger: "Letter," p. 268.
[61]   Heidegger: "Letter," p. 247.

being enacted in its being said. For waiting upon truth in which is love conceived requires that thinking with gender is always to be prayer, attentive to the culture in which its words are formed and its grammar shaped, listening for the heartbeat that keeps the economy of human relationships vibrant, experiencing the world's anguish and its consolations, and asking, always asking at the threshold, how it is that the breath of love, that very breath which must inform an ethics in Christ, may come to matter here, or all is noise and clanging. Such prayer is preliminary to the coming of God even as it bears witness of God's already having come. So our thinking here too is preliminary, reaching out for what has already come among us, making ready for what is here, and in that preparation is the readiness of the soul for a conceiving of the love of God.

Select Bibliography

Adamson, Jane, Richard Freadman, and David Parker, eds. *Renegotiating Ethics in Literature, Philosophy and Theory*. Cambridge: Cambridge University Press, 1998.

Anderson, Pamela Sue. *A Feminist Philosophy of Religion*. Oxford: Blackwell, 1998.

Anderson, Perry. *The Origins of Postmodernity*. London: Verso, 1998.

Austin, J. L. *How to do Things with Words*. Oxford: Oxford University Press, 1962.

Barrett, Michèle. *Women's Oppression Today: Problems in Marxist Feminist Analysis*. London: Verso, 1986.

Barthes, Roland. *Mythologies*. Annette Lavers, trans. London: Vintage, 1993.

Baudrillard, Jean. *Selected Writings*. Mark Poster, ed. Cambridge: Polity Press, 1988.

Bauman, Zygmunt. *Postmodern Ethics*. Oxford: Blackwell, 1993.

Benhabib, Seyla. *Situating the Self: Gender, Community and Postmodernism in Contemporary Ethics*. Cambridge: Polity Press, 1992.

——, and Drucilla Cornell, eds. *Feminism as Critique: Essays on the Politics of Gender in Late-Capitalist Societies*. Cambridge: Polity Press, 1987.

——, Judith Butler, Drucilla Cornell, Nancy Fraser, and Linda Nicholson. *Feminist Contentions: A Philosophical Exchange*. London: Routledge, 1995. (First published as *Der Streit um Differenz*. Frankfurt: Fischer Verlag, 1993.)

Bernstein, Richard J. *The New Constellation: The Ethical-Political Horizons of Modernity/Postmodernity*. Cambridge: Polity Press, 1991.

Berry, Philippa, and Andrew Wernick, eds. *Shadow of Spirit: Postmodernism and Religion*. London: Routledge, 1992.

Bertens, Hans. *The Idea of the Postmodern*. London: Routledge, 1995.

Bly, Robert. *The Pillow and the Key: Commentary on the Fairy Tale of Iron John, Part One*. St. Paul, MN: Ally Press, 1987.

——. *When a Hair Turns Gold: Commentary on the Fairy Tale of Iron John, Part Two*. St. Paul, MN: Ally Press, 1988.

Bons-Storm, Riet. *The Incredible Woman: Listening to Women's Silences in Pastoral Care and Counseling*. Nashville, TN: Abingdon Press, 1996.

Bordo, Susan. *The Flight to Objectivity: Essays on Cartesianism and Culture*. Albany, NY: State University of New York Press, 1987.

Boulton, Wayne G., Thomas D. Kennedy, and Allen Verhey, eds. *From Christ to the World: Introductory Readings in Christian Ethics*. Grand Rapids, MI: William B. Eerdmans, 1994.

Bourdieu, Pierre: *Outline of a Theory of Practice*. Richard Nice, trans. Cambridge: Cambridge University Press, 1977.

Boyle, Nicholas. *Who Are We Now? Christian Humanism and the Global Market from Hegel to Heaney*. Edinburgh: T. & T. Clark, 1998.

Bravmann, Scott. *Queer Fictions of the Past: History, Culture and Difference*. Cambridge: Cambridge University Press, 1997.

Brod, Harry, ed. *The Making of Masculinities: The New Men's Studies*. London: Routledge, 1987.

Buckley, Michael J., SJ. *At the Origins of Modern Atheism*. New Haven, CT: Yale University Press, 1987.

Bulbeck, Chilla. *Re-Orienting Western Feminisms: Women's Diversity in a Postcolonial World*. Cambridge: Cambridge University Press, 1998.

Butler, Judith. *Gender Trouble: Feminism and the Subversion of Identity*. London: Routledge, 1990.

——. *Bodies That Matter: On The Discursive Limits of "Sex"*. London: Routledge, 1993.

——. *Excitable Speech: A Politics of the Performative*. London: Routledge, 1997.

——. *The Psychic Life of Power*. Stanford, CA: Stanford University Press, 1997.

Cahill, Lisa Sowle. *Between the Sexes: Foundations for a Christian Ethics of Sexuality*. Philadelphia, PA: Fortress Press, 1985.

——. *Sex, Gender and Christian Ethics*. Cambridge: Cambridge University Press, 1996.

Caputo, John D. *Against Ethics: Contributions to a Poetics of Obligation with Constant Reference to Deconstruction*. Bloomington: Indiana University Press, 1993.

Cavarero, Adriana. *In Spite of Plato: A Feminist Rewriting of Ancient Philosophy*. Serena Anderlini-D'Onofrio and Áine O'Healy, trans. Cambridge: Polity Press, 1995.

Chopp, Rebecca S. *The Power to Speak: Feminism, Language and God*. New York: Crossroad, 1989.

—— *Saving Work: Feminist Practices of Theological Education*. Louisville, KY: Westminster John Knox Press, 1995.

—— and Sheila Greeve Davaney, eds. *Horizons in Feminist Theology: Identity, Tradition, and Norms*. Minneapolis, MN: Fortress Press, 1997.

Christ, Carol. *Diving Deep and Surfacing: Women Writers on Spiritual Quest*. Boston: Beacon Press, 1980.

Clatterbaugh, Kenneth. *Contemporary Perspectives on Masculinity: Men, Women, and Politics in Modern Society*. Boulder, CO: Westview Press, 1990.

Cocks, Joan. *The Oppositional Imagination: Feminism, Critique and Political Theory*. New York: Routledge, 1989.

Code, Lorraine. *What Can She Know? Feminist Theory and the Construction of Knowledge*. Ithaca, NY: Cornell University Press, 1991.

Daly, Mary. *Beyond God the Father: Toward a Philosophy of Women's Liberation*. Boston: Beacon Press, 1973.

——. *Gyn/Ecology: The Metaethics of Radical Feminism*. London: The Women's Press, 1984.

David, Hugh. *On Queer Street: A Social History of British Homosexuality 1895–1995*. London: HarperCollins, 1997.

de Beauvoir, Simone. *The Second Sex*. H. M. Parshley, trans. New York: Bantam Books, 1961.

Deleuze, Gilles, and Félix Guattari. *What is Philosophy?* Graham Burchell and Hugh Tomlinson, trans. London: Verso, 1994.

——. *Difference and Repetition*. Paul Patton, trans. London: The Athlone Press, 1994.

Derrida, Jacques. *Of Grammatology*. Gayatri Chakravorty Spivak, trans. Baltimore, MD: Johns Hopkins University Press, 1976.

——. *Margins of Philosophy*. Alan Bass, trans. London: Harvester Wheatsheaf, 1982.

——. *Writing and Difference*. Alan Bass, trans. London: Routledge, 1995.

Deutscher, Penelope. *Yielding Gender: Feminism, Deconstruction and the History of Philosophy*. London: Routledge, 1997.

Diprose, Rosalyn. *The Bodies of Women: Ethics, Embodiment and Sexual Difference*. London: Routledge, 1994.

Di Stefano, Christine. *Configurations of Masculinity: A Feminist Perspective on Modern Political Theory*. Ithaca, NY: Cornell University Press, 1991.

Evans, Donald D. *The Logic of Self-Involvement: A Philosophical Study of Everyday Language with Special Reference to the Christian Use of Language about God as Creator*. London: SCM Press, 1963.

Fiorenza, Elisabeth Schüssler. *In Memory of Her: A Feminist Theological Reconstruction of Christian Origins*. London: SCM Press, 1983.

Fiumara, Gemma Corradi. *The Other Side of Language: A Philosophy of Listening*. Charles Lambert, trans. London: Routledge, 1990.

——. *The Metaphoric Process: Connections between Language and Life*. London: Routledge, 1995.

Foucault, Michel. *L'archéologie du savoir*. Paris: Éditions Gallimard, 1969.

——. *Discipline and Punish: The Birth of the Prison*, trans. Alan Sheridan (New York: Vintage, 1979).

——. *Power/Knowledge: Selected Interviews and Other Writings 1972–1977*, ed. Colin Gordon (Brighton: Harvester, 1980).

——. *The Foucault Reader*, ed. Paul Rabinow (Harmondsworth: Penguin, 1986).

——. *The Order of Things: An Archaeology of the Human Sciences*. London: Routledge, 1997.

Fowler, Bridget. *Pierre Bourdieu and Cultural Theory: Critical Investigations*. London: Sage, 1997.

Fuss, Diana. *Essentially Speaking: Feminism, Nature and Difference*. London: Routledge, 1989.

Gardner, Lucy. "Touching upon the Soul: the Interiority of Transcendence after Luce Irigaray." In Parsons, Susan F., ed. *Challenging Women's Orthodoxies in the Context of Faith*. London: Ashgate Press, 2000.

Gatens, Moira. *Feminism and Philosophy: Perspectives on Difference and Equality*. Cambridge: Polity Press, 1991.

———. *Imaginary Bodies: Ethics, Power and Corporeality* (London: Routledge, 1996).

Giddens, Anthony. *The Transformation of Intimacy: Sexuality, Love and Eroticism in Modern Societies*. Cambridge: Polity Press, 1992.

Gill, Robin. *A Textbook of Christian Ethics*. 2nd edition. Edinburgh: T. & T. Clark, 1995.

Gill, Sean. *The Lesbian and Gay Christian Movement: Campaigning for Justice, Truth and Love*. London: Cassell, 1998.

Gillespie, Michael Allen. *Nihilism before Nietzsche*. Chicago: University of Chicago Press, 1995.

Gilligan, Carol. *In a Different Voice: Psychological Theory and Women's Development*. Cambridge, MA: Harvard University Press, 1982.

———, Janie Victoria Ward, Jill McLean Taylor, and Betty Bardige, eds. *Mapping the Moral Domain*. Cambridge, MA: Harvard University Press, 1988.

Gilson, Etienne. *Being and Some Philosophers*. 2nd edition. Toronto: Pontifical Institute of Mediaeval Studies, 1952.

Goldberg, Herb. *The Hazards of Being Male: Surviving the Myth of Masculine Privilege*. New York: Signet Books, 1976.

Goldberg, Steven. *The Inevitability of Patriarchy*. New York: William Morrow, 1974.

Graham, Elaine L. *Making the Difference: Gender, Personhood and Theology*. London: Mowbray, 1995.

———. *Transforming Practice: Pastoral Theology in an Age of Uncertainty*. London: Mowbray, 1996.

Grey, Mary. *The Wisdom of Fools? Seeking Revelation for Today*. London: SPCK, 1993.

Grosz, Elizabeth. *Sexual Subversions: Three French Feminists*. Sydney: Allen & Unwin, 1989.

———. *Jacques Lacan: A Feminist Introduction*. London: Routledge, 1990.

Habermas, Jürgen. *Moral Consciousness and Communicative Action*. Christian Lehnhardt and Shierry Weber Nicholsen, trans. Boston: MIT Press, 1990.

Hamel, Ronald P. and Kenneth R. Himes, OFM, eds. *Introduction to Christian Ethics: A Reader*. New York: Paulist Press, 1989.

Hampson, Daphne. *After Christianity*. London: SCM Press, 1996.

Hauerwas, Stanley. *Sanctify Them in the Truth: Holiness Exemplified*. Edinburgh: T. & T. Clark, 1998.

Heidegger, Martin. *An Introduction to Metaphysics*. Ralph Manheim, trans. Garden City, NY: Doubleday, 1961.

———. *Being and Time*. John Macquarrie and Edward Robinson, trans. London: SCM Press, 1962.

———— . *The Question Concerning Technology and other essays.* William Lovitt, trans. New York: Harper & Row, 1977.

———— . *Nietzsche.* Vols. III and IV. Joan Stambaugh, David Farrell Krell, and Frank A. Capuzzi, trans. New York: HarperCollins, 1991.

———— . *Pathmarks.* William McNeill, ed. Cambridge: Cambridge University Press, 1998.

Hemming, Laurence Paul. "Heidegger and the Grounds of Redemption." In Milbank, John, Catherine Pickstock, and Graham Ward, eds. *Radical Orthodoxy: A New Theology.* London: Routledge, 1999, pp. 91–108.

———— . *Heidegger's Atheism.* Notre Dame, IN: University of Notre Dame Press, 2002.

———— . "After Heidegger: Transubstantiation." *Heythrop Journal* 41:2 (April 2000), pp. 170–86.

———— . "The Nature of Nature: Is Sexual Difference Really Necessary?" In Parsons, Susan Frank, ed. *Challenging Women's Orthodoxies in the Context of Faith.* Aldershot: Ashgate Press, 2000.

Heyward, Isabel Carter. *Touching Our Strength: The Erotic as Power and the Love of God.* New York: HarperCollins, 1989.

Hodge, Joanna. *Heidegger and Ethics.* London: Routledge, 1995.

Hodgson, Peter C. *Winds of the Spirit: A Constructive Christian Theology.* London: SCM Press, 1994.

Hoose, Bernard, ed. *Christian Ethics: An Introduction.* London: Cassell, 1998.

Hughes, Gerard, SJ: "Is Ethics One or Many?" Unpublished paper given to the Association of Teachers of Moral Theology, UK, and available from its secretary.

Irigaray, Luce. "Equal to Whom?" *differences, A Journal of Feminist Cultural Studies* 1:2 (1988), pp. 59–76.

———— . *Speculum of the Other Woman.* Gillian C. Gill, trans. Ithaca, NY: Cornell University Press, 1974.

———— . *This Sex Which is Not One.* Catherine Porter, with Carolyn Burke, trans. Ithaca, NY: Cornell University Press, 1977.

———— . *An Ethics of Sexual Difference.* Carolyn Burke and Gillian C. Gill, trans. London: The Athlone Press, 1993.

———— . *Sexes and Genealogies.* Gillian C. Gill, trans. New York: Columbia University Press, 1987.

———— . *Elemental Passions.* Joanne Collie and Judith Still, trans. London: The Athlone Press, 1992.

———— . *je, tu, nous: Toward a Culture of Difference.* Alison Martin, trans. London: Routledge, 1993.

———— . *Thinking the Difference: For a Peaceful Revolution.* Karin Montin, trans. London: The Athlone Press, 1994.

Jaggar, Alison M., ed.: *Living with Contradictions: Controversies in Feminist Social Ethics.* Boulder, CO: Westview Press, 1994.

Jameson, Fredric. *Postmodernism or, the Cultural Logic of Late Capitalism.* London: Verso, 1991.

Jantzen, Grace M. *Julian of Norwich: Mystic and Theologian*. London: SPCK, 1987.

——. *Power, Gender and Christian Mysticism*. Cambridge: Cambridge University Press, 1995.

——. *Becoming Divine: Towards a Feminist Philosophy of Religion*. Manchester: Manchester University Press, 1998.

Johnson, Elizabeth. *She Who Is: The Mystery of God in Feminist Theological Discourse*. New York: Crossroad, 1997.

Jordan, Mark D. *The Invention of Sodomy in Christian Theology*. Chicago: University of Chicago Press, 1997.

Kant, Immanuel. *Critique of Practical Reason*. Lewis White Beck, trans. New York: Bobbs-Merrill, 1956.

——. *Groundwork of the Metaphysic of Morals*. H. J. Paton, trans. New York: Harper Torchbooks, 1964.

Kearney, Richard. *Modern Movements in European Philosophy*. Manchester: Manchester University Press, 1994.

Kelly, Kevin T. *New Directions in Moral Theology: The Challenge of Being Human*. London: Geoffrey Chapman, 1992.

——. *New Directions in Sexual Ethics: Moral Theology and the Challenge of Aids*. London: Geoffrey Chapman, 1998.

Kerr, Fergus, OP. *Immortal Longings: Versions of Transcending Humanity*. London: SPCK, 1997.

Kierkegaard, Søren. *Concluding Unscientific Postscript*. David F. Swenson, trans. Princeton, NJ: Princeton University Press, 1968.

Kim, C. W. Maggie, Susan M. St. Ville, and Susan M. Simonaitis, eds. *Transfigurations: Theology and the French Feminists*. Minneapolis MN: Fortress Press, 1993.

King, Ursula, ed. *Religion and Gender*. Oxford: Blackwell, 1995.

Kristeva, Julia. *Desire in Language: A Semiotic Approach to Literature and Art*. Leon S. Roudiez, ed. Thomas Gora, Alice Jardine and Leon S. Roudiez, trans. Oxford: Blackwell, 1993.

Lacan, Jacques. *Ecrits: a Selection*. Alan Sheridan, trans. London: Tavistock, 1977.

——. *Le moi dans la théorie de Freud et dans la technique de la psychanalyse*: Le séminaire II, 1954–55. Paris: Seuil, 1978.

LaCugna, Catherine Mowry. *God For Us: The Trinity and Christian Life*. New York: HarperCollins, 1991.

——, ed. *Freeing Theology: The Essentials of Theology in Feminist Perspective*. San Francisco: HarperCollins, 1993.

Laqueur, Thomas. *Making Sex: Body and Gender from the Greeks to Freud*. Cambridge, MA: Harvard University Press, 1992.

Le Doeuff, Michèle. *Hipparchia's Choice: An Essay Concerning Women, Philosophy, etc.*, Trista Selous, trans. Oxford: Blackwell, 1991.

Lerner, Gerda. *The Creation of Patriarchy*. Oxford: Oxford University Press, 1986.

——. *The Creation of Feminist Consciousness*. Oxford: Oxford University Press, 1993.

Levinas, Emmanuel. *Totality and Infinity: An Essay on Exteriority*. Alphonso Lingis, trans. Pittsburgh, PA: Duquesne University Press, 1969.

——. *Otherwise than Being: or Beyond Essence*. Alphonso Lingis, trans. Dordrecht: Martinus Nijhoff, 1981.

——. "God and Philosophy." Richard A. Cohen and Alphonso Lingis, trans. In Graham Ward, ed. *The Postmodern God: A Theological Reader*. Oxford: Blackwell, 1997. pp. 52–73.

Lévi-Strauss, Claude. *Structural Anthropology*. Vol. 1. Claire Jacobson and Brooke Grundfest Schoepf, trans. London: Penguin, 1993.

Lloyd, Genevieve. *The Man of Reason: "Male" and "Female" in Western Philosophy*. London: Methuen, 1984.

Lyotard, Jean-François, *The Postmodern Condition: A Report on Knowledge*. Geoff Bennington and Brian Massumi, trans. Manchester: Manchester University Press, 1997.

MacIntyre, Alasdair. *A Short History of Ethics: A History of Moral Philosophy from the Homeric Age to the Twentieth Century*. London: Routledge & Kegan Paul, 1967.

Macmurray, John. *The Self as Agent*. London: Faber & Faber, 1969.

——. *Persons in Relation*. London: Faber & Faber, 1991.

Mahoney, John, SJ. *The Making of Moral Theology: A Study of the Roman Catholic Tradition*. Oxford: Clarendon Press, 1989.

McFadyen, Alistair I. *The Call to Personhood: A Christian Theory of the Individual in Social Relationships*. Cambridge: Cambridge University Press, 1990.

McFague, Sallie. *Models of God: Theology for an Ecological, Nuclear Age*. Philadelphia, PA: Fortress Press, 1987.

——. *The Body of God: An Ecological Theology*. London: SCM Press, 1993.

——. *Super, Natural Christians: How We Should Love Nature*. London: SCM Press, 1997.

Marks, Elaine and Isabelle de Courtivron, eds. *New French Feminisms: An Anthology*. Brighton: Harvester, 1986.

Martineau, Harriet. *Society in America*. Seymour Martin Lipset, ed. Garden City, NY: Anchor Doubleday, 1962.

Midgley, Mary. *Beast and Man: The Roots of Human Nature*. London: Methuen, 1980.

Nietzsche, Friedrich. *The Genealogy of Morals*. Francis Golffing, trans. Garden City, NY: Doubleday Anchor, 1956.

——. *The Gay Science*. trans. Walter Kaufmann. New York: Vintage. 1974.

——. *Human, All Too Human: A Book for Free Spirits*. R. J. Hollingdale, trans. Cambridge: Cambridge University Press, 1986.

——. *Thus Spoke Zarathustra*. Thomas Common, trans. Ware: Wordsworth Editions Ltd., 1997.

Norris, Christopher. *The Truth About Postmodernism*. Oxford: Blackwell, 1993.

——. *Truth and the Ethics of Criticism*. Manchester: Manchester University Press, 1994.

——. *New Idols of the Cave: On the Limits of Anti-realism*. Manchester: Manchester University Press, 1997.

Nussbaum, Martha C. and Amartya Sen, eds. *The Quality of Life*. A study prepared for the World Institute for Development Economics Research (WIDER) of the United Nations University. Oxford: Clarendon Press, 1993.

——. "The Professor of Parody: The Hip Defeatism of Judith Butler." *The New Republic* (February 22, 1999), pp. 37–45.

——. and Jonathan Glover, eds. *Women, Culture and Development: A Study of Human Capabilities*. Oxford: Clarendon Press, 1995.

Okin, Susan Moller. *Justice, Gender and the Family*. New York: Basic Books, 1989.

Parsons, Susan Frank *Feminism and Christian Ethics*. Cambridge: Cambridge University Press, 1996.

——. "The Dilemma of Difference: A Feminist Theological Exploration." *Feminist Theology* 14 (January 1997), pp. 51–72.

——. "The Boundaries of Desire: A Consideration of Judith Butler and Carter Heyward." *Feminist Theology* 23 (January 2000), pp. 90–104.

——, ed. *Challenging Women's Orthodoxies in the Context of Faith*. Aldershot: Ashgate Press, 2000.

Rawls, John. *A Theory of Justice*. Oxford: Oxford University Press, 1972.

Riley, Denise. *Am I That Name? Feminism and the Category of "Women" in History*. New York: Macmillan, 1988.

Rorty, Richard. *Contingency, Irony, and Solidarity*. Cambridge: Cambridge University Press, 1989.

Rossi, Alice S. *The Feminist Papers*. New York: Bantam Books, 1973.

Rowbotham, Sheila. *Woman's Consciousness, Man's World*. London: Penguin, 1973.

——. *Women, Resistance and Revolution: A History of Women and Revolution in the Modern World*. New York: Vintage, 1974.

Ruether, Rosemary Radford. *Sexism and God-Talk: Towards a Feminist Theology*. London: SCM Press, 1983.

——. "Dualism and the Nature of Evil in Feminist Theology." *Studies in Christian Ethics* 5:1 (1992) pp. 26–39.

——. *Women and Redemption: A Theological History*. London: SCM Press, 1998.

Samuels, Andrew, ed. *The Father: Contemporary Jungian Perspectives*. London: Free Association Books, 1985.

Sartre, Jean-Paul. *Being and Nothingness: An Essay in Phenomenological Ontology*. Hazel E. Barnes, trans. New York: The Citadel Press, 1965.

Schiebinger, Londa. *The Mind has no Sex? Women in the Origins of Modern Science*. Cambridge, MA: Harvard University Press, 1989.

Schweiker, William and Charles Hallisey. *Companion to Religious Ethics*. Oxford: Blackwell, forthcoming.

Sedgwick, Eve Kosofsky. *Epistemology of the Closet*. Berkeley: University of California Press, 1990.

Seidler, Victor J. *Recovering the Self: Morality and Social Theory*. London: Routledge, 1994.

Seidman, Steven. *Difference Troubles: Queering Social Theory and Sexual Politics*. Cambridge: Cambridge University Press, 1997.

Selden, Raman. *A Reader's Guide to Contemporary Literary Theory*. Brighton: Harvester, 1985.

Singer, Peter, ed. *A Companion to Ethics*. Oxford: Blackwell, 1994.

Skinner, Quentin, ed. *The Return of Grand Theory in the Human Sciences*. Cambridge: Cambridge University Press, 1985.

Snodgrass, Jon, ed. *A Book of Readings for Men Against Sexism*. Albion, CA: Tunes Change Press, 1977.

Sölle, Dorothee: *Thinking About God: An Introduction to Theology*. London: SCM Press, 1990.

Sontag, Susan, ed. *A Roland Barthes Reader*. London: Vintage, 1993.

Soper, Kate. *Humanism and Anti-Humanism*. London: Hutchinson, 1986.

——. *What is Nature?* Oxford: Blackwell, 1995.

Sturrock, John, ed. *Structuralism and Since: From Lévi-Strauss to Derrida*. Oxford: Oxford University Press, 1979.

Sweasey, Peter. *From Queer to Eternity: Spirituality in the Lives of Lesbian, Gay and Bisexual People*. London: Cassell, 1997.

Taylor, Charles. *Sources of the Self: The Making of the Modern Identity*. Cambridge, MA: Harvard University Press, 1989.

——. *The Ethics of Authenticity*. Cambridge, MA: Harvard University Press, 1991.

Thatcher, Adrian and Elizabeth Stuart, eds. *Christian Perspectives on Sexuality and Gender*. Leominster: Gracewing, 1996.

Thiselton, Anthony C. *Interpreting God and the Postmodern Self: On Meaning, Manipulation and Promise*. Edinburgh: T. & T. Clark, 1995.

Tolson, Andrew. *The Limits of Masculinity*. New York: Harper & Row, 1977.

Tronto, Joan C. *Moral Boundaries: A Political Argument for an Ethic of Care*. London: Routledge, 1993.

Van Heijst, Annelies. *Longing for the Fall*. Kampen: Kok Pharos, 1995.

Vanhoozer, Kevin. "Human being, individual and social." In Gunton, Colin E., ed. *The Cambridge Companion to Christian Doctrine*. Cambridge: Cambridge University Press, 1997, pp. 158–88.

Vardy, Peter and Paul Grosch. *The Puzzle of Ethics*. London: HarperCollins, 1994.

Walker, Michelle Boulous. *Philosophy and the Maternal Body: Reading Silence*. London: Routledge, 1998.

Ward, Graham. *Barth, Derrida and the Language of Theology*. Cambridge: Cambridge University Press, 1995.

——, ed. *The Postmodern God: A Theological Reader*. Oxford: Blackwell, 1997.

Weeks, Jeffrey. *Sexuality and its Discontents: Meanings, Myths & Modern Sexualities*. London: Routledge, 1985.

Welch, Sharon. *Communities of Resistance and Solidarity: A Feminist Theology of Liberation*. New York: Orbis Books, 1985.

——. *A Feminist Ethic of Risk*. Minneapolis, MN: Fortress Press, 1990.

West, Angela: *Deadly Innocence: Feminism and the Mythology of Sin*. London: Mowbray, 1995.

——. "Justification by Gender – Daphne Hampson's *After Christianity*." *Scottish Journal of Theology* 51:1 (1998). (Reprinted in Parsons, Susan F., ed. *Challenging Women's Orthodoxies in the Context of Faith*. London: Ashgate Press, 2000.)

Wollstonecraft, Mary. *A Vindication of the Rights of Woman*. (Reprinted in Alice S. Rossi, ed. *The Feminist Papers*. New York: Bantam Books, 1973.)

Wood, Julia T. *Gendered Lives: Communication, Gender and Culture*. Belmont, CA: Wadsworth, 1994.

Wyschogrod, Edith. *Saints and Postmodernism: Revisioning Moral Philosophy*. Chicago: University of Chicago Press, 1990.

Young, Ian. *The Stonewall Experiment: A Gay Psychohistory*. London: Cassell, 1995.

Young, Robert J. *Torn Halves: Political Conflict in Literary and Cultural Theory*. Manchester: Manchester University Press, 1996.

Zizek, Slavoj. *The Ticklish Subject: The Absent Centre of Political Ontology*. London: Verso, 1999.

Zizioulas, John D. "On Being a Person. Towards an Ontology of Personhood." In Schwöbel, Christoph and Colin E. Gunton, eds. *Persons, Divine and Human*. Edinburgh: T. & T. Clark, 1991, pp. 33–46.

Index